Palgrave Studies in European Union Politics

Edited by: **Michelle Egan**, American University USA, **Neill Nugent**, Manchester Metropolitan University, UK, **William Paterson**, University of Birmingham, UK
Editorial Board: **Christopher Hill**, Cambridge, UK, **Simon Hix**, London School of Economics, UK, **Mark Pollack**, Temple University, USA, **Kalypso Nicolaïdis**, Oxford UK, **Morton Egeberg**, Oslo University, Norway, **Amy Verdun**, University of Victoria, Canada

Palgrave Macmillan is delighted to announce the launch of a new book series on the European Union. Following on the sustained success of the acclaimed *European Union Series*, which essentially publishes research-based textbooks, *Palgrave Studies in European Union Politics* will publish research-driven monographs.

The remit of the series is broadly defined, both in terms of subject and academic discipline. All topics of significance concerning the nature and operation of the European Union potentially fall within the scope of the series. The series is multi-disciplinary to reflect the growing importance of the EU as a political and social phenomenon. We will welcome submissions from the areas of political studies, international relations, political economy, public and social policy and sociology.

Titles include:

Heather Grabbe
THE EU'S TRANSFORMATIVE POWER
Europeanization Through Conditionality in Central and Eastern Europe

Justus Schönlau
DRAFTING THE EU CHARTER
Rights, Legitimacy and Process

Forthcoming titles in the series include:

Ian Bache and Andrew Jordan *(editors)*
THE EUROPEANIZATION OF BRITISH POLITICS

Lauren McLaren
IDENTITY INTERESTS AND ATTITUDES TO EUROPEAN INTEGRATION

Karen Smith and Katie Verlin Laatikainen *(editors)*
THE EUROPEAN UNION AND THE UNITED NATIONS

Morten Egeberg *(editor)*
MULTILEVEL COMMUNITY ADMINISTRATION

Palgrave Studies in European Union Politics
Series Standing Order ISBN 1–4039–9511–7 (hardback) and 1–4039–9512–5 (paperback)

You can receive future titles in this series as they are published by placing a standing order. Please contact your bookseller or, in case of difficulty, write to us at the address below with your name and address, the title of the series and the ISBN quoted above.

Customer Services Department, Macmillan Distribution Ltd, Houndmills, Basingstoke, Hampshire RG21 6XS, England

Books by the same author

Heather Grabbe (2004), *The Constellations of Europe: How Enlargement will Transform the EU*, London: Centre for European Reform.

Katinka Barysch and Heather Grabbe (2002), *Who's Ready for EU Enlargement?* London: Centre for European Reform.

Heather Grabbe and Wolfgang Münchau (2002), *Germany and Britain: An Alliance of Necessity*, London: Centre for European Reform.

Heather Grabbe (2001), *Profiting from EU Enlargement*, London: Centre for European Reform.

Heather Grabbe and Kirsty Hughes (1998), *Enlarging the EU Eastwards*, London: RIIA/Continuum.

The EU's Transformative Power

Europeanization Through Conditionality in Central and Eastern Europe

Heather Grabbe

First published 2006 by
PALGRAVE MACMILLAN
Houndmills, Basingstoke, Hampshire RG21 6XS and
175 Fifth Avenue, New York, N. Y. 10010
Companies and representatives throughout the world

PALGRAVE MACMILLAN is the global academic imprint of the Palgrave Macmillan division of St. Martin's Press, LLC and of Palgrave Macmillan Ltd. Macmillan® is a registered trademark in the United States, United Kingdom and other countries. Palgrave is a registered trademark in the European Union and other countries.

ISBN-13: 978–1–4039–4903–5   hardback
ISBN-10: 1–4039–4903–4   hardback

This book is printed on paper suitable for recycling and made from fully managed and sustained forest sources.

A catalogue record for this book is available from the British Library.

Library of Congress Cataloging-in-Publication Data
Grabbe, Heather.
    The EU's transformative power : Europeanization through conditionality in Central and Eastern Europe / Heather Grabbe.
        p. cm. – (Palgrave studies in European Union politics)
    Includes bibliographical references and index.
    ISBN 1–4039–4903–4
    1. European Union–Europe, Eastern. 2. European Union–Europe, Central. 3. European cooperation. I. Title: European Union's transformative power. II. Title. III. Series.
HC240.25.E852G72 2005
341.242′2′0947–dc22   2005051279

Printed and bound in Great Britain by
CPI Antony Rowe, Chippenham and Eastbourne

For my parents, Elizabeth and Lester

Contents

List of Tables

Abstract

This book examines how the European Union (EU) uses its conditions for membership to influence the policy choices made by candidate countries. The author argues that the EU has enormous potential influence on public policy in candidate countries, but that its influence in Central and Eastern Europe did not fulfil this potential because of the inconsistency and lack of precision in the Union's membership criteria.

The EU had many specific routes of influence through which it could shape policies and institutions in candidate countries, as well as the general and powerful attraction of membership. To explore the way that EU influence worked in detail, the author presents case-studies of how the EU actively sought to shape policy-making on regulating the movement of persons. The EU did not use its full potential to shape outcomes effectively because its influence was diffuse – partly owing to the diversity of its current member-states – and because of the multiple kinds of uncertainty that characterised the accession process. However, the accession process had a long-term impact because it embedded 'Europeanisation' processes in the candidate countries.

About the Author

Dr Heather Grabbe is a member of the Cabinet of Olli Rehn, the European Commissioner for enlargement. When this book was written, she was Deputy Director of the Centre for European Reform, an independent think-tank based in London. She is also an Associate Fellow of the European Institute at the London School of Economics and member of the Senior Common Room of St Antony's College, Oxford University. She has worked extensively on EU enlargement and its implications, as well as on other European issues and questions of conditionality. Her publications include 'The Constellations of Europe: How Enlargement will Transform the EU' (2004, CER); 'Who's Ready for EU Enlargement?' (written jointly with Katinka Barysch, 2002, CER); 'Germany and Britain: An Alliance of Necessity' (written jointly with Wolfgang Münchau, 2002, CER), 'Profiting from EU Enlargement' (2001, CER) and 'Enlarging the EU Eastwards' (written jointly with Kirsty Hughes, 1998, RIIA/Continuum). She was previously Research Fellow at the Royal Institute of International Affairs and she has been a visiting fellow at the European University Institute (Florence), the European Union Institute for Security Studies (Paris) and the Centre for International Relations (Warsaw). She was educated at Oxford and Birmingham universities.

Acknowledgements

The author would like to thank all the people who took the time to discuss ideas and comment on drafts of this book, including Giuliano Amato, Graham Avery, Judy Batt, Renata Dwan, Brigid Fowler, Klaus Goetz, John Gould, Charles Grant, Jim Hughes, Kirsty Hughes, Sandra Lavenex, Richard Mash, Anand Menon, Willie Paterson, Claudio Radaelli, Martin Rhodes, Thomas Risse, Jacques Rupnik, Uli Sedelmeier, Yasemin Soysal, Paul Taggart, Boyko Todorov, Loukas Tsoukalis, Helen Wallace, William Wallace, Antje Wiener, Stephen Wilks, Andrew Wilson, Kasia Wolczuk, Stewart Wood, Ngaire Woods and Marcin Zaborowski. Many policy-makers were very generous in helping me with the research and sharing their insights – but they prefer to remain anonymous.

Several institutions provided vital practical support while I was undertaking research. Janusz Reiter kindly offered me the facilities of the Centre for International Relations in Warsaw while I was doing fieldwork in Poland, and he and his family were extremely generous in accommodating me. Piotr Buras and Olaf Osica went out of their way to help with my research in Poland, as well as with my Polish. Renata Dwan freely offered accommodation and office space while I was working in Budapest – as well as ideas and encouragement – and I am grateful to the staff at the EastWest Institute in Budapest for their assistance.

Abbreviations

AP – Accession Partnership
CDU/CSU – Christian Democratic Union/Christian Socialist Union
CEC – Commission of the European Communities
CEE – Central and East European
CFSP – Common Foreign and Security Policy
CIS – Commonwealth of Independent States
COMECON – Council for Mutual Economic Assistance
COREPER – Committee of Permanent Representatives
DCP – draft common position
DG – Directorate-General
EA – Europe Agreement
EBRD – European Bank for Reconstruction and Development
ECOFIN – Council of Economics and Finance Ministers
ECOSOC – Economic and Social Committee of the European Union
EFTA – European Free Trade Area
EMU – Economic and Monetary Union
EU – European Union
FDI – foreign direct investment
FMP – free movement of persons
GDP – Gross Domestic Product
IFI – international financial institution
IGC – inter-governmental conference
IMF – International Monetary Fund
JHA – justice and home affairs
MFA – Ministry of Foreign Affairs
NATO – North Atlantic Treaty Organisation
NGO – Non-Governmental Organisation
NPAA – National Programme for Adoption of the *Acquis*
OECD – Organisation for Economic Cooperation and Development
SIS – Schengen Information System
SMWP – Single Market White Paper

Chronology

	Events in EU	Events in Central and Eastern Europe	Development of EU accession policy	Development of policies on movement of persons
1985				Schengen Accord signed between Belgium, France, Germany, Luxembourg and Netherlands
1989		Fall of the Berlin Wall, collapse of communist regimes across CEE	EU sets up Phare aid programme for CEE; European Commission starts coordinating aid to CEE from the G24	
1990				Schengen Accord becomes the Schengen Convention
1991	Completion of programme to create the single market	Independence of Estonia, Latvia and Lithuania from the Soviet Union; independence of Slovenia from Yugoslavia	EU starts to sign Europe Agreements bilaterally with CEE countries, starting with Hungary and Poland	
1992	Maastricht Treaty signed			
1993	Copenhagen European Council	'Velvet divorce' of the Czech Republic and Slovakia	EU sets conditions for membership for the first time	
1994	Essen European Council	Hungary and Poland are the first CEE countries to apply for membership	EU establishes eastern accession policy	
1995	Austria, Finland and Sweden join EU		Commission issues Single Market White Paper on sequencing of legislation to be adopted by applicants	Abolition of controls at common frontiers between Schengen members
1996	Inter-governmental conference begins on institutional reforms for enlargement			

Chronology – *continued*

	Events in EU	Events in Central and Eastern Europe	Development of EU accession policy	Development of policies on movement of persons
1997	Amsterdam Treaty signed; Luxembourg European Council	Bulgarian Socialist Party voted out of office	Commission publishes 'opinions' on readiness for membership of 12 applicants, and 'Agenda 2000' pre-accession strategy; EU offers candidate status to 12 countries	
1998		Mečiar government voted out in Slovakia; EU cuts Phare assistance to Poland because of non-fulfilment of conditions	EU opens accession negotiations with Cyprus, Czech Republic, Estonia, Hungary, Poland and Slovenia; Commission issues first Regular Reports and Accession Partnerships; Catch-Up Facility established for Bulgaria and Romania	
1999	Single currency launched; Helsinki European Council; Lisbon European Council establishes 10-year economic reform programme	NATO bombs Serbia after Serbian troops enter Kosovo; Slovakia meets political conditions, opening the way to negotiations; candidates establish first national programmes for adoption of the *acquis*	EU offers candidate status to Turkey and accession negotiations to remaining applicants; start of 'twinning' programme	Schengen Convention incorporated into EU treaties; EU publishes Schengen *acquis* for first time
2000	Nice Treaty signed; new EU budget begins for 2000–2006; Lisbon process begins		EU opens accession negotiations with Bulgaria, Latvia, Lithuania, Malta, Romania and Slovakia	Commission puts forward initial draft common position on free movement of persons

Chronology – *continued*

	Events in EU	*Events in Central and Eastern Europe*	*Development of EU accession policy*	*Development of policies on movement of persons*
2001	Gothenburg European Council		EU decides on 'big bang' enlargement to ten new members	Commission presents full draft common position on free movement of persons; Schengen members liberalise visa regime with Bulgaria
2002	Copenhagen European Council; Convention on the Future of Europe begins		EU concludes accession negotiations with ten candidates	Schengen members liberalise visa regime with Romania
2003	Draft constitution completed by European Convention	Accession treaties approved in referenda in nine candidate countries	All accession treaties ratified by national parliaments and European Parliament	
2004	Ten new members join EU on 1 May; European Parliament elections; inter-governmental conference approves constitution		EU concludes negotiations with Bulgaria and Romania; EU sets dates for Croatia and Turkey to begin accession negotiations	12 of the 15 member-states decide to restrict access to their labour markets for CEE workers

1
Introduction

This book is concerned with how the process of accession to the European Union (EU) shaped public policy-making in the Central and East European (CEE) candidate countries from 1989 to 2004. It analyses in detail how the EU used its accession conditions to exercise influence, and it investigates specifically how mechanisms of Europeanisation worked. The analysis is organised around case-studies of two policy areas concerned with regulating the movement of persons.

The case-studies seek to explain two puzzles: in 2001, the EU closed a key chapter in accession negotiations with several CEE applicants for membership. In doing so, it secured their agreement on a transition period of up to seven years before citizens of new member-states could work freely anywhere in the 15 existing member-states. This outcome was clearly against the interests of the CEE countries, and it also contradicted the EU's own single market policy on labour mobility. The second puzzle arose when the EU put forward a negotiating position on justice and home affairs (JHA) that required the applicants to implement its border policies prior to accession, but which did not make any reciprocal commitment that the existing member-states would remove frontier controls with the new members immediately after enlargement. In both cases, the candidates agreed to an EU position which explicitly denied them the benefits accorded to existing members on accession.

Why did the candidates accept an outcome which was blatantly against their interests? An obvious answer is that the applicants were in a weak position *vis-à-vis* the Union owing to their asymmetrical dependence on it. They wanted membership far more than the current member-states wanted to accept them. Indeed, the Union's own collective ambivalence about enlargement strengthened its negotiating power. Moreover, EU accession was a package deal. The EU negotiators could put bargains on the table which were unattractive to the candidates, but which the CEE negotiators accepted because the overall attraction of joining the Union outweighed the disadvantages of parts of the deal. 'Ultimately, accession on any terms is better than no accession', as one Hungarian official remarked to the author in 1997.

The EU's relative power in negotiations and the nature of the accession conditionality are important parts of the explanation for this outcome. But these factors are insufficient to explain the applicants' behaviour in the domestic accession preparations running in parallel with negotiations. The CEE policy-makers knew at least several years in advance that the EU was likely to put forward such negotiating positions. Yet they responded positively to demands from the EU that they implement parts of the EU's policy agenda for regulating free movement, even though there would probably be no reciprocal benefits. Why did they comply? Why did they not use strongly what negotiating power they had, to argue that they would not prepare for policies from which they would not benefit immediately on accession? Why did they not stall or delay implementation, or try to mitigate the impact of these measures? This book seeks to answer these questions by exploring the process of Europeanisation in the CEE countries.

Studies on international negotiations suggest that negotiators can behave in ways that seem not to accord with their interests, but which are explicable through rationalist frameworks. A number of influential studies have sought to explain such cases: Robert Putnam (Putnam 1988 and Putnam *et al.* 1993) famously argued that parallel domestic political games shape outcomes in international negotiations – and *vice versa*. George Tsebelis (1990) created an elaborate framework to explain why political actors accept sub-optimal outcomes by analysing how different political games in multiple arenas affect one another. These kinds of rationalist frameworks can explain parts of the negotiating process. But this book argues that additional variables must be introduced to explain fully the behaviour of the applicant countries, and chief among them are processes of Europeanisation. Europeanisation can certainly include calculations of material interest, but it also involves changes in the logic of behaviour of domestic actors and institutions that are driven by the absorption of EU norms.

This book argues that EU accession preparations and negotiations are linked processes, but each is distinct and has its own logic. Negotiations are about 'us and them', a process in which each side seeks the best possible deal. But accession preparations are about 'the future us', a process in which the candidates align with EU norms and try to become like member-states. Europeanisation involves both.

To investigate how Europeanisation works in practice in would-be members of the EU, this book presents two case-studies of the enlargement of the EU to CEE: free movement of persons in the single market; and control of movement of people across the external borders of the Union under the Schengen regime. These case-studies investigate why the applicants adopted EU policies even in areas where the EU's policy logic was contradictory and where the candidate countries had little immediate incentive to comply. Arguments based on material interests cannot fully explain why the candidates continued with processes of Europeanisation in their domestic institutions. The case-studies are concerned with the interface between two processes: the process of Europeanisation through accession preparations, and the process of negotiations. The two cases are of related policy areas in which the EU's negotiating position conflicted with the candidates' interests.

Based on an analysis of the accession conditionality and two case-studies, this book makes the following claims:

- The EU's exercise of influence in the CEE region since 1989 worked principally through the conditionality for accession, which provided a number of different methods of 'Europeanising' the candidates.
- The EU had enormous potential influence in CEE, but its impact was constrained by diffuseness and uncertainty.
- A power-politics explanation is inadequate to account for the outcome of negotiations in two policy areas: free movement of persons, and justice and home affairs. The case-studies present evidence of behaviour that was not based on material interests. In the EU, that behaviour comprised allowing trade-offs in other areas in the negotiations despite its enormous asymmetry of power. It suggests a diffuse norm of accommodating CEE interests was at work.
- For the CEE candidates, the puzzle lies in their continued implementation of EU policies despite the imposition of a transition period and despite high levels of uncertainty. The missing part of the explanation can be accounted for by examining how a logic of adapting to the EU became embedded in domestic policy-making in CEE. The applicants became locked into a process of Europeanisation which had a momentum and logic that existed independently of negotiations.

Their policy-makers became committed to the process because they had already invested considerable sunk costs and political capital into aligning with EU policies, so it became very expensive to withdraw. Moreover, the top-level actors in CEE also became part of the EU political space, which gave them incentives to behave as willing partners to the existing member-states, and socialised them in the political discourse of the Union.

1.1   Europeanisation

This book's approach to studying the EU's effects in the eastern applicant countries uses as its starting-point the growing literature on Europeanisation, but it is not confined to the frameworks developed for studying the EU. Europeanisation is an area of enquiry as much as a concept, and this study is about Europeanisation in the sense that it is concerned with how the EU influenced three particular nation-states – Bulgaria, Hungary and Poland. There are two very important determinants of how these countries reacted to adaptational pressures from the EU: their status as candidates and not full members, and their background as post-communist political systems and economies. The intention in this study is not to define the scope of the enquiry by reference to the existing literature, or to look simply for the same phenomena in Central and Eastern Europe as have been observed within the EU. Rather, it is to use concepts, ideas and methods from the Europeanisation literature.

This book argues that the literature on Europeanisation in the EU is relevant to studying the CEE candidates because they are affected by substantially the same independent variable as the member-states (i.e. the *acquis communautaire*). However, although Europeanisation is a relevant approach, specific features of the EU-CEE relationship must be taken into account, particularly power and uncertainty. Moreover, this study supplements the Europeanisation literature with concepts from elsewhere in political science to provide a full explanation.

'Europeanisation' is a useful term, but also a potentially misleading one. It is a term used in the literature on European integration to mean both the 'downloading' of EU policy into the national polity, and sometimes also the 'uploading' of national preferences to EU level (Börzel 1999). In the case of the CEE countries, the asymmetrical power relationship that they had with the Union as applicants for membership meant that they were mainly downloading policy, with few opportunities for uploading. In the context of post-communist transition, the term

'Europeanisation' is ambiguous, because it implies both the process of joining the EU and also the much wider process of the 'return to Europe' after the revolutions of 1989. This study confines itself to investigating the part of these processes that was driven by accession requirements. As others have observed, this might be more properly called 'EU-isation'. However, there was a very widespread perception in Central and Eastern Europe that the process of 'EU-isation' – meaning the meeting of accession requirements and the adoption of EU norms, policies and institutional models – was strongly connected to the wider processes of modernisation and post-communist transition. For many people in the region, EU-isation was part of, and even a pre-requisite for, the wider Europeanisation of their countries, which meant moving beyond communist legacies and regaining a full role in the European political and economic space. The ambiguity of the term 'Europeanisation' thus usefully captures an important ambiguity in the CEE candidates' attitudes towards alignment with EU norms. It is thus an appropriate concept to use as a starting-point in studying the candidates' relationships with the EU.

EU policies obviously penetrated political systems, but what were the effects of this process? Did the EU change domestic political structures and public policy? If so, what were the mechanisms of change? The literature on Europeanisation seeks to address these questions in the context of the existing EU, so it provides an ideal starting-point for investigating the candidates. There is a lively debate about the impact of 'Europe' on the EU member-states, and a body of empirical research on its effects. This book asks similar questions about the impact of 'Europe' on CEE.

1.2 The structure of this book

This book asks: What was the nature and extent of the accession conditionality for the CEE candidates? How did they respond to the incentives and constraints established by the accession process? How did the EU influence CEE policy and policy-making? What were the limits on this influence? We are concerned here with where conditionality operated, how it worked, and the conditions that determined its success in effecting changes in institutions and public policies in CEE. We are not aiming directly to explain the behaviour of the EU or the evolution of its eastern accession policy. Hence the reader should not expect a detailed analysis of the politics of enlargement among the EU's member-states, or of the policy-making processes by which the EU arrived at its conditions for membership. Instead, this study focuses on what happened after the conditions had been set, analysing the process from the point of view of the applicant countries. However, the accession conditionality requires considerable explanation if its effects are to be understood, so it is analysed in detail from the candidates' perspective.

Chapter 2 provides an overview of eastern accession policy by examining the conditionality, in order to identify how the EU sought to change the CEE candidates. Chapter 3 sets out the analytical framework for the whole study, reviewing the literature on Europeanisation, and introduces the main explanatory concepts which will be used in the case-studies. Chapter 4 analyses the EU side in detail, discussing how the accession process provided the EU with potential routes of influence in CEE and the variables at work on the EU side. Chapter 5 sets out a framework for the case-studies and explains the variables on the CEE side, particularly the experience of post-communist transition and the candidates' strategies. Chapters 6 and 7 present case-studies of two policy areas, respectively free movement of persons under the single market, and regulating movement of persons through the Schengen *acquis*. The substance of the two policy areas covered the same issue (movement of persons in the enlarged EU), but they differed in their degree of political controversy, the policy agenda (both the substance of the agenda and the detail in which it was presented to CEE), and the routes of Europeanisation used. Chapter 8 compares the cases explicitly and explains how EU influence worked. Chapter 9 presents the conclusions.

2
Accession Conditionality and its Implications[1]

The aim of this chapter is to define 'EU influence' as it was exerted through the conditions set by the EU for the CEE candidates. The evolving relationship between the EU and the CEE applicants for membership had three broad phases: the post-1989 trade and aid programmes; then the first pre-accession strategy that began with the Copenhagen commitment to enlargement and ended with the Commission's publication of its opinions (*avis*) on the applicants in 1997; and finally the Accession Partnerships and negotiations from 1998 to 2002. In this third phase, substantive negotiations began in November 1998 with five of the countries (Czech Republic, Estonia, Hungary, Poland and Slovenia), while the other five candidates (Bulgaria, Latvia, Lithuania, Romania and Slovakia) finally joined negotiations in March 2000. All the candidates also went through a process of 'screening' to assess the compatibility of their legislation with EU requirements. All of the CEE candidates finished negotiations in 2002.

However, membership conditionality is not the only way that the EU exerts influence on third countries, so Chapter 4 considers all the other Europeanisation mechanisms that the EU can employ.

2.1   The first phase of EU eastern accession policy 1989–97

1989–93: Trade and aid

In this first phase, relations moved from traditional third-country relations based on aid and trade conditions to the prospect of membership. The EU created the Phare[2] aid programme in 1989, as an aid programme intended to support post-communist transformation in CEE. The EU's initial focus was on economic transition rather than political development. On its establishment in 1989, Phare's primary instrument was direct grants, used to fund technical assistance in a very wide range of areas. Following revision of the pre-accession strategy in 1997, its focus was narrowed to funding accession preparations alone. Initially, the EU used Phare funds to channel advice on economic transformation, with the Commission deliberately confining its conditionality to market-developing measures; however, from 1992 to 1997 a budget line was built in for a democracy programme as well. Conditionality for Phare funds and the technical assistance it provided reinforced the generally neo-liberal agenda that the EU put forward; however, the programme was fragmented as a result of its dependence on consultants under contract, and Phare's overall lack of coherence limited the extent to which it could be used to guide CEE consistently toward particular policy prescriptions.

In 1989, the European Commission was also given the task of co-ordinating aid from the G24 (including the OECD, World Bank, IMF and Paris Club), an unexpected extension of its mandate that it used actively (Sedelmeier and Wallace 1996). The assistance provided included elimination of trade barriers and export promotion for CEE; the Commission also coordinated macroeconomic assistance from other institutions, including medium-term financial assistance for currency stabilisation and balance of payments assistance, and also debt relief (in cooperation with the Paris Club). Through the Commission's role in aid coordination, the EU was thus in a position to channel a wide range of policy advice about transition, both from its own resources and also the international financial institutions and other bodies. This was also the start of a larger role for the Commission than in previous enlargements, as it took responsibility for a major aid programme as well as accession preparations.

The trade side started with the granting of preferential concessions to CEE, followed by different forms of association with the EU devised from the late 1980s, resulting in a hierarchy of new forms of partnership with the CEE countries.[3] Trade and cooperation agreements had been concluded with most CEE countries and the Soviet Union between 1988 and 1990, covering trade and commercial and economic cooperation. Their main importance was symbolic, in removing historical trade discrimination, and the substance of the trade concessions and cooperation was limited (Sedelmeier and Wallace 1996). The agreements bound the CEE countries to progressive abolition of quantitative restrictions on import of EU goods, although they were already in the process of liberalising trade owing to membership of the General Agreement on Tariffs and Trade (GATT, later the World Trade Organisation). For the applicants for membership, these agreements were superseded by the 'Europe Agreements' signed bilaterally from 1991 onwards, which provided a more comprehensive form of partnership than the Association Agreements previously signed with Turkey, Malta and Cyprus.

The main innovation in EU conditionality during this period was the addition of a suspension clause to all Europe Agreements concluded after May 1992 that linked trade and cooperation agreements to five conditions: rule of law, human rights, a multi-party system, free and fair elections, and a market economy. Europe Agreements can be suspended if these conditions are not maintained, but no suspensions have occurred, even after the EU publicly criticised undemocratic practices in Slovakia in 1994 and 1995, reflecting the fact that suspension is seen by the EU as a very last resort.

The content of the Europe Agreements was a set of formally structured trade relations, with a mixed content of both political and economic provisions (see Box 2.1). The Europe Agreements were intended to create a free trade area and to implement the four freedoms of the single market (free movement of goods, services, capital and labour) over a ten-year timetable, and they also provided a general framework for political and economic cooperation, including approximation of legislation; they thus started the process of introducing the EU's legislation and policies to the applicants. The liberalisation was asymmetric, with the EU opening markets for industrial goods within five years and the CEE countries within ten. The Europe Agreements made specific policy demands on CEE through the chapters on trade, on competition, on free movement of workers, and on establishment and supply of services. The trade chapters were the most comprehensive,

---

Box 2.1   Content of the Europe Agreements

1. political dialogue
2. 10-year timetable for liberalisation of trade in industrial goods, on an asymmetric basis and in two stages
3. complex rules for trade in agricultural products
4. titles on movement of workers, freedom of establishment, and supply of services
5. liberalisation of capital movements
6. competition policy
7. 'cooperation' on other economic issues, from energy to education to statistics (areas for technical assistance).[4]

with the annexes to the Europe Agreements giving schedules for removal of trade barriers, including special protocols on 'sensitive' sectors (textiles, iron, coal and steel) and complex restrictions on agricultural trade.

The agenda set by the Europe Agreements was thus generally liberalising, although EU agriculture markets remained protected until accession. The emphasis of the agreements on free movement of the factors essential for the operation of the single market was developed further in the Commission's Single Market White Paper, published in 1995.

1993–97: The Copenhagen conditions and the first pre-accession strategy

The conditions set out at the Copenhagen European Council in 1993 (see Box 2.2) were designed to minimise the risk of new entrants becoming politically unstable and economically burdensome to the existing EU. The conditions were formulated as much to reassure reluctant member-states as to guide CEE, and this dual purpose to conditionality continued to play an important role in the politics of accession within the EU. The fourth condition (quoted in Box 2.2) reflected member-state anxieties about the impact that enlargement might have on EU institutions and policies because of the increase in numbers and diversity, apart from the specific problems that CEE members might bring in; it was a condition for enlargement, whereas the others were conditions for entry.

Box 2.2   The Copenhagen conditions

'Membership requires
▶ that the candidate country has achieved stability of institutions guaranteeing democracy, the rule of law, human rights and respect for and protection of minorities,
▶ the existence of a functioning market economy as well as the capacity to cope with competitive pressure and market forces within the Union.
▶ Membership presupposes the candidate's ability to take on the obligations of membership including adherence to the aims of political, economic and monetary union.
▶ The Union's capacity to absorb new members, while maintaining the momentum of European integration, is also an important consideration in the general interest of both the Union and the candidate countries.'

The Copenhagen conditions were followed by the formal launch of a 'pre-accession strategy' at the Essen European Council in December 1994. The prospect of integrating so many and such different countries provoked a more comprehensive policy approach to enlargement than in previous accessions, although this was slow to evolve.[5] The strategy incorporated earlier agreements and commitments (through the Europe Agreements and Phare) and added some new elements (the Single Market White Paper and the Structured Dialogue). The first two elements set a general framework for adapting to EU requirements, while the latter two were intended to facilitate this process by providing aid and a forum for multilateral discussion.

The pre-accession strategy provided detailed legislative measures for the CEE countries to adopt, but in a limited range of policy areas. It began the process of elaborating the conditions for membership in terms of specific requirements, but in a selective fashion, putting forward only some of the EU's body of law and dealing with the other Copenhagen conditions *ad hoc*. The strategy's content was primarily concerned with liberalisation of external economic relations and creating the conditions for free movement of industrial goods, services and, to some extent, capital; however, it left out the fourth factor of production, labour, and also agricultural policy. The other parts of the legislation which governs the single market were given less attention, and the timetable for taking them on was left unclear, introducing the principle of phased adoption of EU rules. This was a new approach in the EU's history, because the *acquis communautaire* for the single market had previously been regarded as indivisible.[6]

In providing specific demands and aid for changing legislation, the pre-accession strategy had a strong impact on a range of policy processes in CEE. The speed with which different applicant countries met the formal aspects of EU demands through the pre-accession strategy varied, and the extent of implementation was hard to gauge, but the demands set out a policy agenda of sorts for CEE. That agenda was then developed further with publication of the Commission's Opinions on readiness for membership in 1997, and the refocusing of the pre-accession strategy following the publication of 'Agenda 2000' – the Commission's framework from accession policy from 1997 onwards.

The 1995 Single Market White Paper set out the key legislation governing trade in goods and services in the EU's Internal Market. It took the EU's agenda a stage further than the Europe Agreements by introducing measures in a large number of new policy areas. Again, the content set a policy agenda that was generally liberalising (see Box 2.3), although some provisions have been criticised as suboptimal for CEE countries in the process of liberalising their economies; for example, the competition policy provisions are more restrictive than some existing CEE policies (Wilks 1997). In each sector, the White Paper divided the legislation into 'Stage 1' measures, which set out the basic policies essential to the functioning of the single market and the instruments required to implement them, and then 'Stage 2' detailed the implementing rules. The White Paper did not provide an overall prioritisation between sectors, although it made suggestions about sequencing; countries had to make their own distinctions between measures that were required simply for accession and those that were also of immediate benefit to their economies.

Unlike the Europe Agreements, the White Paper was not a legally binding agreement. Nevertheless, the regulatory alignment policy it outlined was a central concern of CEE policy-makers because it gave them a framework and set of concrete measures to implement. Moreover, progress in taking on the measures in the White Paper was judged in the Commission's Opinion as a key element in assessing ability to take on the obligations of membership. The White Paper thus became *de facto* a part of EU conditionality for the applicants, despite its status as a document for guidance rather than a legal framework for relations. The White Paper was also an important step in developing the EU's approach to regulatory harmonisation in CEE. The two-stage approach taken in the White Paper – of allowing the CEE candidates to take on some parts of the regulatory framework before others – was at odds with the internal market's 'policy paradigm' of alignment

---

Box 2.3   Content of the Single Market White Paper

1. free movement of capital
2. free movement and safety of industrial products
3. social policy and action
4. agriculture
5. transport
6. audiovisual
7. environment
8. telecoms
9. taxation
10. free movement of persons
11. public procurement
12. financial services

(Sedelmeier 2001). It left decisions about transition periods after accession to negotiations, and so allowed countries to take on aspects of the single market regulation selectively, and potentially after accession.

1997–98: A reinforced pre-accession strategy and the start of negotiations

The brief overview of the original pre-accession strategy provided above indicates the main thrust of EU demands on applicants in the early years of transition: liberalisation and regulatory harmonisation. In July 1997, a new phase began when the Commission published its Opinions (or *avis* in French) on the applicants' progress in meeting the Copenhagen conditions, and put forward proposals for a 'reinforced' pre-accession strategy based on the Accession Partnerships in 'Agenda 2000', its blueprint for enlargement. The accession part of 'Agenda 2000' was largely endorsed at the Luxembourg European Council of December 1997, although the Community budget proposals were later changed as part of the overall budget negotiations in 1998–99.

The Commission's Opinions gave an overview of the political and economic situations in the ten countries up to May 1997, and also an assessment of how close each might come to being ready to join in five years' time. These Opinions were thus unique in the history of EU enlargements in not merely judging applicants' readiness for membership at that moment, but assessing whether they would be able to meet the conditions for membership within the timespan of negotiations. Each Opinion covered all of the Copenhagen conditions, so there were chapters on the political criteria, the economic criteria, adoption of EU legislation and other aspects of the applicants' ability to 'assume the obligations of membership'. They were based on judgements by the Commission, with little argumentation or evidence presented for the conclusions about readiness.

The Opinions were an important step forward in EU conditionality in two respects: both as a first active application of conditionality and also as an elaboration of the economic conditions to join. First, they provided the basis for the first active application of conditionality on involvement in the accession process, by providing assessments that allowed differentiation between the applicants according to how near they were to meeting the Copenhagen conditions. None of the applicants was judged to have met the economic criteria fully by 1997, but the Council concurred with the Commission's recommendation that negotiations should start with only five of the CEE candidates plus

Cyprus. The 1997 Luxembourg European Council therefore provided the first instance that benefits were granted to or withdrawn from an applicant country explicitly on the basis of the Copenhagen conditionality. Slovakia was the only country excluded on political grounds, although its economy was assessed relatively favourably; Bulgaria, Romania, Latvia and Lithuania were judged not to have met the economic conditions, although the problems of the first two countries were assessed as more serious than the latter two.

Secondly, the Opinions provided an interpretation of the Copenhagen conditions that elaborated the Commission's view (later endorsed by the Luxembourg European Council) of the requirements for becoming an EU member-state. The *avis* judged candidates' progress in conforming to the pre-accession strategy set out by the EU so far, and also in meeting the Copenhagen conditions. In addition, the *avis* were the basis for the priorities elaborated in the Accession Partnerships, and hence the objectives for which the EU would grant aid. They were thus an important step in elaborating the EU's policy agenda for CEE.

2.2   Tightened conditionality 1998–2002

The previous section has shown how EU conditionality for the CEE candidates changed after it was first set in 1993, in both nature and scope. The Copenhagen conditions set in 1993 were very general and open to interpretation, and they were then made progressively more specific and explicit through the pre-accession strategy. The main actor shaping these conditions and defining the requirements in detail was the Commission rather than member-states.

The EU set out its most explicit list of tasks to be undertaken by the candidates in the Accession Partnerships. These resolved a number of questions about what the applicants had to do to make themselves acceptable to the EU, but they also raised further questions. Most important in considering their impact on CEE is the way that the Accession Partnerships limited the scope of negotiations by making a number of potentially negotiable areas part of the conditions, and how they increased the scope of EU involvement in domestic policy-making both relative to the EU's previous role in CEE and also relative to its role in the existing member-states.

The first Accession Partnerships were presented to the applicants in March 1998. New Accession Partnerships were then published in 1999, which were subsequently updated in 2000 and 2001. These documents made the EU's requirements more explicit, and focused aid more closely on accession requirements rather than general development goals. The Accession Partnerships were intended to make conditionality stricter, both on financial assistance through Phare and ultimately on accession itself, by uniting all EU demands and assistance for meeting them in a single framework. They set priorities for policy reforms on a timetable of short- and medium-term priorities. Applicants then prepared 'National Programmes for Adoption of the *Acquis*', which set timetables for achieving the priorities. The Commission subsequently published annual Regular Reports on each candidate's preparations for accession.

The Commission managed the Accession Partnership programmes and monitored implementation; however, member-states insisted that (contrary to the original proposals in Agenda 2000) the Council rather than the Commission should ultimately decide on the application of conditionality. The Council could at any time take 'appropriate steps with regard to any pre-accession assistance granted to any applicant State', acting by qualified majority on a proposal from the Commission, where 'the commitments contained in the Europe Agreements are not respected and/or the progress towards fulfilment of the Copenhagen criteria is insufficient ...'.[7] On the EU side, application of conditionality was complicated by the Accession Partnerships' lack of a specific legal base in the Treaty. The Accession Partnerships were not legally binding for applicant states, as they were unilateral EU measures. However, they made the Copenhagen conditions a quasi-legal obligation by establishing a control procedure and system of sanctions (Hillion 1998), and they rapidly became the main instrument governing EU-CEE relations, making them a strong influence on CEE policy-makers.

The Accession Partnerships also changed conditionality for the Phare programme: before 1998, priorities had been 'demand-driven' and conditionality depended on meeting very general economic and political objectives. However, with the Accession Partnerships, Phare became much more explicitly driven by the Commission, with funds geared specifically towards meeting the priorities set out in the Accession Partnerships. Aid was tied to conditions for accession, not more general transition and development goals; as a result, EU aid policy for CEE moved towards privileging the third Copenhagen condition (the obligations of membership) over the first two (political and economic). Whereas the Phare programme was originally concerned with economic reform and democratisation, under the Accession Partnerships it became primarily concerned with taking on EU legislation and policies.

The Accession Partnerships left the rules of the game uncertain for applicants: what exactly would count as a 'failure to respect the Europe Agreements' or to make progress in fulfilling the Copenhagen criteria? The EU was still left with a large margin in interpreting whether applicants had met the conditions and whether or not relations were satisfactory in the period prior to accession.

The Accession Partnerships also changed the scope of the accession conditionality. Their contents covered a huge range of policy areas, and set a very ambitious agenda for the applicant states, given their financial and administrative resources. They united all the EU's demands, covering not only all of the EU's legislation (as defined by the Commission), but also the other political and economic conditions. The breadth of the agenda set out for the CEE countries is illustrated in Table 2.1, which lists just a small part of the priorities: the economic reform tasks set in the 1998 Accession Partnerships for the short term (to be completed or taken forward in the same year). In addition, applicants had to establish, review or update medium-term economic policy priorities within the framework of the Europe Agreements.[8]

In addition to these economic priorities, there were objectives for the short and medium term in the following areas in 1998:

1. Political criteria. Short-term priorities were set here only for Slovakia (on elections, opposition party participation and minority languages) and Estonia and Latvia (integration of non-citizens and language training); all applicants had some medium-term objectives, such as improving the judicial system and prison conditions (Latvia), protection of individual liberties (Bulgaria) and integration of minorities.
2. Reinforcement of institutional and administrative capacity, including many areas of policy reform, from banking supervision to internal financial control.
3. Internal market. This objective continued many of the measures detailed in the Single Market White Paper, and pushed reform in areas such as liberalisation of capital movements (Poland and Slovenia), adoption of a competition law (Estonia), and adoption of anti-trust laws (Slovenia).
4. Justice and Home Affairs. A priority for all applicants was effective border management with their eastern neighbours, but there were few specific tasks until the 1999 Accession Partnerships (as discussed in Chapter 7).

Table 2.1 Economic reform priorities for the short term

Bulgaria	• privatise state enterprises and banks transparently • restructure industry, financial sector and agriculture • encourage increased foreign direct investment
Czech Republic	• implement policies to maintain internal and external balance • improve corporate governance by accelerating industrial and bank restructuring; implementing financial sector regulation; enforcing Securities and Exchange Commission supervision
Estonia	• sustain high growth rates, reduce inflation, increase level of national savings • accelerate land reform • start pension reform
Hungary	• advance structural reforms, particularly of health care
Latvia	• accelerate market-based enterprise restructuring and complete privatisation • strengthen banking sector • modernise agriculture and establish a land and property register
Lithuania	• accelerate large-scale privatisation • restructure banking, energy and agri-food sectors • enforce financial discipline for enterprises
Poland	• adopt viable steel sector restructuring programme by 30 June and start implementation • restructure coal sector • accelerate privatization/restructuring of state enterprises (including telecoms) • develop financial sector, including banking privatisation • improve bankruptcy proceedings
Romania	• privatise two banks • transform *régies autonomes* into commercial companies • implement foreign investment regime • restructure/privatise a number of large state-owned industrial and agricultural companies • implement agreements with international financial institutions
Slovakia	• tackle internal and external imbalances and sustain macroeconomic stability • make progress on structural reforms • privatise and restructure enterprises, finance, banking and energy-intensive heavy industries
Slovenia	• act on market-driven restructuring in the enterprise, finance and banking sectors • prepare pension reform

5. Environment. All of the candidates had to continue transposition of legislation, and to commence detailed approximation programmes and implementation strategies.

In addition, some candidates had priorities for industrial restructuring, agriculture, property rights, nuclear security and energy. For the medium term, there were additional priorities for fisheries, transport, employment and social affairs, and regional policy and cohesion. The priorities were similar, despite the applicants' different problems, raising the question of how precisely measures had been targeted to individual countries' circumstances.

2.3   Negotiations 1998–2002

Eight of the ten eastern applicants completed accession negotiations at the Copenhagen European Council in December 2002; Bulgaria and Romania completed their negotiations in 2004. The five countries that began in 1998 (Czech Republic, Estonia, Hungary, Poland and Slovenia) made solid progress from the start, forming a 'front-runner group' in the accession marathon. The European Council in Helsinki (December 1999) then decided that the EU should open negotiations with all of the remaining candidates in 2000. This was a surprising outcome, because only Latvia, Lithuania and Slovakia were considered to be making solid progress by the Commission in its Regular Reports of the time.

One reason why the EU was motivated to start negotiations with the second group was in order to reward countries for their support of the NATO operation in Kosovo in Spring 1999. That explanation makes sense in a foreign policy perspective: the coalition of western countries that supported the bombing of Serbia that year needed to reward Bulgaria and Romania for their support of the Kosovo military operations in April 1999, including use of their airspace for bombing raids. This argument was used by some EU politicians as a reason why the two countries at the bottom of the list should be invited to join negotiations. Officials and commentators pointed to the sacrifices that the Bulgarian government had made, particularly maintenance of the economic sanctions and oil embargo on the Federal Republic of Yugoslavia, which had a serious impact on the Bulgarian economy. The Bulgarian government continued its support even in the face of anti-NATO demonstrations in Sofia and widespread public opposition to the bombing campaign. The argument was that Bulgaria should be rewarded, not just through increased levels of international aid, but also politically through the start of accession negotiations. This argument was also used for Slovakia, whose government had been more politically supportive of the Kosovo operations than the Czech Republic, even though the latter was a new NATO member.

It is difficult to assess the counter-factual to this explanation – that is, the question of when the rest of the applicants might have joined negotiations if the bombing of Yugoslavia had not happened. However, the view of many policy-makers involved (and interviewed by the author at the time) was that it tipped the balance in favour of starting negotiations with the remaining candidates. Whatever its overall significance in the accession process, the 'Kosovo reward' factor was certainly important in ensuring that Bulgaria in particular was invited to join negotiations in 2000.

It was unusual for the EU to use accession policy strategically to achieve a foreign policy goal. Moreover, by 2000, the EU's accession policy was already firmly set, owing to the structure of the negotiations and the rules governing Phare and other aid funds. It is generally difficult for the EU to use progress in negotiations or aid strategically to encourage or reward countries for reasons that are not directly related to accession. The Regular Reports in 1999 and 2000 used encouraging language about Bulgaria, and Bulgaria's prospects were improving owing to greater macroeconomic stability, so it was possible for the Commission to argue that Bulgaria had made sufficient progress to warrant negotiations. Romania had made very little progress, and its economy was getting worse, but the Union found it politically difficult to leave only one candidate out of negotiations. Romania's economic and political situation was worsening, but its government was still promising progress. Moreover, the Romanian opposition parties looked even worse in the eyes of EU member-states, which were therefore unwilling to use the gate-keeping sanction against the Romanian government, and hence isolate it.

However, the EU did stick to its principles of readiness, in that it set extra conditions to be met before Bulgaria and Romania could start negotiation: Bulgaria had to set a date for closing down the Kozloduy nuclear power plant, while Romania had to reform its state childcare institutions and improve its macroeconomic situation. The decision to let the two most lagging countries into negotiations was thus partly motivated by political considerations that were not related directly to the accession process, but the EU did use its conditionality to pressure these two candidates to make specific changes to remedy the most pressing problems that had kept them outside.

Readiness for accession by 2002

By 1999, all ten central European candidates had been judged to have met the first political conditions – which were then set as an explicit pre-requisite for starting negotiations at the Helsinki European Council that year. Some of the candidate countries had also made quick progress towards meeting the economic and *acquis* conditions. By 2000, the European Commission's annual 'Regular Reports' on the candidate countries showed that eight out of the ten east European countries were making steady progress towards meeting the economic conditions. In particular, all five countries that started negotiations in 1998 had become functioning market economies and were close to becoming competitive in the single market.

The EU was able to conclude negotiations at the end of 2002 because Latvia, Lithuania and Slovakia caught up fairly quickly with the front-runners, despite starting negotiations two years later. However, Bulgaria and Romania lagged behind, although the Sofia government made better progress than its counterpart in Bucharest. The final two years of negotiations were slowed by hold-ups over the free movement of persons and the allocation of regional funds. Moreover, the member-states started discussing the budgetary costs of enlargement in earnest in Spring 2001 – even though this was not officially on the agenda until the following year. The Commission had previously been left to manage the accession process, but from mid-2001 onwards the member-states started to declare their positions and defend key interests. Once the member-states started entering the end-game of negotiations, the negotiating process became much more unpredictable and subject to domestic politics.

The 31 chapters in negotiations are set out in Table 2.2. However, the chapters were not opened for negotiation in the order listed. Instead, negotiations started with the easiest chapters (such as science and research) and worked up to the most difficult. The five front-runner countries reached the really difficult points in the accession negotiations only in 2001. In the relatively easy chapters completed in 1998–2000, there were many technical issues to be resolved, but no major stumbling-blocks emerged. However, issues such as competition policy, free movement of services, energy and transport all posed problems. Moreover, as previous enlargements had shown – even the relatively smooth accession negotiations with Austria, Finland and Sweden – unexpected difficulties were bound to arise even in seemingly uncontroversial areas.

Table 2.2   The 31 chapters in negotiations

1. Free movement of goods	13. Social policy and employment	23. Consumer and health protection
2. Free movement of persons	14. Energy	24. Justice and home affairs
3. Freedom to provide services	15. Industrial policy	25. Customs union
4. Free movement of capital	16. Small and medium-sized enterprises	26. External relations
5. Company law	17. Science and research	27. Common foreign and security policy
6. Competition and state aids	18. Education, training and youth	28. Financial control
7. Agriculture	19. Telecommunications and information technologies	29. Financial and budgetary provisions
8. Fisheries		30. Institutions (of the Union)
9. Transport policy	20. Culture and audiovisual policy	31. Other
10. Taxation	21. Regional policy and coordination of structural instruments	
11. Economic and monetary union	22. Environment	
12. Statistics		

At the Nice European Council in December 2000, the EU's member-states expressed the hope that the first accessions could take place in time for new members to participate in the next European Parliament elections in June 2004. But this was not a firm commitment to a target-date, as German and French policy-makers were quick to point out: a protocol to the Treaty on European Union allowed applicants to take part in European elections before accession. The Gothenburg European Council in June 2001 removed this ambiguity and potential excuse for delay, stating the EU's 'objective' that some candidates participate in the 2004 elections 'as members'. The Gothenburg conclusions also re-affirmed the goal of concluding negotiations with the best-prepared candidates in 2002. The Swedish Presidency had to fight hard at Gothenburg to overcome German and French opposition to setting a firmer target-date. Both countries were facing elections in 2002, and were nervous about declining public support for enlargement. The German government was also concerned about the impact of a firmer date on Poland's prospects for early membership. The Gothenburg conclusions officially re-affirmed the principle of 'differentiation', whereby each applicant country should proceed at its own pace. But a number of senior German policy-makers were concerned that Poland should not be left behind in the first accessions as a result of such differentiation. A large majority of the other member-states supported the firmer date commitment, partly because they were rattled by the negative

Table 2.3   **Referendum results (per cent of valid votes cast)**

	Yes	No	Turnout (per cent of electorate)
Malta	54	46	91
Slovenia	90	10	60
Hungary	84	16	46
Lithuania	91	9	63
Slovakia	93	7	52
Poland	77	23	59
Czech Republic	77	23	55
Estonia	67	33	64
Latvia	67	33	73
Cyprus	No referendum on membership		

result of the Irish referendum on the Treaty of Nice. The re-affirmation of the timetable and the clearer target-date were an attempt by the member-states to keep up the momentum of the accession process.

However, the timing of enlargement remained uncertain even after the EU set a date for the first accessions: 1 May 2004. After the successful completion of negotiations, every member-state parliament and the European Parliament had to approve each accession treaty. The whole process could have been blocked by just one member-state's parliament if it threw out the accession treaty. In the event, all of the member-states ratified the accession treaties for the ten countries which entered in 2004.

The candidates had to approve the accession treaty as well, and all of them except Cyprus decided to have a referendum on EU membership. However, the rejection of membership by one candidate country's public would not have stopped the process; it would just have ruled out that country's participation in the 2004 enlargement. This fact made for a major asymmetry of power between the electorates of the candidate countries and member-states. In the event, all of the candidate countries passed their accession treaties in the referenda of 2003 – with only Malta doing so by a small margin (as shown in Table 2.3).

2.4   Deconstructing the EU's accession agenda

The Accession Partnerships opened up a large policy-making agenda that pushed through some fundamental reforms relatively quickly. For most of the applicants, their introduction meant that the EU started taking over as the key external driver of reform. Until 1997, there had been a widespread perception in CEE that the EU was not having much of an impact on fundamental parts of the transition process – such as privatisation and budgetary consolidation – in comparison with the international financial institutions (IFIs – principally the World Bank and International Monetary Fund) and domestic factors. However, the more specific and wide-ranging agenda set out by the Accession Partnerships, and the closer conditionality of EU financing on these objectives, changed this situation from 1998 onwards by increasing the EU's influence on the process of institutional and policy reform in CEE. For the first five CEE applicants that started negotiations in 1998, the IFIs' role was diminishing at the same time as the EU's role started growing. In any case, the IFIs had more limited policy aims for post-communist countries, such as macroeconomic stabilisation (in the case of the IMF) or development goals (in the case of the World Bank) than did the EU. IFI policies generally restrain the redistributive functions of states, but they are not so concerned with regulatory functions; by contrast the EU started with the latter and rapidly began to cover the former as well.

The Accession Partnerships extended EU-level influence over policy-making to an extent that went beyond the EU's role in the domestic policy processes of its member-states. These documents covered EU-level policies that had not been adopted by all member-states (such as Schengen and monetary union) and their content went beyond the *acquis*, because they also included the first two Copenhagen conditions (political and macro-economic). Although only some policy domains have moved to supranational level in the EU (Stone Sweet and Sandholtz 1997), in the agenda presented to CEE the distinctions between Community and national competences that are constantly debated within the EU were not acknowledged. Indeed, the Accession Partnerships covered several areas where member-states had long been very resistant to extending Community competence. The political criteria took the EU into areas such as judicial reform and prison conditions; the economic criteria were interpreted to include areas such as reform of pension, taxation and social security systems, and corporate governance; and the measures for 'administrative capacity to apply the *acquis*' brought EU conditions to civil service reform in CEE. The EU also had an impact on the applicants' foreign policies – especially towards their eastern neighbours – owing to the justice and home affairs measures in the Accession Partnerships and separate readmission agreements (as discussed in Chapter 7).

Through the Accession Partnerships, the EU started influencing both regulation and redistribution, which are normally policy preserves of the nation-state. However, it covered the first far more than the second. The pre-accession strategy as a whole (from the Europe Agreements to the Single Market White Paper to the Accession Partnerships) set out a detailed regulatory agenda for CEE, reflecting the fact that the EU's own key governance function is regulating social and political risk rather than resource redistribution (Hix 1998). The CEE accession policies were much less detailed in areas that lie outside regulatory policy; for example, the content frequently comprised exhortations for 'major efforts' to improve or strengthen policies and institutions, without the means being specified. The emphasis at this stage was on having coherent policies and functioning institutions, rather than the EU specifying prescriptions for policy content. The detail was then filled in by each country's authorities in the 'National Programme for Adoption of the *Acquis*' which it prepared; this method put the onus on the applicants to decide how to meet the objectives specified by the EU. However, the EU's preferences in policy content did emerge through which projects received Phare funding and in the Commission's annual Regular Reports on each country's progress.

Despite their lack of detail, however, the Accession Partnerships did contain implicit policy models for CEE. This was most evident on the economic side, where the thrust of the agenda was neo-liberal, emphasising privatisation of the means of production, a reduction in state involvement in the economy (particularly industry), and further liberalisation of the means of exchange. Considering the variety of models of capitalism to be found among EU member-states, the Accession Partnerships promoted a remarkably uniform view of what a 'market economy' should look like. The socio-economic system they implicitly endorsed had a more 'Anglo-Saxon' flavour than the 'Rhenish' social market economies of France or Germany or the 'Latin' economic systems in the southern EU.[9] There was little attention to the role of networks between social partners in the economy or to industrial policy, for example. The priorities were largely anti-interventionist, although the role of appropriate regulation was recognised in response to the inadequacies that had emerged over the previous few years in CEE, particularly in corporate governance.

However, no explicit rationale was presented for this agenda, even though it covered so many functions of the modern state. The conditions were presented as if they were self-evident, with no acknowledgement of the policy debates going on in the EU and outside about the appropriate role of the state in the economy and alternative models of corporate governance. It would have been possible to make convincing arguments as to why many of the Accession Partnership measures were necessary in CEE; for example, the need to reduce the power of social networks to promote competition, and the problems caused by lack of appropriate regulation of the financial sector in several countries. However, no such rationale was presented publicly. Even though this was such a wide agenda from such an important external influence, there was no detailed justification for these demands beyond the fact that they came in the name of joining the EU.

2.5 The political context for accession policy in the EU

This section gives an overview of the political dynamics at work in the late 1990s among the principal EU actors involved in accession policy. More detailed analyses of the development of eastern accession policy in the 1990s are provided by Mayhew (1998), Sedelmeier (1998), Sedelmeier and Wallace (2000) and Sedelmeier (2000).

The more detailed accession conditions that emerged after 1997 were designed during a period of debate among EU member-states that was not characterised by enthusiasm for a large increase in the policy areas covered by Community competence. The Inter-governmental Conference (IGC) of 1996–97 was intended to decide on institutional reforms to prepare the Union for enlargement; however, its deliberations demonstrated the lack of consensus among member-states over institutional reform as a whole, and the final phase of negotiations showed a decreasing willingness on the part of even traditionally integrationist member-states to increase the powers of EU institutions.[10] The subsequent European Councils did not indicate any increase in member-states' willingness to give the Commission new powers. As one commentator on the Amsterdam Treaty put it, 'The overall impression left by the Treaty is ... that the Commission is still not entirely trusted to observe the rules of the game.' (Ludlow 1997).

However, in policy towards CEE candidates, member-states continued to prefer that the Commission take the lead in formulating the pre-accession strategy even after 1997, with the important exception of the most sensitive area of justice and home affairs. The rotating presidency of the Union continued to set the priorities for the Union every six months – including in enlargement policy – but the day-to-day management of the accession process was largely left to the

European Commission. The member-states played a role in the process sporadically, and they took an increasing interest in it in the last two years of the accession negotiations. However, for seven years or so, the principal agent in accession policy was the Commission, and it had a wide margin for interpreting the very general conditions set by the European Council through the pre-accession conditionality. From 2001 onwards, however, the member-states came back into the process because the negotiations reached the most politically sensitive areas for the EU, such as free movement of labour and common policies with budgetary implications (particularly the Common Agricultural Policy).

Why did the member-states sanction such an increase in the Commission's mandate in this area? This section explores the various factors which led to this outcome, most of which relate to the member-states' interests in the enlargement process.

The Commission's role in the accession process

An important innovation in eastern enlargement policy was the degree to which the EU developed a pre-accession strategy well before the negotiations began. In previous enlargements, the main focus of preparations for membership was the accession negotiations themselves. However, in the case of the eastward enlargement, the large number of candidates, their state of political and economic development, and their distance from EU norms necessitated a much more elaborate pre-accession strategy than in previous enlargements, and this meant a correspondingly greater role for the Commission. The Commission was the actor which mainly devised and managed the pre-accession policies that preceded and ran in tandem with the formal negotiations.

In accession negotiations, the Commission has no formal role in legal terms. A bilateral Inter-governmental Conference between the member-states and a candidate country carries out the accession negotiations. The member-states ask the Commission only to facilitate the negotiations, particularly by submitting draft common positions (DCPs) to the Council Working Group on Enlargement; the member-states then define EU Common Positions based on these draft positions from the Commission. Normally, the DCPs are drafted by DG Enlargement, based on input from the relevant line DG(s). The Commission services typically have close informal contacts with both the candidate country and the member-states. The Commission is duty-bound to protect the Community interest, but it also looks for solutions that take due account of the specific circumstances of the candidate country. This is the most concrete aspect of the Commission's facilitation role.

The Commission has no formal power to withdraw its proposal or to stop the member-states from adopting a position with which the Commission disagrees. The Commission only has the 'soft power' of its technical expertise and knowledge of the candidate countries. To preserve this power, the Commission has to win over the member-states time and again, by demonstrating its expertise is superior to that of the member-states. During the eastward enlargement process, the Commission succeeded in demonstrating its added value, and the member-states did not adopt positions to which the Commission was opposed. Moreover, the Commission managed to gain a vastly increased role in the accession conditionality through its management of the pre-accession strategy, again because it demonstrated its greater knowledge of the candidate countries.

The Commission's functional argumentation

The member-states seem largely to have accepted the Commission's argumentation that functional reasons as well as institutional ones required a new approach to accession based on stricter conditionality and a closer linking of the different elements of the pre-accession strategy. The Commission thus remained at the centre of the growing enlargement process, resulting in a degree of 'mission creep'.

Similarly, the extension of the Commission's mandate can be interpreted as a functional response to the increasing complexity of the conditionality. The task of preparing these accessions presented an unprecedented technical challenge: it involved preparing twelve sets of negotiations and monitoring all the applicants' preparations, stretching Commission resources both in Brussels and in the delegations in the applicant countries. The solution to the problem of an increasingly diverse agenda was the linking together of the tasks of setting conditions, monitoring preparations and disbursement of aid, which itself favoured concentrating responsibility for the whole process in a single agency.

A further factor favouring the emergence of a single coordinating instrument was the need to remedy perceived weaknesses of the original pre-accession policy. There was support both within the Commission and among member-states for re-focusing the pre-accession strategy. Criticism of the original pre-accession strategy, and particularly the Phare programme, from within the Union and from the applicants had led to calls for EU aid to be focused more carefully, with greater policy coherence and a more 'efficient' use of funds. A logical way to achieve this was to focus Phare more closely on accession issues, steering away from the previous problems of fragmentation and dependence on western consultants. The Commission found the solution in the Accession Partnerships, which linked aid to accession conditions directly and set priorities at the EU end rather than through the 'demand-driven' process that had previously operated.

The Accession Partnerships extended the Commission's mandate further by giving it responsibility for setting priorities, reviewing the applicants' progress in meeting objectives, and recommending whether candidates should be in negotiations or not. Although final decisions on applying conditionality (either on aid or accession) were left to the Council, the Commission largely determined the agenda by overseeing the whole process and managing the programmes. Responsibility for aid programmes effectively put at least some of the conditionality in the Commission's hands; for example, in 1998 the Commission decided to cut Phare assistance to Poland by 34 million euro, having rejected proposed projects as not meeting the priorities set out in the Accession Partnership for Poland.[11] In this way, the parallel operation of the Accession Partnerships alongside negotiations gave the Commission a much larger influence over accession terms than had been the case in previous enlargements. Partly because the Commission was largely responsible for managing the enlargement process, accession policy became increasingly technical in nature – focused on meeting EU norms and standards. As discussed in the next chapter, this approach affected the 'goodness of fit' between EU policies and pre-existing CEE policies and institutions, and therefore the effects of Europeanisation in different policy areas.

Ambivalence about enlargement

From the beginning of eastern accession policy, there was a lack of strategy and coherence in the EU's approach, largely because of the dearth of political leadership in the EU on how to deal with the aftermath of 1989. The EU was slow to respond to the end of the Cold War and many member-states were reluctant to commit themselves to the accession of post-communist CEE. This unwillingness to take political responsibility for enlargement led the member-states to delegate much of accession policy-making to the Commission in practice.

During the IGC and after Amsterdam, several key member-states became increasingly ambivalent about the social and economic effects of enlargement, and the impact on EU policies and institutions. Most importantly, the driver of the enlargement project in the early 1990s, Germany, saw increasing public debate about the potentially negative effects of enlargement on the German economy, labour markets and agriculture. The federal election campaign of 1997–98 included the issues of migration from CEE, wage competition, and the budgetary implications of enlargement. The response from the Kohl government was proposals to restrict movement of workers after accession, and further reassurances that enlargement should not result in an increase in German contributions to the Community budget (see Bulmer, Jeffery and Paterson 2000). Similarly, the Austrian debate became increasingly preoccupied with the issues of migration and border control, and correspondingly more hostile towards enlargement.

There was a parallel debate about the impact of enlargement on the Community budget and EU institutions. Net recipients from EU policies also became more openly opposed to the prospect of losing budgetary transfers. Proposals for reform of the regional funds and the common agricultural policy in Agenda 2000 galvanised lobbying efforts and intensified debate about the costs of enlargement. At the same time, member-states were reluctant to address institutional reform. Difficult decisions were postponed by adding a protocol to the Amsterdam Treaty requiring another IGC before the number of new member-states exceeded five, although several member-states (Belgium, France and Italy) immediately argued for further institutional reform as a prerequisite for even the first accessions.[12]

This reluctance to confront the challenges posed by enlargement led the member-states to favour ever stricter accession conditionality. By arguing that the CEE countries had to be ready to join, the member-states put the emphasis on the applicants conforming to the EU, rather than the EU reforming itself to fit new members. Fears of the consequences of enlargement also encouraged an approach based on reducing its social and economic impact by demanding full compliance by the applicants in advance of accession. This approach also implied that there was less to negotiate, if the priority was on minimising the implications for the EU rather than for CEE.

At the same time, there was a sense that there was no reason to hurry the process of enlargement. The alternative of a rapid accession process and long transitional arrangements had been rejected in the early 1990s, partly as a result of CEE insistence on full rather than partial membership, and the Commission's technocratic approach prevailed rather than one based on geo-strategic considerations. The difficult negotiations on institutional reform at the end of the IGC in 1997 encouraged member-states to plan a longer timetable for the first accessions, to give the EU longer to prepare itself. As a result, when the Commission put forward Accession Partnerships which emphasised implementation of the whole *acquis communautaire* and strict conditionality, it did not meet with opposition from the member-states that wished to hurry the whole process along.

Consensus on the agenda for the candidates

The extension of the Commission's role in setting such a wide political and economic agenda for CEE went unopposed for another reason: the content of the Accession Partnerships generally accorded with the member-states' interests. There was no significant disagreement in the Council with the Commission's draft Accession Partnerships, although some minor adjustments to their content were made in the Council of Ministers. According to an account prepared by the French parliament (Assemblée Nationale 1998), seven of the then 15 member-states approved the drafts submitted by the Commission. Germany (supported by France) proposed further provisions on justice and home affairs cooperation. Likewise, France (supported on some points by the Netherlands) argued in favour of sharpening a number of points in the draft Accession Partnerships, including a greater stress on measures to combat corruption and crime, on restructuring of metallurgy, coal and agriculture, and on respect for the constitution and independence of the media in Slovakia. Overall, however, there were no strong objections to the contents, and amendments proposed by the member-states tended to reinforce rather than ease demands on the candidates.

The content of key documents like the Accession Partnerships coincided with the member-states' interests in three spheres: the first was the broad consensus about the desirable shape of political and economic systems in CEE. In so far as they speeded transition, the Accession Partnerships accorded with the goal of increasing stability and prosperity in CEE. Throughout the pre-accession phase, member-states rarely disagreed with the Commission's interpretation of the Copenhagen conditions; for example, in 1997, the European Council at Luxembourg accepted the Commission's recommendations to start negotiations with only five CEE applicants plus Cyprus. This agreement to differentiate between candidates in negotiations was not reached without controversy – for example, Denmark and Sweden opposed the exclusion of Latvia and Lithuania from the first group to start negotiations. However, the Commission's overall ranking of the applicants' readiness to join was accepted by member-states; it accorded both with the consensus about progress in transition and also with general geo-political priorities among the applicants. Germany's priority to the accession of Poland, Hungary and the Czech Republic coincided with their perceived front-runner status in transition, while Estonia and Slovenia were seen as small and relatively uncomplicated to integrate.

The second interest was the desire to avoid long transition periods on the CEE side. A widespread view was that derogations or long transition periods of the kind negotiated by the Mediterranean applicants should not be on offer. As the French parliament report put it on transition periods, '... l'Union ... ne concédera pas dix-sept ans comme elle l'avait fait pour l'Espagne ... mais tout au plus cinq ans ... dans quelques secteurs bien délimités', and for this reason, '[les candidats] devront faire l'effort essentiel pendant la période de pré-adhésion ...'.[13] This was a common view among EU policy-makers, but it was not a sufficient justification in itself. Why should CEE candidates not receive the same latitude as previous applicants in taking on obligations after accession? The scale of the challenge that these applicants faced in transition provided an argument that they should be given additional concessions, not fewer than those enjoyed by previous joiners.

Thirdly, a number of member-states wanted faster movement from the CEE candidates in addressing issues such as nuclear safety and border controls – which caused concern in member-states bordering the candidates, such as Austria. Some member-states thus welcomed the chance to increase pressure on the CEE countries to act more rapidly in these areas; in turn, that raised the support for stricter conditionality and a focus on EU priorities rather than the overall economic transition of the region.

2.6 Analytical difficulties in interpreting the EU's accession conditionality

The moving target problem: what exactly do applicants have to do before they can join?

The Copenhagen conditions were not a straightforward case of conditionality, and they differed from the traditional conditionality used by IFIs such as the development banks. In its simplest formulation, IFI conditionality links perceived benefits to the fulfilment of certain conditions. In the case of IMF and World Bank finance, conditionality is primarily linked to the implementation of specific economic policies, such as structural adjustment, and the main benefit is financial. It is a means of ensuring the execution of a contract, 'a promise by one party to do something now in exchange for a promise by the other party to do something else in the future', as an analysis of World Bank conditionality puts it (Mosley *et al.* 1991, p. 65). By contrast, the EU's demands on the CEE applicants were not just a set of conditions to receive defined benefits, but an evolving process. The linkage between fulfilling particular tasks and receiving particular benefits was much less clear than in IFI conditionality because the tasks were complex and many of them were not amenable to quantitative targets that showed explicitly when they had been fulfilled. This added to the uncertainties inherent in the accession process, discussed in Chapter 4.

The moving target problem existed in all the Copenhagen conditions for entry. The first two required definitions of what constituted a 'democracy', a 'market economy' and 'the capacity to cope with competitive pressure and market forces' – all highly debatable and slippery concepts. The EU never provided an explicit definition of these concepts, although there were implicit assumptions about their content in the Commission's formal 'Opinions' on each candidate's readiness for membership (published in 1997) and annual reports on their progress. There was thus no published rationale for how various EU demands would bring applicants closer to West European political and economic norms. The third condition on the 'obligations of membership' was problematic because of the question of what exactly the form and content of the accession *acquis* would be in the final stages of negotiations – as discussed below. Formal alignment with the *acquis* in legal and institutional terms was the most measurable dimension of the accession process, because observers could count how many laws had been rewritten or introduced. Likewise, they could see how many chapters had been opened, provisionally closed, or 'set aside' for later consideration. The media, particularly in the candidate countries, often focused on these measurable dimensions of the process in their coverage as a result. This focus reinforced the candidate countries' efforts on getting chapters provisionally closed, and opening new ones, in order to demonstrate their progress – even though closing chapters did not guarantee an earlier date for accession, and provisionally closed chapters could be re-opened later in negotiations.

The EU influenced policy-making at different levels of government through multiple channels, and it was far from being a unitary actor in the CEE countries. Different parts of the EU – both its institutions and member-states – gave different advice and signals, and different actors even in the same institution did so as well (for example, individual directorates-general within the European Commission stressed different tasks). At the same time, CEE policy-makers were dealing with pre-accession advisors from national administrations, Commission officials, national experts from the Council, and civil servants and politicians from individual member-states, plus a range of joint parliamentary committees, and representatives from the European Parliament and the Economic and Social Committee. It was thus hardly surprising that they were often unsure exactly what the EU's requirements were and who really spoke for the Union.

What is the accession *acquis*?

Even the supposedly firm *acquis* attached to the third condition, on the 'obligations of membership', was open to interpretation. In previous enlargements, the obligations of membership were solely the implementation of the existing '*acquis communautaire*.' For the 1995 EFTA enlargement, the 'obligations of membership' were to take on the *acquis communautaire* as it applied to the present member-states.[14] The term '*acquis communautaire*' had been used in previous accessions to refer to 'the whole body of EU rules, political principles and judicial decisions which new Member-states must adhere to, in their entirety and from the beginning, when they become members of the Communities' (Gialdino 1995, p. 1090). Similarly, the *acquis* had been defined for this enlargement by the Commission as 'all the real and potential rights and obligations of the EU system and its institutional framework'.[15] The total was more than 80,000 pages of legislative texts, but the *acquis* was not clearly defined and it implied an evolving set of demands.

This policy became known as 'the *acquis*, the whole *acquis* and nothing but the *acquis*' among policy-makers; but it was never really credible. François Lamoureux, a senior Commission official, was widely reported to have commented in 1993 that no member-state had implemented more than 80% of the *acquis*. This statistic was often quoted by CEE policy-makers, many of whom asked 'How can the EU ask us for 100% compliance prior to accession, when the much richer member-states have not managed it?'

Moreover, the *acquis* is a dynamic concept because the body of legislation grows all the time through Treaty change, adoption of legislative measures (including resolutions, declarations and other measures, including inter-governmental agreements), international agreements and the jurisprudence of the European Court of Justice. In addition, the edges of the *acquis* remain fuzzy in legal terms because parts of it are open to interpretation. It is more than just its formal institutional framework; it develops as a result of processes that inform debates over policy substance and agenda-setting, such as policy practices (Wiener 1998). It is thus open to minimalist and maximalist interpretations, and these in turn affected the demands made on CEE applicants.

Presentation of the substance of the *acquis* was critical to defining the conditions for entry. In previous enlargements, the room for interpreting the *acquis* allowed a margin for negotiating what were effectively derogations, but not called as such (Nicolaides and Boean 1997). The EU presented a maximalist interpretation to the applicants. For example, the Commission argued that the social dialogue was part of the *acquis* for the applicants, even though not all member-states accept it.[16] The candidates also had to take on the EU's 'soft law' of nonbinding resolutions and recommendations. Moreover, CEE countries had no possibility of negotiating opt-outs such as those which applied to some member-states on Schengen and Stage 3 of monetary union.

Interpretation of this third condition, like the others, was mostly left to the Commission. However, there were some areas deemed too politically sensitive by the member-states to be left to the Commission; for example, the Council of Ministers set up its own working group to establish the accession *acquis* in the area of justice and home affairs (discussed further in Chapter 7).

Insistence on maintaining the integrity of the *acquis* had made the EU a tough and unyielding negotiating partner for previous applicants (Michalski and Wallace 1992), and a widespread view among EU officials was that CEE applicants had to join the EU club on this same principle. But in policy debates in the 1990s, others argued that this 'club membership' view of eastward enlargement was an inadequate response by the EU to the unprecedented challenge of post-communist transition, because the CEE candidates needed more help than previous joiners.

However, the Copenhagen conditions implied that applicants had to meet higher standards than did present member-states. Current members had not been judged on these conditions, and they had been able to negotiate opt-outs from parts of the *acquis* which were not available to CEE applicants. By contrast, CEE candidates were expected to meet the conditions fully, in advance, without opt-outs, and in the absence of reciprocal commitments from the EU to prepare for enlargement. This opening stance was a negotiating position, of course, intended to encourage compliance by CEE, and in practice both sides wanted transition periods on different issues. However, the EU's inflexible stance raised a question of double standards that aroused resentment in CEE, and later played a role in their domestic political debates about EU accession in the early 2000s.

The EU's twofold role in CEE: aid donor and club owner

The EU played a twofold role in the process of post-communist transformation in CEE: on the one hand, the EU was an aid donor imposing conditions on relations with third countries that were intended to benefit them by supporting post-communist transformation of economies and societies. Yet on the other hand, it was guiding these countries towards membership, which required creating incentives and judging progress in taking on specific EU models.

How compatible were these goals? The assumption in much of the language used in official EU publications on enlargement was that accession and transition were part of the same process and that preparations to join the EU were coterminous with overall development goals. There are reasons to be sceptical about this assumption: EU policies and regulatory models were created to fit economies and societies at a very different level of development, and they contain anomalies that are the outcome of a bargaining process between different interests and traditions. They were not designed for countries in transition, and they often require a complex institutional structure for implementation that was little developed in CEE. EU models in at least some policy areas were sub-optimal for the applicants; for example, the competition policy model implied by the EU's conditions for CEE was probably not appropriate for post-communist countries, given the forms of corporate governance emerging in the region (Wilks 1997). Moreover, the EU's emphasis on regulatory alignment had potential contradictions with the process of economic restructuring. Politically, the EU was moving in the 1990s towards taking regulation of the single market as its primary role, and relying on coordination in most other areas (McGowan and Wallace 1996). It thus lacked the wide experience of a development agency role that would have been more suitable to guiding CEE transition.

Implications of the Accession Partnerships for negotiations

The Accession Partnerships were the first list of specific demands that the EU put forward for the accession of the CEE candidates, and also for interim benefits in the accession process such as aid and participation in negotiations. They therefore provided an elaboration and clarification of the conditions for membership; however, they also affected interpretation of the accession conditions and negotiations.

The first issue is the impact of the Accession Partnerships on the process of negotiations and the relative bargaining power of the EU and the applicants. Because their implementation ran in parallel with the screening and negotiating processes, they downgraded the status of bilateral negotiations. Having an annual programme running in parallel reduced the negotiators' flexibility in deciding what might be subject to compromise on both the CEE and EU sides, because the Accession Partnerships presented the conditions as a package which was difficult to take apart in negotiations. The CEE applicants had little power to argue against EU demands, because there was a pre-set EU agenda on which aid was already conditional. Although the Accession Partnerships were supposed to be 'partnerships', decided in collaboration with each applicant, in practice the process of consultation involved only cursory attention to CEE objections to either the content or sequencing of demands. Effectively, the Accession Partnerships added further and more specific conditions to the EU's list of demands, and they gave the EU an even stronger position in the event of a conflict of interests by adding sanctions in the form of withdrawal of aid funds.

In previous enlargements, accession terms had been a bargained outcome, and negotiations resulted in special arrangements in areas such as external trade conditions and aid to third countries (Redmond and Rosenthal 1998). But in the eastward enlargement, the Accession Partnerships set detailed objectives for CEE that pre-judged the negotiations. Partly this was because of the expansion of the *acquis* to cover many more policy areas than in previous enlargements; however, the Accession Partnerships pre-judged the accession terms in areas outside the *acquis* as well, reducing the scope of negotiations to agreeing transition periods.

The second issue is the scope of EU policy. Through the Accession Partnerships, member-states gave the Commission competences in CEE that they had never accepted for themselves, as discussed above. Moreover, these competences were extended without any of the justificatory and restraining principles that apply in the EU, such as subsidiarity, proportionality and competence, or the involvement of restraining institutions. The only monitoring function for accession policy during negotiations was performed by the Council, with no role for the European Court of Justice, very little for the European Parliament (until the assent procedure for the accession treaties) or national parliaments (until ratification of the treaties). Despite the EU's insistence that applicants must be democracies, the EU itself had very little democratic accountability built into the accession process until after treaties had already been signed with CEE – at which point parliaments had a right of veto. Accession policy was still treated as an aspect of external relations with third countries, even though its effects in CEE were much more like the EU's relationship with existing member-states. There was thus a paradox in EU-CEE relations: applicants were treated like member-states in the extent of their obligations under the Accession Partnerships, but as applicants they had no rights and little say in determining the substance of relations, leaving the EU as an increasingly hegemonic actor in the region.

Conclusions

This chapter has investigated and analysed the EU's policy agenda for CEE, in order to define the pressures for Europeanisation created through the accession process. The EU's policy agenda for CEE was innovative in the history of European integration in that it went further than the agenda for any previous applicant. However, its development was an iterated process whereby the conditions were changed and reshaped over the pre-accession period. It was an often ambiguous conditionality, because the EU is a complex constellation of actors who often maintain ambiguity to gain agreement among themselves. For these two reasons, the conditionality was difficult to interpret for the applicants, and the researcher has to go to some lengths to 'deconstruct' the EU's agenda for the candidates before trying to analyse its impact.

The conditions for joining the EU looked deceptively straightforward: an aspirant member had to be a stable democracy and competitive market economy, and demonstrate it was willing and able to take on all EU policies, both present and future. These conditions might seem self-evident, a set of 'motherhood and apple pie' criteria to which no European could object. But it was evident that one of their aims was to reassure EU states that the eastern candidates would look like familiar, West European countries, not bringing instability, authoritarianism or economic collapse into the Union.

The independent variable described in this chapter is a complex one, because the accession *acquis* was defined broadly, and its implications for conditionality and the scope of EU influence in CEE raise a number of questions for investigation in the case-studies. In addition to the implications for the accession process discussed above, there is the question of what room for manoeuvre the applicants had in implementing the Accession Partnerships. Although the priorities were listed and the timetable for implementing the short-term ones was set clearly, the EU still had considerable scope for interpretation in deciding whether or not they had been fulfilled.

On the CEE side, there was also scope for countries to vary the speed with which they acted on some of the priorities. For example, in 1998, Romania was told to 'privatise two banks' by the end of that year (so it was fairly straightforward to judge how much progress had been made), but the Czech Republic was told to 'improve corporate governance' (progress was much harder to gauge, and clearly 1998 could only be the start of a longer-term process). Hence the level of detail at which the EU specifies its agenda is an important determinant of the extent of EU influence.

3
Europeanisation, Negotiations and Influence

The previous chapter has shown that the EU mattered in central and eastern European policy-making. But how? The applicants had to take on all the obligations of EU membership. Therefore the transfer of EU policies and institutions was likely to have comparable domestic effects in the applicant countries to those in the existing member-states even though the political relationship was different. This chapter provides the analytical framework for the book, situating the approach used in the case-studies within the literature on 'Europeanisation'.

The chapter proceeds as follows: Section 3.1 sets out a *prima facie* case for comparing the study of Europeanisation within the Union with the EU's effects in CEE, arguing that the effects are likely to have been similar in nature to those in the existing member-states, but broader and deeper in scope. The Europeanisation literature is used as the starting-point for building a conceptual framework to examine the EU's effects on the CEE candidates, because these countries were already subject to substantially the same pressures of adaptation to EU policies as current member-states. The term 'Europeanisation' is used throughout this book in the sense of the EU's impact on countries, not bilateral pressures between states.

Section 3.2 summarises academic research on Europeanisation and discusses how it should be applied as a conceptual framework to studying CEE accession. Europeanisation mechanisms identified in the literature on the EU are likely to have operated for applicant countries too, given that the same policy structures and implementation procedures were used; formally, the main independent variable (the *acquis communautaire*) is the same in both cases.

However, there were two major differences in the case of CEE: the first was the wider scope of the EU's agenda in the first eastward enlargement, which went far beyond the *acquis* because there were also political and economic conditions attached to membership for the CEE countries, unlike for previous applicants. The second was the political context of a power relationship between the EU and the individual countries that was based on conditionality. Section 3.3 analyses the relationship between the EU and the candidates. The accession process gave the EU more coercive routes of influence in domestic policy-making processes in CEE (because the applicants faced conditionality) than it had in the existing member-states. Section 3.4 introduces further concepts that are used in the case-studies to clarify and explain the EU's approach and the response of the CEE candidates. These concepts are policy transfer, goodness of fit, policy type, institutional isomorphism, policy paradigms, and agenda-setting.

Chapter 4 will then discuss in more detail the main routes by which the EU could influence public policy-making in the candidate countries, and the constraints on that influence. Chapter 5 then sets out the structure of the case-studies that follow.

3.1   The case for comparability with the existing EU

This analysis takes a Europeanisation perspective in so far as it is concerned with the impact of the EU accession process on national patterns of governance. It might be more accurate to call it an exploration of 'EU-isation' in CEE, in that it is looking just at EU influence in the region, not at all the influences from the whole of Europe. The two concepts are not the same, either in the EU or in the candidate countries. However, this study calls it 'Europeanisation' because it draws on a literature that refers to EU influence in its current member-states by that name. Moreover, in CEE political and academic debates, the two concepts of EU influence and the 'return to Europe' after 1989 have often been conflated. Processes of EU-isation (i.e. becoming like the EU and joining the Union) were often justified as being part of, or essential to, modernisation and post-communist transition. These processes were often presented together as interwoven and cotermi-nous. This book confines itself to examining the 'EU-isation' component of Europeanisation, looking only at the formal accession process. But of course this process interacted with the many other political processes at work in both the candidate countries and the Union itself.

This study aims to connect the Europeanisation debate with the growing literature on enlargement, by identifying the specific modes and processes of Europeanisation at work in CEE. Most previous studies of Europeanisation have dealt only with countries that had already joined the EU (Goetz 2000 is a welcome exception), yet the EU exerted similar pressures on the CEE applicant countries. Indeed, the pressures on the CEE candidates for adaptation and policy convergence are more comparable with those on member-states in the 1990s than on Mediterranean applicants in the 1970s and 1980s because of the development of eastern accession conditionality. These pressures were also greater than those on previous applicants owing to the Union's much more advanced state of policy development – because of the completion of the single market in 1992, the integration of the Schengen area of passport-free movement into the EU's Treaty framework in 1997, and the launch of the single currency in 1999.

The creation of formal accession conditions gave the EU much wider leverage to get these applicants to comply with its demands than previous ones. It also reduced the ability of applicants to negotiate concessions such as transition periods and derogations in comparison with previous enlargements. The EU applied the accession conditions for CEE in a way more similar to the Maastricht convergence criteria for monetary union than to its approach in previous enlargements. The conditions were set in advance and national governments had to meet them before they could join – as with the convergence criteria – although the participants had less power to negotiate with their fellow-members about whether they were ready to join than did the would-be members of the euro-zone.

Many of the phenomena identified in the Europeanisation literature could also be seen in CEE, but the EU's influence on applicants had the added dimensions of conditionality and a negotiating process. However, this book does not make strong claims for the use of Europeanisation indiscriminately as a theoretical framework. In using the term with reference to the CEE region, it is particularly important not to over-estimate the EU's influence. It is easy to do so when a study is looking for evidence of the EU's effects. Moreover, there is already a tendency in parts of the literature on transition to exaggerate the EU's impact. For example, scholars working on democratisation have tended to assume that the EU vigorously encouraged democratisation by pressing the CEE countries into implementing democratic human rights regimes and open political systems (e.g. Linz and Stepan 1996, Kopecký and Mudde 2000). However, this book suggests that although the EU had enormous potential influence, scholars should not pre-judge the extent to which the EU actually shaped governance overall. Indeed, a systematic examination of the limits of the EU's impact as well as its extent is essential, because the effects may not have been as great as commonly supposed.

The *prima facie* case for EU influence

What kind of convergence between EU and CEE policies should we expect? This is a difficult question because we lack the concepts, methodology and data to study convergence properly even within the old EU-15 (Olsen 2003). Moreover, the experience of the EU's old member-states would suggest the scope is not wide. However, this book will argue that it was considerably greater for CEE.

Within the pre-2004 Union, there had been only limited convergence of policies and institutions, and the continuing diversity of member-states has been well documented (Cowles *et al.* 2001, Héritier *et al.* 2001, Kohler-Koch and Eising 1999). For example, there has been little convergence towards a European 'model of capitalism' (Berger and Dore 1996, Crouch and Streeck 1997, Rhodes and Apeldoorn 1998, among others). National economic systems have remained diverse partly because of the characteristics of EU policy-making. In particular, the EU's key governance function is regulating social and political risk rather than resource redistribution (Hix 1998). Secondly, the EU's policy framework for regulating the single market – which is one of its most extensively developed policy areas – remains a patchwork (Héritier 1996). Moreover, member-states can mitigate the impact of regulatory alignment on their domestic political economies, leading to uneven implementation and hence differentiated effects on national regimes (McGowan and Wallace 1996).

However, four factors give grounds for a hypothesis that the EU accession process pushed the applicant countries towards greater convergence with particular policy models than had occurred within the existing EU.[17] The first factor is the speed of adjustment. The formal accession process set out to adapt CEE institutions and policies to the EU much faster and more thoroughly than the EU-15 members had done. It took Greece well over a decade to adapt to the EU's single market norms (Featherstone 1998). By contrast, prospective CEE members were expected to orient their institutions and policies to the EU prior to membership, which meant only just over a decade after the accession conditions were set in 1993. Moreover, they did so from a much lower starting-point and with very limited scope for negotiating transition periods. The EU was able to push CEE policy reforms faster than they would otherwise have gone because of the priority accorded to accession by their governments and because of the institutional lacunae resulting from the communist era. After 1989, most of the candidates built a system of market regulation on only the most basic of foundations, and introduced many policies where there had been none – in areas like competition, migration, asylum and the protection of minorities.

The second factor is the openness of CEE to EU influence owing to the process of post-communist transformation and the weakness of state administrations. The CEE applicants were working from different starting-points in terms of institutional development, with gaps left by communist systems (Batt and Wolczuk 1999). They were at a critical juncture in their history, because of the weakness of the successor administrations just after the collapse of communism. They were wide open to external influence because they had few established public policies that commanded widespread support and their political leaders were seeking external legitimation for their policy choices. The EU was one of the most important sources of that legitimation.

The candidates did not start with an institutional *tabula rasa* – far from it (see Lijphart and Crawford 1995) – but the communist legacy meant that EU policies generally met with less institutional resistance than in the old member-states. What was called 'deregulation' under the single market programme meant radical re-regulation in the CEE case, and sometimes imposing regulation where there had been none – for most financial services, for example. The candidates were in the process of throwing off communist-era legislative frameworks and creating new ones for a capitalist market economy. This process made them more receptive to regulatory paradigms than the EU's member-states were, because EU models were being presented at the same time as CEE policy-makers were seeking a model to implement in many areas. Moreover, it was more difficult for applicant countries to soften the impact of EU policies than it was for states that had already gained membership, owing to the continuous monitoring of implementation of every part of the *acquis*, including annual reports from the Commission.

The European 'regulatory state'[18] may still be embryonic, but it was the key starting-point for the development of national models of economic governance in CEE. EU competition policy, sectoral policies and industrial standards formed the core building-blocks for the construction of market regulation. This is a core issue for the study of political economy; for example, Fligstein (1996) argues that the 'rules' of market-building and market intervention are key to understanding how new markets develop in a society. In CEE, the EU established or changed many of these rules. This is also an issue at the heart of the literature on European integration. For example, Wilks (1996) argues that in the EU, European regulation affected the evolution or choice of a model of capitalism by shaping the creation of markets, given that 'markets are social institutions governed by a set of rules, many of which are framed by the public authorities' (Wilks 1996, pp. 538–9). If one applies this argument to countries in transition, the EU had an extraordinary opportunity to shape the rules that constitute and define the development of new market economies. However, the extent to which the EU used this opportunity is another question, one that needs empirical investigation.

The third factor was the breadth of the EU's agenda in CEE. The CEE applicants had no possibility of opt-outs from parts of the agenda, such as the Social Chapter or EMU opt-outs obtained by the UK. Hence the applicants were committed to converging with a maximalist version of the EU's policies. In areas like social policy, where there is resistance to greater integration from some member-states, the Commission tended to define a 'maximalist' version of the *acquis communautaire* for CEE (Brusis 1998).

The fourth factor is that the EU's economic governance agenda in CEE became wider than that for current member-states through the membership conditions established for the eastern applicants. The conditions set at Copenhagen in 1993 went beyond those for any previous applicant, stating that not only do prospective members have to take on the 'obligations of membership' – i.e. the *acquis communautaire* – but they also have to have a 'functioning market economy' and 'the capacity to cope with competitive pressure and market forces within the Union' (as discussed in Chapter 2). Conditionality for accession thus extended the reach of EU influence considerably more deeply into domestic policy-making in CEE than it had done in the member-states, which only had to implement policies resulting from 'the obligations of membership' (the third condition) and were never judged on the first two conditions.

3.2   Using Europeanisation as a conceptual framework

The previous section has argued that we may expect the EU's influence in CEE to have been similar in nature to that in the EU-15, but wider and deeper in scope. This section explains how the concept of 'Europeanisation' can be used to investigate the effects that the EU had on public policy in the candidate countries. It categorises the different mechanisms of Europeanisation at work in CEE public policy, distinguishing between those that were similar to the mechanisms in the EU-15 and those that were particular to the accession process.

We have a *prima facie* case for comparing the CEE applicants directly with member-states because the EU had similar mechanisms of influence on both. The degree of Europeanisation in a policy area provides a guide to the relative effectiveness of EU conditionality in that area, so Europeanisation can be used as an analytical framework to assess how conditionality worked and the conditions for its success in effecting domestic policy change. We need an analytical framework similar to that used to analyse the EU, but one that takes into account the particular characteristics that were critically different for CEE.

Europeanisation: one concept or several?

The concept of 'Europeanisation' has recently received increasing attention in the field of European studies. There is considerable debate about how to conceptualise Europeanisation, and several scholars have asked whether it is different in degree or in kind from other processes such as policy transfer (Bomberg and Peterson 2000, Bulmer and Lequesne 2002). Recent reviews of the literature have distinguished two different approaches to Europeanisation originating from policy analysis and international relations, which have different core interests and should therefore be kept separate (Kohler-Koch 2000). Study of the Europeanisation of CEE lies more with the approach of policy analysis and comparative government studies, which are concerned with the 'varying impact of European integration on domestic arrangements and structures' (Knill and Lehmkuhl 1999). In this approach, the level of analysis is the domestic system and the main analytical construct is exploring the impact of the EU. In this study of CEE, we are less interested in the concern of international relations with Europeanisation, which is the transformation of formerly sovereign states into a new and distinct kind of political integration (Cowles *et al.* 2001), and hence the nature of the EU rather than its effects on other countries.

Beate Kohler-Koch uses a broader definition of Europeanisation, as processes that enlarge the scope of the relevant unit of policy-making (Kohler-Koch 1999), and hence not only transform economic governance, but also push social actors out of the scope of the nation state. In applying the concept of Europeanisation to CEE, we need both to broaden and to narrow Kohler-Koch's conception of potential effects. The conception needs to be broadened to encompass processes that *change* the boundaries of the relevant political space, potentially either enlarging them or closing them down. The EU can *reduce* policy spaces by foreclosing certain policy options, although it can also open up others. Conceptualising Europeanisation in this study of CEE also requires a narrower definition because it leaves out dynamics that are not exclusively triggered by EU-level policies. Kohler-Koch's model includes dynamics that originate from other European countries, as well as those specifically triggered by EU-level policy-making processes. Here we are concerned only with the latter, and have to leave out dynamics that are disseminated through transnational processes in order to keep the study to manageable size. This analysis of Europeanisation effects in CEE is confined to the effects of the formal accession process; however, the processes of bilateral and transnational influence in CEE that accompanied EU conditionality are obviously an important subject for future research.

The most precise and useful definition of Europeanisation for our purposes is the one put forward by Claudio Radaelli (2000a):

> Europeanisation consists of processes of (a) construction (b) diffusion and (c) institutionalization of formal and informal rules, procedures, policy paradigms, styles, 'ways of doing things' and shared beliefs and norms which are first defined and consolidated in the EU policy process and then incorporated in the logic of domestic (national and subnational) discourse, identities, political structures and public policies.

This definition stresses the importance of change in the logic of political behaviour, which is a useful way of distinguishing Europeanisation effects from the many other processes of change at work in the post-communist political context. In applying this heuristic concept to CEE, we are primarily investigating (b) and (c), looking at how the outcomes of EU policy processes were diffused and institutionalised in CEE. The typology of Europeanisation mechanisms presented below is primarily concerned with 'hard transfer', that is, how the EU transferred rules, procedures and policy paradigms to CEE. However, the importance of soft transfer – of styles, 'ways of doing things', and shared beliefs and norms – is also increasingly evident (as pointed out by Sedelmeier 2001 and Schimmelfennig 2001).

This study is confined only to certain dimensions of Europeanisation: its main subject is public policy, not political structures, structures of representation, or cognitive and normative structures (to use a typology of potential subjects put forward by Radaelli 2000a). The EU undoubtedly had an effect on political structures in CEE, as early work on the Europeanisation of interest groups (Fink-Hafner 1998) and political parties (Pridham *et al.* 1997, Taggart and Szczerbiak 2001) shows. Moreover, there is an interaction between policy dynamics and political structures in the EU (Héritier and Knill 2000) to be investigated in CEE. However, these lie beyond the scope of this enquiry, which is confined to the effects on public policy – the area which the EU most obviously sought to affect in CEE prior to accession.

Using this framework for Europeanisation in CEE is in the tradition of 'second image' (Waltz 1959) and 'second image reversed' (Gourevitch 1978) research design. That is, it looks at the impact of domestic factors on international relations and *vice versa*, and the interaction between exogenous and endogenous processes of change. Where the Europeanisation framework adds value to such a research design is in highlighting the particularities of EU policies and methods of effecting domestic change, as well as providing a framework that allows comparison with empirical work and theoretical insights about the existing EU.

What Europeanisation is – and is not – in the case of the candidate countries

Before proceeding with the above definition, we must define what Europeanisation is not, lest it become a catch-all for any process of domestic change. In studying the EU, Radaelli (2000a) makes a series of analytical distinctions between Europeanisation and convergence, harmonisation and political integration, while recognising that in the real world Europeanisation and EU policy formation are interconnected. In our investigation, we must similarly distinguish between the process leading to the formation of a certain policy within the EU and the reverberation of that policy in domestic arenas in CEE.

Three further distinctions are needed when applying Europeanisation to the candidate countries:

1. *Europeanisation is not a theory of EU enlargement.* Theories of enlargement address the question 'Why did the EU decide to enlarge and why did CEE countries want to join?' (e.g. Fierke and Wiener 1999, Schimmelfennig 1999). They seek to explain why the enlargement process is happening, that is, the ontological stage of research, whereas Europeanisation is post-ontological in being concerned with the effects of the enlargement process. This distinction parallels that made by Caporaso (1996) between EU ontology and post-ontological perspectives in Europeanisation and political integration in the EU. Clearly Europeanisation is linked to the politics of enlargement in practice,

through a two-way process that causes feed-back effects from Europeanisation in CEE onto reformulation of accession policy. However, formation of enlargement policy and Europeanisation should be kept separate at a conceptual level.

2. *Exploring Europeanisation requires discrimination between differences of kind as well as differences of degree.* Radaelli (2000a) draws on Sartori (1991) to remind us of the danger of 'degreeism': if we are unable to tell the difference between a cat and a dog, we end up talking of different degrees of cat-dog. If we are always looking at the extent of Europeanisation, we may fail to notice that other processes are producing the effects. It is easy to over-stress the role of the EU when we are looking for it as a specific variable.

This is a particular danger in studying the accession process, because both EU and CEE policy-makers tended to exaggerate the extent of EU influence for political purposes. Both the main sources for evidence of Europeanisation (i.e. actors in EU institutions and candidate country governments) had a vested interest in claiming that the EU was the principal driver of most reforms. CEE officials tended to talk up the EU's role to emphasise the scale of preparations and how ready they were, and to blame the EU for unpopular reforms. On the EU side, both officials and politicians liked to promote enlargement as a commitment device in post-communist transition, claiming that the Union was the principal driver of beneficial political and economic reforms in CEE. As is the case in the EU, institutional isomorphism was used as a source of legitimacy (Radaelli 2000b).

Both sets of claims were justified to some extent, but they often exaggerated the EU's specific influences in any given policy area. There were many other exogenous forces and endogenous processes of change at work in post-communist contexts. It is particularly important to distinguish Europeanisation from globalisation (a powerful exogenous process) and from transition (endogenous factors). CEE domestic structures and public policies were very different from EU norms at the start of the accession process, and the simultaneous processes of political and economic transition interacted with the accession process as well as with each other (see Offe 1991 on the 'triple transition'). At the same time, it is important to resist assuming that changes in political behaviour were the same as those identified in the member-states, given the candidates' very different starting circumstances and the context of post-communist reforms.

The distinction between these processes is difficult to maintain in practice because these three variables interacted; Europeanisation was an important intervening variable in the processes of modernisation and post-communist reform, and the interaction between Europeanisation dynamics and transition processes is an interesting research area to explore. Moreover, Europeanisation effects are a continuum, and work on the EU has shown the importance of parallel processes of national and EU-level reforms (e.g. Héritier and Knill 2000 on transport, Radaelli 1997 on taxation).

3. *Distinguishing between intentional and unintentional effects of the EU.* We cannot assume that the EU achieved the effects it explicitly aimed for just because of its power relationship through conditionality and the breadth of its agenda. 'EU influence' operated through many different actor constellations and its goals were often unclear, so the overall impact could have been very diffuse (as discussed in Chapter 4). One must therefore look carefully at whether EU pressures actually had their intended effects. It is equally important to be sensitive to unintended consequences, because the EU can effect change by example-setting and unintended policy transfer. The EU was a significant source of models for political actors seeking outside guidance on policy and institutional change. 'European' norms and models are frequently cited in CEE political debates to legitimate political choices of various kinds (see, for example, Fowler 2001 on regional reforms). However, 'EU norms' were also invoked in contexts where the EU had not asked for compliance, such as constitutional models.

Studying the EU's effects: mechanisms of Europeanisation

Studies of EU influence on particular policies or institutions in CEE have often tended to make uncritical assumptions about the EU's routes of influence, without examining its influence relative to other pressures and relative to other items on its agenda. One of the aims of this book is to show the need for empirical studies on eastward enlargement to put EU influences in context by establishing a consistent framework for analysing the processes at work. There is scope for a number of different analytical frameworks to be used, depending on what aspect of the eastern accession process is under examination.

A major methodological problem in all studies of Europeanisation is trying to build a test of EU influence. It seems to defy measurement precisely because EU influence is interwoven with domestic politics and other external influences. Moreover, in many studies of Europeanisation, the boundaries between cause and effect, independent and dependent variables are blurred (Bulmer and Radaelli 2004). The distinguishing feature of Europeanisation is that it changes the logic of political behaviour, and policy-makers often cease to be aware of what is EU as opposed to national policy. However, this book tries to see how EU influence works by identifying the adaptational pressures, even if we cannot reach a firm conclusion about how different the outcome is from what would have resulted without the EU. In other words, we can study the process systematically even if we lack a counter-factual.

The aim of using the Europeanisation literature is to distinguish different mechanisms identified in studies of the member-states and to see if their insights are relevant in CEE. In summary, four dimensions of Europeanisation have been highlighted by empirical work on the impact of the EU on member-states (summary from Harcourt 2002):

1. How member-states have adapted economically to Europe (e.g. Featherstone 1998, Ladrech 1994).
2. How member-states have adapted institutionally to Europe (Héritier 1998, Ladrech 1994, Cowles *et al.* 2001). Here authors such as Börzel (1999) and Cowles *et al.* (2001) have explored the extent to which policy choices presented by EU institutions are compatible with the institutional and administrative culture and policy styles of member-states – what they call 'goodness-of-fit'.
3. The type of discourse used to justify and provide legitimacy for Europeanisation (Schmidt 1997) – that is, processes of 'cognitive adaptation' to the EU.
4. Specific mechanisms of Europeanisation (Knill and Lehmkuhl 1999, Radaelli 2000b).

This book is primarily concerned with the last of these: mechanisms of Europeanisation. Mechanisms of Europeanisation of public policy identified in the literature on the existing EU include coercion, mimetism (i.e. mimicry or imitation), normative pressures and cognitive convergence, all of which are useful in analysing effects in CEE. Several recent studies (Börzel 1999, Cowles *et al.* 2001) stress 'goodness-of-fit' (i.e. degree of institutional compatibility) as a key mechanism of Europeanisation. In the conception of Europeanisation used here, goodness-of-fit is not a mechanism in itself, but rather it is an intervening variable that affects how Europeanisation mechanisms work (intervening variables are discussed in Section 3.4 below). The emphasis on goodness-of-fit was previously challenged by Knill and Lehmkuhl (1999) who point to the effects of policy structure on the domestic impact of different EU policies. In particular, they point to the significance of some policies' impact on domestic opportunity structure and of the beliefs and expectations of domestic actors. Goodness-of-fit is just one variable, and its explanatory value varies according to the distinctive Europeanisation logic underlying the policy in question. Kohler-Koch (1996) also points to Europeanisation effects that go beyond the impact of EU policy, affecting the balance of power in the EU and hence its pattern of governance. In the longer term, the accession of the CEE candidates is likely to affect governance patterns in the enlarged EU, so enlargement will itself have feed-back effects on Europeanisation mechanisms. This is an area for future research.

What Europeanisation effects should we expect?

The literature on Europeanisation in West Europe suggests several potential effects that might emerge in the candidate countries. First, Europeanisation entails *absorbing EU imperatives, logic and norms into domestic policy*, so that the distinction between EU and domestic policy requirements disappears (Anderson and Eliassen 1993, Ladrech 1994). However, the domestic impact of EU adaptation varies across institutional and policy dimensions (Mény *et al.* 1996, Kassim and Menon 1996, Featherstone 1998, Forder and Menon 1998, Hine and Kassim 1998).

Secondly, Europeanisation has the effect of *empowering modernisers* to change specific policies (particularly macro-economic policies) and also to reform political institutions; this effect has been observed not only in the case of later acceders to the EU like Greece (Featherstone 1998), but also in founder-members like France (Ladrech 1994) and Italy (Francioni 1992, Amato 1996). 'Europe' has been claimed and used by elites as an external constraint to bypass national political and administrative systems and to enforce decisions and policies that would not otherwise have been agreed upon or accepted. But at the same time, membership of the EU has been an integral part of the reassertion of the nation-state as an organisational unity, with the integration process strengthening the ability of national actors to develop bundles of domestic policies to satisfy coalitions of political interests (Milward 1992).

Thirdly, the EU has the effect of *creating policy space* for new initiatives on the political agenda by causing institutional adaptations that have permanent effects on the policy-making process. Organisations respond to changes in the perceptions of interest and value that occur in the principles, norms and institutional design of the regime in which they are embedded (Haas 1990). EU political and economic dynamics thus become part of the organisational logic of national politics and policy-making; however, the pre-existing national framework mediates this process of adjustment in both formal and informal ways (Ladrech 1994). In the case of CEE, this mediation could have been particularly affected by the institutional legacies of the communist era.

Each of these phenomena could be evident in CEE. Hence we may expect a large number of parallels with the impact that Europeanisation had on less-developed member-states, but also some contrasts. Particularly important are the potential parallels with the literature on southern EU member-states. However, contrasts immediately arise too: global forces had more impact in CEE than in the Mediterranean countries, because of the much greater extent of globalisation through liberalisation of trade and capital movements in the 1990s compared with when Greece, Portugal and Spain were preparing to join the EU. For the CEE applicants, it was not just the EU that forced liberalisation, although in some areas the EU may have been the key influence. Moreover, EU agencies in government were not so integrated or influential prior to the start of negotiations as they were for the existing member-states. Finally, flows of aid to CEE were much less than those to the main recipient member-states as a proportion of GDP.

3.3   Characterising the EU-CEE relationship

The EU-candidate relationship was one of obvious asymmetry of interdependence, an evident source of power.[19] The EU had all the benefits to offer (principally accession, trade and aid), and far from all of its component member-states were sure they wanted all the CEE countries to join. The CEE countries, by contrast, had little to offer the EU, given their tiny economic size. They also had little to bargain with because of the strong desire of their political elites to join – even if public opinion was subject to greater fluctuation. This asymmetry of interdependence allowed the EU to set the rules of the game in the accession conditionality.

However, incentives were much more effective than constraints in this relationship because the accession process is voluntary. The EU generally had more carrots at its disposal than sticks, as will be shown in Chapter 4. But carrots can be very effective, and the prospect of EU membership provided a strong incentive to implement difficult reforms, and to modify specific policies in order to attain membership. The EU also influenced democratisation in CEE through 'leading by example'. During the Cold War, the EU offered a showcase of stability and prosperity based on liberal democracy and market economics that was influential in encouraging the idea of 'returning to Europe' that was such an important theme of post-1989 CEE politics: the goal of joining the EU was not just based on a calculated motivation of receiving specific benefits, but was seen as a way of becoming 'modern' and 'civilised'. Identification with 'Europe' as an ideal of civilisation, embodying a distinct set of values and standards of political behaviour and socio-economic organisation, provided a crucial component of the motivation to press on with painful and divisive reforms (see Kumar 1992). In this respect, the EU reinforced political will for reforms and its demands provided ammunition to governments that needed to overcome the resistance of interest groups.

Yet for the dynamic to work, membership had to be a realistic goal: it had to look probable that the institution would expand and that the candidates would be able to fulfil the requirements. Hence the external influence of the EU depended on a certain tension between confidence that membership would be secured and fear of rejection owing to inadequate reforms. This did not always work: for example, in the Czech Republic under the Klaus government, over-confidence about getting into the EU and NATO undermined comprehensive domestic reforms and a rational foreign policy (Vachudová 2001). Similarly, the EU faced difficulties in steering some of the CEE candidates in particular directions where there was a more coercive than cooperative relationship, as was the case with Slovakia until the September 1998 elections (Bútorová 1998).

Using membership conditionality for precise policy influence requires willing, not reluctant partners: in considering the coercive/voluntary mix, the voluntary cooperation is critical because the EU's coercive power is very limited. As coercive sanctions against undemocratic practices in CEE, the EU had only exclusion from various parts of the accession process: it could suspend the Europe Agreements and the Phare aid programme, and it could exclude a country from negotiations. The value of these sanctions relied entirely on how desirable inclusion in the process was to a country's political elite; hence the EU had leverage only where a regime had at least partly bought into the aims of integration.

This lack of coercive tools is hardly surprising, given the EU's history and purpose: it was established as a vehicle for the economic and political integration of willing states, not as a force for transition in unwilling regimes. The EU lacks the IMF's leverage because it is unable to offer assistance in a crisis or a clear set of policy prescriptions on which aid is precisely conditional. The situation is quite the opposite: EU membership is offered only to countries that are already out of crisis. Moreover, its conditions are broad, imprecise and shifting, as indicated in Chapter 2. That makes it difficult to posit a precise causal relationship between success in democratic transition and the EU accession process. For this reason, researchers should be cautious about the assumption frequently made by transitologists looking at democratisation in CEE that the EU was an unquestionably beneficial influence in transition to democracy. The EU rarely used its conditionality negatively – in the sense of withdrawing a reward – and although the EU shaped governance in CEE countries indirectly, it rarely did so directly (see Grabbe 2001a).

In the negotiations, the central source of power for the EU in getting deals on particular chapters was the political sensitivity of particular issues in existing member-states. Even after the completion of the accession negotiations, the candidates faced 18 potential vetoes over their applications. The accession treaty had to be ratified by every member-state's parliament, so the negotiators were seeking an outcome that they calculated would not be rejected by any of the 15 national parliaments. The European Parliament could also reject the treaties. Then, a few months before the date of accession, the Commission had to give its blessing to each candidate's progress in preparations after the conclusion of negotiations. Although the European Council might not accept the Commission's recommendations, it was unlikely to accept that a candidate was ready if the Commission argued strongly that it was not. This daunting gamut of potential vetoes put the EU negotiators in a strong position to argue that some unattractive deals had to be accepted or else the whole treaty might be rejected after the conclusion of the negotiations.

There are many useful insights to be gained from studies of international bargaining, particularly with regard to how implementation can be used to mitigate the impact of the deals reached in negotiations. However, this book is concerned with other questions as well. It investigates how the EU caused Europeanisation effects in CEE through the accession process, which requires a different set of conceptual tools from those needed for a study of negotiating dynamics. Investigating these questions requires a detailed examination of CEE policy-making, and tools from political science disciplines such as comparative politics, organisational analysis and public policy analysis. But the nature of the relationship between the EU and the applicants still needs scrutiny in terms of international relations because it affected the ways in which the EU can cause Europeanisation effects – the EU's 'routes of influence' in CEE discussed in Chapter 4.

The process under investigation is how the CEE candidates tried to meet the conditions and how that started a process of Europeanisation. In methodological terms, the EU's accession policy is the independent variable, and the dependent variable is the extent of Europeanisation that it caused in different policy areas. However, although accession policy is an independent variable, it requires considerable analysis in order to understand how and how far it can influence policy in the candidate countries – hence the need for the detailed analysis of accession policy that was presented in Chapter 2.

3.4 Moving towards explanation: Six concepts

In this chapter, Section 3.1 has made a case for a very wide and deep influence from the EU in CEE, Section 3.2 has discussed how Europeanisation can work as a conceptual framework to analyse this influence, and Section 3.3 has introduced the argument that the EU-candidate relationship is characterised by power, but that relative negotiating power alone cannot explain the extent of EU influence in CEE. The accession process is voluntary, and the EU's coercive power is very limited. Moreover, the explanation also has to involve mechanisms of Europeanisation. Section 3.4 introduces six concepts from the political science literature that will be used in the case-studies to clarify the Europeanisation processes that occurred in two policy areas, and to guide us towards an explanation of the outcomes in Chapter 8.

The following section sets out some concepts that will be used in the case-studies to explain the EU's approach and the candidates' reaction. These concepts do not in themselves explain the outcomes, but they help in understanding the processes at work and identifying intervening variables. The concepts are drawn from several different literatures: comparative politics (policy transfer), European integration (goodness of fit), international relations (policy paradigms), and organisational behaviour (institutional isomorphism).

Policy transfer

Policy transfer is one of the principal mechanisms of Europeanisation, and it is one of the processes at the heart of the case-studies. As Claudio Radaelli concludes, summarising the EU literature, 'The quasi-federal EU (Sbragia 1992, Majone 1992) is most of the time a massive policy transfer platform from dominant countries (Héritier, Knill and

Mingers 1996) and/or winning advocacy coalitions (Sabatier 1998, Radaelli 1999) to other countries and coalitions.'[20] The conditionality for eastward enlargement involves an even greater scale of policy transfer, because it goes beyond the *acquis* agreed by member-states, as we saw in Chapter 2.

The framework of policy transfer thus provides part of the conceptual framework for the cases, but it is just one of several mechanisms at work in the case of EU enlargement (in Chapter 4). There is a substantial literature on policy transfer already, but only parts of it are relevant to the study of EU influence in candidate countries. This section discusses the insights that the literature offers, and the analytical problems in applying it to the case of EU influence. The chief shortcomings of most existing approaches in using them to analyse the EU-CEE case are that they focus on why policies are transferred, rather than how, and that most present a crude distinction between voluntary and coercive conditions of transfer.

The literature on policy transfer encompasses a number of different phenomena, such as recent work by Coleman (1994) on policy convergence, Majone (1991) on policy diffusion, Haas (1992) on policy learning, and Rose (1991) on lesson-drawing. Dolowitz and Marsh have drawn together this literature in a synthetic framework (1996 and 2000). Policy transfer analysis has the advantage of bringing together both domestic and international politics under a single lens, and it is specifically geared to dealing with transnational processes that involve both international agencies and states, as in the case of EU-CEE integration. Moreover, it can be used as an analytical tool rather than a causal model (see Evans and Davies 1999). Using policy transfer as an analogy allows us to look at how the EU transfers policies as well as why this happens. It is a 'meso-level' concept that provides a link between micro-level analysis, of particular policy decisions, and macro-level analysis, in this case the broader question of the power relationship between the EU and the candidate states. Operating at the meso-level helps to ensure that we do not lose sight of either micro or macro questions in this multi-layered process of Europeanisation.

The case-studies explore the explicit agenda for policy transfer taking place under the pre-accession strategy – hence primarily the 'hard transfer' discussed below – although it also included the transfer of policy assumptions (the 'policy paradigms' discussed below). The analysis addresses what was being transferred, which mechanisms were used, and what were the outputs. A central problem in the literature on policy transfer is usually determining *why* policies are being transferred, but in these cases the motivation was relatively clear: the EU used accession conditionality to transfer its policies to would-be member-states, and the CEE countries agreed to it because of the powerful attraction of EU membership. However, although the 'why' question is more straightforward than in many cases, the issues of *how* it occurred – and how complete the transfer was at the end – are more complex. Several dimensions of EU-CEE transfer are not satisfactorily explained by the analogical models proposed in the literature so far. Three analytical problems are identified – hard and soft transfer, completeness of transfer, and the blurred line between coercion and voluntarism – which leads us to consider further analytical tools to supplement policy transfer.

Hard and soft transfer

The EU accession process produces two varieties of policy transfer: 'hard' transfers of programmes and implementation, and also 'soft' transfers of ideas, concepts and attitudes (to adopt the distinction suggested by Evans and Davies 1999). 'Hard transfer' of policy programmes has been a key condition for admittance to the EU since its first enlargement in 1973. The EU requires that any new applicant take on the same range of policies that its members have already agreed to. The difference in the case of the eastern applicants was that the EU imposed additional political and economic conditions that required them to do more than just adopt the EU's existing rules. As a result, EU influence penetrated almost every part of public policy-making in the CEE applicant countries.

Table 3.1 summarises the main routes of potential policy influence from the EU to CEE. These contacts all have the potential to influence the policies adopted in CEE. Dolowitz and Marsh (1996) identify seven objects of transfer between states: policy goals; structure and content; policy instruments or administrative techniques; institutions; ideology; ideas, attitudes and concepts; and negative lessons. All of these were potentially transferred from the EU to CEE because of the 'teaching' role adopted by the EU for public and private sector actors in CEE. The official routes, including aid, policy documents, legal agreements, and institutional contacts, were all used actively to transfer policies. The agenda for 'hard' transfer was fairly fixed, as indicated above, and these multiple points of contact provided many opportunities for the EU to reinforce its message about transferring the *acquis*. Beyond the *acquis*, however, the consistency of the policy advice given through these routes is uncertain, as the different EU agencies and bilateral contacts

58

Table 3.1 The EU's hard and soft routes for policy transfer in CEE
The darkly shaded boxes are the official routes of 'hard' transfer of policies at state level, while the lightly shaded boxes are 'soft' transfer effects.

Route	Examples (when introduced)	Type of influence	Leverage exerted on policy	Limits on influence and issues for analysis
Aid and technical assistance	Phare (1989), bilateral aid programmes	Policy conditionality for financial and other benefits. Transfer of practices and assumptions into national bureaucracies.	EU offered tested policy options at the start of transition when CEE were seeking models. EU aid became accession-focused from 1998.	The Phare programme's overall lack of coherence and dependence on consultants under contract probably limited the extent to which it could be used to guide CEE consistently toward particular policy prescriptions.
Policy documents from the EU for domestic implementation	Single Market White Paper (1995), Accession Partnerships (1998 onwards)	Guidelines for specific adoption of policies are not legally binding but directly related to conditionality for next stage in the accession process.	Directly linked with meeting accession conditions.	Depth of implementation and effectiveness of enforcement of regulation need closer investigation to gauge impact.
Legally binding agreements	Europe Agreements (in effect from 1993 onwards)	Legal obligations to liberalise trade on a specified timetable, subject to enforcement through trade sanctions.	Very influential in implementation because they could be publicly enforced through the Association Council.	CEE able to procrastinate in implementation (hence trade disputes with the EU), but forced to comply eventually.
Multilateral institutional contact	Structured Dialogue (1993-97), European Conference (1998 onwards)	High-level political contact, multilateral meetings.	Influence primarily through high-level political contacts, not specific policies.	Effects depended on the attention the meetings were accorded by EU policy-makers, and the level of ministerial attendance.

Table 3.1 The EU's hard and soft routes for policy transfer in CEE – *continued*
The darkly shaded boxes are the official routes of 'hard' transfer of policies at state level, while the lightly shaded boxes are 'soft' transfer effects.

Route	Examples (when introduced)	Type of influence	Leverage exerted on policy	Limits on influence and issues for analysis
Bureaucracy-to-bureaucracy contacts	TAIEX, twinning of officials (1999 onwards)	Routinisation of practices; absorption of EU ideas and norms by CEE officials working with EU officials.	Long-term indirect influence, taking EU practices to the heart of policy-making.	Depended on the officials taking part, varied by country and policy area.
Leading by example/ anticipatory adjustment	CEE started voluntary emulation of EU policy models that were not part of formal accession conditionality, e.g. aiming for EMU convergence criteria, using DM/ euro as peg in currency boards (Bulgaria, Estonia)	CEE officials adopted EU policy models even when these were not imposed by EU.	Only a few clear examples; analysing influence requires systematic process-tracing across numerous policy areas.	Rhetorical commitment to EU models often not matched by substantive implementation.
Private sector actors	Foreign direct investors, banks, intra-firm contacts	CEE private sector adopted EU practices because of competition in home market (efficiency gains, technology transfer) or in EU markets (product and process standards).	Studies of foreign direct investment suggest a 'learning process' operated, but it is very hard to measure.	Influence depends on sector, and type and intensity of competition.

could give contradictory messages about implementation of policies that were not clearly defined under the *acquis*.

It is problematic to analyse this second category of non-*acquis* policies as 'policy transfer', because there was no precise set of stated programmes to be adopted, as there was with the *acquis communautaire*. Policies for CEE were much less detailed in areas that lie outside regulatory policy: the content consisted of exhortations for 'major efforts' to improve or strengthen policies and institutions, without the means being specified. The emphasis in accession policy during negotiations was on having coherent policies and functioning institutions, rather than on specific prescriptions for policy content. Differences in policy structure and their role as variables are discussed below.

In analysing 'hard' and 'soft' transfers, we need to make clear distinctions to determine the evidence required for showing these different types of transfer. Dolowitz and Marsh rightly stress the need for a clear scheme for measuring the occurrence of policy transfer, but this is much harder to provide for 'soft' transfer than for 'hard' transfer, which can be demonstrated by looking at changes in CEE legislation.

In the CEE context, identifying the causal chain for EU influence is further complicated by pre-1989 contacts. The EU had an indirect influence on some policies, for example in the Hungarian economic reforms of the 1980s (see Bohle 1996, Tóth 1998). Moreover, the EU's 'twinning' projects which started in 1999 took EU influence deep into state administrations in CEE. Member-state officials working within CEE ministries through 'twinning programmes' could bring EU practices and norms directly into the policy-making process. Whereas the Phare aid programme's effect on policy-making had been blunted by the use of consultants as advisers, twinning meant that EU bureaucrats assisted with implementation from within CEE governmental structures. They took in their own countries' methods of working and assumptions about policies and policy-making processes, but here again, the consistency and effectiveness of their influence may have varied greatly.

The case-studies aim to assess the scope of EU influence in CEE ministries through interviews with policy-makers that ascertain how much their views and interpretations of policy needs were affected by the EU. However, the role of ideas, examples and practices is hard to trace because there is no counter-factual to judge how policy would have been different if the EU had not been there. Ultimately, we can only speculate how far the ideology, ideas, attitudes and concepts that emerged in the CEE countries would have been different if they had not been next door to the EU, and what the negative lessons of European integration were for these countries. Exploration of this question has to lie beyond the scope of this book, although it is an area for further research.

Completeness of transfer

The *prima facie* case presented above in Section 3.1 and the analysis of accession policy in Chapter 2 suggest that large-scale policy transfer occurred from the EU to CEE. But how complete was it? To what extent did CEE policies actually become 'Europeanised'? Was it only the political rhetoric that was Europeanised? Here we are trying to measure 'outputs' rather than 'outcomes', to use the policy analysis language of Putnam (1993, derived from Pennock 1966). In essence, we are looking at how the policies themselves resemble EU policies, rather than whether these policies resulted in similar economic or social conditions to those in the EU. For example, measuring outputs involves assessing whether CEE market regulation was similar in form and content to single market regulation, rather than whether CEE markets started to converge with EU markets. In other words, outputs are the rules that result, whereas outcomes are the effects of those rules on economies or societies.

There are several problems with trying to measure policy outputs. The first is the absence of a counter-factual. The second issue is how to gauge the depth of Europeanisation: the parts of a ministry that are in contact with the EU may talk the language of Brussels and aim at full compliance in implementing policies, but that does not necessarily mean that their colleagues in other parts of the ministry pay much attention to EU demands in formulating policy. So attention has to be paid to how far the whole policy chain is affected by EU demands.

Coercive versus voluntary transfer: a false dichotomy

In looking at the politics of aid conditionality, 'the central theoretical and empirical problem in analysing compliance is to distinguish between underlying interests and strategic interaction, between consent and coercion', according to Haggard and Moravcsik (1993, p. 272). There is a similar analytical problem in relations between CEE and the EU because they involved a mixture of conflict and consensus, making it difficult to distinguish sharply between governments complying with conditions because they accepted the underlying goals, or because the conditions were linked to external inducements or sanctions. Unlike relations with other international bodies like the IMF, whose remit is narrower and whose clients are often forced to comply through financial desperation, relations with the EU were largely permissive. Indeed, the EU cannot use conditionality to force policy change in countries that refuse to comply because its sanctions are primarily carrots rather than sticks (as discussed in Chapter 2).

EU-CEE policy transfer was coercive in Dolowitz and Marsh's terms, as it involved 'one government or supra-national institution pushing, or even forcing, another government to adopt a particular programme' (1996, p. 344). However, this policy transfer process was not wholly coercive, because there was also a strong demand-pull for policy learning from the applicants (as discussed in Chapter 2). This implies a combination of voluntary and coercive transfer conditions, whereas the literature on policy transfer has often tended to assume that the two are mutually exclusive conditions. However, recent work has begun to acknowledge that there can be a range; for example, Dolowitz and Marsh (2000) move towards looking at voluntary-to-coercive as a continuum, while Bulmer and Padgett (2005) set out a range of possible transfer outcomes, assessed on a scale from emulation to influence.

In fact, motivations for policy transfer in the EU-CEE case were highly complex, and the process involved a degree of 'locking-in' that makes it hard to say exactly whether a given instance of policy transfer was voluntary or coercive. All the CEE countries acted voluntarily in applying for EU membership and agreeing to meet the general conditions; but on the other hand, conditionality for aid and interim benefits required them to meet detailed conditions. In interviews with the author, policy-makers themselves were at times uncertain about what was clearly coercive (i.e. policy transfer would not have taken place without the EU having imposed accession conditions) and what was voluntary (i.e. CEE policy-makers were looking for models in a particular policy area and decided to adopt EU models because that also fitted their foreign policy goal of joining the Union). It is thus very difficult to assess where consent ended and coercion began. Indeed, one of the effects of Europeanisation is to blur that distinction, because policy-makers started to behave in ways that followed EU policy logic.

In the EU-CEE relationship we find many different conditions of transfer. It is far more appropriate to plot them along a scale of consent-to-coercion, rather than trying to categorise each policy area as either one or the other. Moreover, what was coercively forced on one country may have been voluntarily adopted by another, depending on the degree of domestic opposition to it; for example, the Czech Republic adopted EU state aid rules quite willingly, whereas Poland was reluctant to do so and procrastinated in their implementation. In addition, hybrid phenomena arose such as 'anticipatory adjustment', whereby countries adjusted to what policy-makers presumed would be future EU demands, such as the Maastricht convergence criteria for monetary union. Here they were neither responding to coercion (because the EU had not asked them to meet these criteria before joining) nor voluntarily adopting policies simply because they thought such policies fitted their domestic needs. Rather, the EU was providing a template for policies that were adopted on the basis that they were 'European' instead of on the basis of a simple cost-benefit calculation. Hence normative pressures such as legitimacy played an important role, as discussed below in the section on institutional isomorphism.

The implementation phase in policy transfer

What occurred (if anything) between the EU's demands and the outcomes in CEE? This is a key question in examining the EU's effects in CEE. One way to approach it is to consider the role of implementation in a 'two-level game' (to use the language of Putnam). Studies of international bargaining suggest that implementation can be used to mitigate the impact of conditionality. EU actors (particularly the Commission) laid increasing stress on the effective implementation of EU rules, not just writing them into national law. We need to consider whether the degree of Europeanisation was affected by the way policies were implemented, and how to measure how much this occurred. The implementation stage is critical to understanding how the EU affected policy and policy-making in CEE: it is the interface between domestic and foreign policy, and it determines the impact of conditionality. The EU's influence on detailed policy formation and implementation is mediated by domestic actors; determining the manner and the extent of this mediation requires empirical enquiry. EU member-states have frequently used partial implementation to mitigate the impact of EU-level policies on their domestic political economies. The tight conditions for accession and continuous monitoring by the Commission meant there were fewer opportunities to do so in CEE than there were for the EU-15 (McGowan and Wallace 1996), but opportunities nevertheless existed.

The focus of analysis in policy transfer is usually the spatial dimension – i.e. whence and to where policy is transferred (Evans and Davies 1999). But in the EU-CEE case, the issue is more what happens *after* policies were transferred from one body to another. Large-scale transfer of EU rules into national law in CEE certainly occurred, but what happened when the policies were implemented? Which levels of government were involved and how did they interact? The EU affected relations between central and local government, and blurred the line between foreign and domestic policy in CEE. Did this interaction itself affect completeness of transfer? These areas all need investigation, so the model has to be expanded in the implementation phase, moving beyond its current focus on the emergence of transfer networks to encompass the phase between process and outcome.

An initial question is how to measure whether transfer was complete or only partial. An obvious place to start is to use the EU's own interim assessments of how far candidates had met the Copenhagen conditions for accession year by year. Each Autumn from 1998 to 2003, the Commission presented Regular Reports on the candidates' progress in complying with the conditions across the range of policy areas. However, there are two reasons to take care in using the Commission's views as a method of measuring compliance: the first is that the Commission's judgements were general and often vague, both in the macro-assessments and discussion of particular policy areas. For example, the Commission stated in its 1997 Opinion on Slovakia's ability to meet the economic criteria that 'Slovakia has introduced most of the reforms necessary to establish a market economy', and in its 1998 Regular Report on Hungary that 'Although the current state of implementation is broadly satisfactory, considerable progress still needs to be made' in agricultural policy (CEC 1998b, p. 30). These comments are so general as to be almost meaningless; their main purpose was to establish a relative scale of progress when the language in each report was compared with that in the reports of different years and on the other applicants. At micro level, the Commission's standards of measurement were never published and seem to have been somewhat *ad hoc*, at times making them inconsistent across policy areas and countries (see Grabbe and Hughes 1998).

Secondly, the macro-assessments made by the Commission were not just technical reports on compliance with the Copenhagen criteria, but were opinions about whether a country was ready to start negotiations, which was a highly politicised judgement. The Commission was a political player in the enlargement process, and it was subject to influence from the member-states. Other standards of measurement are thus needed, to be used in conjunction with the Commission's assessments of compliance. Cross-checking with the views of other international institutions and aid providers in CEE can help to uncover inconsistencies, as do the views of CEE policy actors, as they were very sensitive to any possibility of bias in comparative assessments of their progress with that of other countries. Academic studies of compliance also offer additional ways of measuring compliance in different areas and more detail (e.g. Carlin *et al.* 1999, Mayhew and Orlowski 1998). However, the lack of systematic cross-policy and cross-country studies makes overall assessments inevitably somewhat subjective.

Goodness of fit

The concept of 'goodness of fit' has been used in several recent studies of the domestic impact of Europeanisation in the EU (Risse and Börzel 2003, Cowles *et al.* 2001, Börzel 1999). In studying policies, politics, or polities, these authors argue that a misfit between European-level and domestic processes, policies, or institutions constitutes the necessary condition for expecting *any* change. Europeanisation must be 'inconvenient', in some way. There must be some degree of 'misfit' or incompatibility between European-level processes, policies and institutions, on the one hand, and domestic-level processes, policies and institutions, on the other. This degree of fit or misfit constitutes adaptational pressures. However, adaptational pressures are a necessary but insufficient condition for expecting change. The second condition is that there must be some facilitating factors – actors or institutions – that are responding to the adaptational pressures. These mediating factors enable or prohibit domestic change, and they account for the empirically observable differential impact of Europe. Europeanisation might lead to convergence in policy outcomes, but at best to 'clustered convergence', and continuing divergence with regard to policy processes and instruments, politics, and polities (Risse and Börzel 2003).

Chapter 4 of this book identifies five different 'routes of influence' by which the EU can cause Europeanisation to take place in CEE domestic policy-making. However, there were mediating factors at work in CEE as well, and they account for the variance in the outcomes of EU pressure across countries and policy areas. These mediating factors are also set out in Chapter 4: on the EU side, they are diffuseness of influence and uncertainty. On the CEE side, there are the political context and salience of the issue, and the macro-strategy of adaptation to the EU, as well as interaction. This last factor – the interaction of EU pressures with other processes of change and institutional capacity – is one of the central determinants of the goodness-of-fit between the EU pressures and the CEE context in which they work.

Policy types

In order to investigate systematically the impact of EU policies in CEE, we need to distinguish between the different types of policy that the

Union produces. The policy type affects what kind of impact it has at domestic level, and hence it tells us what to look for in seeking to discern the EU's impact.

Some initial work on policy in the existing EU provides a useful starting-point. Knill and Lehmkuhl (1999) and Knill (2001) identify three different types of European policy-making, which they call 'positive', 'negative' and 'framing' integration. Positive integration is where the EU prescribes concrete institutional requirements with which member-states must comply; examples are environmental protection, health and safety at work, and consumer protection. Negative integration is where the EU puts pressure on governments to change institutional arrangements through mechanisms of 'regulatory competition'; the example the authors use is road haulage policy. Framing integration is where the EU alters the beliefs and expectations of domestic actors, changing their 'cognitive logic'; their example is railways policy.

Knill and Lehmkuhl's distinction is based on the study of regulatory policy-making for the single market. Their definitions thus need some adaptation for other policy areas, because they do not clearly express the differences between EU policies outside the single market *acquis*, where there are many more hybrid forms of integration. Knill and Lehmkuhl acknowledge the existence of such hybrids, but their framework cannot easily take account of them.

Nevertheless, their approach is very helpful for this study, and a modified version of these distinctions can be applied to the policies that the EU transferred to CEE. The types of policy that the EU produces could be grouped into three similar but looser categories:

- *Prescriptive policies*: The EU prescribes institutional requirements which are explicitly directed at replacing existing domestic arrangements in terms of institutions and legislation. The EU uses models and templates to effect institutional and policy change.
- *Prohibitive policies*: The EU prohibits the use of particular measures that prevent action. The main aims are liberalisation and deregulation. The EU forces countries to abolish arrangements that are in conflict with the single market, but does not prescribe in detail what arrangements must replace them. In the existing member-states, domestic actors have more discretion because the requirements are less demanding than when the EU prescribes an institutional requirement. However, in CEE this was not the case where the EU pushed the domestic actors to demonstrate compliance in order to gain concessions – an example is visa policy.

- *Framing policies*: The EU alters the beliefs and expectations of domestic actors, so the domestic impact is based on changing a cognitive logic. The EU activity is intended to prepare the ground for subsequent policies of positive or negative integration: changing the domestic political climate by stimulating and strengthening the overall support for broader European reform objectives. For the member-states, framing integration emerges where the EU decision-making context allows for the adoption of only vague and more or less symbolic policies, given the underlying conflicts of interests between member-states – for example, in economic reform through the 'open method of coordination' introduced at the 1999 Lisbon European Council. In CEE, candidate-country policy-makers were strongly encouraged to adopt EU framing policies, even if they were not formally part of the *acquis*.

We will see in Chapter 6 that the case of free movement of persons (FMP) within the single market contained EU policies of all three types. However, the case presented in Chapter 7 – movement of persons across external borders – consisted primarily of prescriptive policies, with some framing policies as well. The value of using this distinction in the case-studies is that we can identify what kind of pressures the EU exerted by looking at whether the Union had an institutional template to present to CEE and whether the policy was prescriptive or prohibitive. Where there is a prescriptive policy, the domestic impact will be discernable by looking at new legislation and institutions. Where there is a prohibitive policy, changes in legislation aimed at liberalisation should be evident. Where a framing policy is used by the Union, there will be changes in the discourse of policy-makers, and the effects on legislation and institutions will be indirect. Identification of the type of policies involved in a Europeanisation process thus enables the researcher to pinpoint where to look for the effects at domestic level.

Policy paradigms

Policy paradigms are distinctive features within the normative institutional structure of each particular policy area. The concept of policy paradigms was developed for the accession context by Sedelmeier (1998), building on the work of Hall (1993). Hall uses the term 'policy paradigm' to refer to the interpretative framework within which policy-makers work. The policy paradigm is the 'framework of ideas and standards that specifies not only the goals of policy and the kind of instruments that can be used to attain them, but also the very nature of the problems that need to be addressed. Like a *Gestalt*, this framework is embedded in the very terminology through which policymakers communicate about their work, and it is influential precisely because so much of it is taken for granted and unamenable to scrutiny as a whole' (Hall 1993, p. 279). Hall argues that policy paradigms are a feature of the overall terms of political discourse, and they can structure the policy-making process just as institutions can.

In the case-studies, we will investigate the policy paradigms underlying the policies transferred to CEE because they affected how the EU determined the standards for compliance with its demands in that area. The role of policy paradigms is particularly interesting in the case of regulating movement of people, because although the same policy area appears in two different cases (the single market and Schengen), the underlying policy paradigms in the two cases are different. In the case of FMP, the policy paradigm is liberalising the free flow of labour around the single market by removing impediments to the ability of individuals to travel, work and establish themselves anywhere in the Union. The goal is economic and the instruments used are regulatory. By contrast, the policy paradigm for regulating movement of persons in Schengen is control and monitoring of travel across borders, and restricting the movement of non-EU nationals. The goal here is security and the instruments are border controls. Each of these policy paradigms is composed of different ideas and standards which define the nature of the problem to be addressed by the policy: for FMP, that is liberalising the movement of persons, whereas for Schengen it is restricting the movement of persons. The policy-makers involved in each of these areas rarely talk to one another, and use very different terminology to discuss their work. As a result, the two policy paradigms are sometimes in conflict.

Institutional isomorphism

Institutional isomorphism is a concept adapted from organisational theory that has been used to analyse how policy is transferred in the EU. Essentially, it means that political institutions become more like one another. Radaelli (2000b) makes the case that institutional isomorphism has considerable potential for the analysis of policy diffusion. He draws on the work of organisational theorists DiMaggio and Powell (1991), whose concept of institutional isomorphism is based on the premise that 'organizations compete not just for resources and customers, but for political power and institutional legitimacy' (DiMaggio and Powell 1991, p. 66). Hence 'copying organizational structures is not a process driven by efficiency considerations, but a way of securing legitimacy in political life.' (Radaelli 2000b, p. 27). Radaelli argues that European institutions stimulate policy transfer in the existing member-states by catalysing isomorphic processes such as coercion, mimetism and normative pressures. The accession process in CEE provides examples of several different kinds of isomorphism; competition authorities, environmental agencies, agriculture ministries and border protection regimes showed different degrees of convergence with EU models. The case-studies examine how the institutions regulating the movement of persons were structured and operated in ways more like those in the EU-15 countries.

The encouragement of isomorphism is an important mechanism by which EU policies and institutions could be transferred because of CEE policy-makers' desire to gain political legitimacy for their institutional and policy changes during post-communist transition. In particular, it is useful in analysing how policy transfer can be used as a political vehicle. As Robertson (1991) puts it, 'policy lessons from abroad often are put forward as politically neutral truths. Beneath this ... adversaries are just as often using such lessons as political weapons' (p. 55). CEE policy-makers could claim to be copying EU institutions in order to gain legitimacy for their activities, and to counter domestic political resistance.

The uncertainty about standards can be an incentive towards institutional isomorphism. In the absence of any objective set of standards for different policy areas, it was very important for CEE to look like the member-states, and not to use different means to achieve the same goals. 'Deviating from traditional or familiar methods and models will provoke the scrutiny, if not the outright suspicion, of the EU.' (Nicolaides 1999, p. 3). Even if the EU specified no precise model or method to achieve the goal it had set, the candidates had a strong incentive to find some familiar 'EU-look' way of achieving it in order to reassure the EU. The EU generally has an aversion to innovation in would-be member-states because one of the aims of accession policy is to make candidates look as much like member-states as possible.

This need to 'look familiar' was especially important in single market policies, because of the concern of the Commission to ensure that enlargement did not disrupt the functioning of the internal market. CEE policy-makers often claimed that they were being forced to comply more strictly with the *acquis* than current member-states had done. This is a difficult claim to corroborate. A rough estimation on single market compliance can be gained by comparing the Commission's annual Internal

Market Scorecard on the existing member-states with comments in the Regular Reports on the applicants, but this does not provide a rigorous methodology because the Commission's comments were so general and often vague. Nicolaides (1999) has done some initial conceptual work on defining implementation capacity and the problems inherent in determining rules for it, but this has not yet resulted in a systematic methodology. Unsurprisingly, the Commission often used institutional isomorphism as a substitute: its lack of comprehensive measures of compliance led it to look at similarity of institutional structures.

For the candidates to look familiar was even more important in the case of justice and home affairs, where the most important hurdle to cross was not a technical assessment by the Commission, but gaining the confidence of the member-states in the capacity of CEE countries to control movement across their eastern borders. It was very difficult for non-members to gain the confidence of the member-states' interior and justice ministers in this area, given the absence of clear criteria for measuring border management capacities. The Commission did not set up benchmarking standards, and it based its assessments on the qualitative reports of EU-appointed missions sent to assess border management. Indeed, some EU actors relied on the twinning agents to perform the unpublished function of reassuring their home governments about the abilities of their host countries to guarantee internal security. For candidates, an important way of reassuring the member-states was to involve the twinning agents in implementing policies and installing technology and practices on the borders that were explicitly modelled on those of key EU member-states (e.g. Germany).

However, there may be costs to such institutional isomorphism too, where they lead to 'functional dualism' (as Jacoby 1999 calls it), whereby their institutions have the formal characteristics of EU ones, but do not function well. This is always a risk with policy transfer, as Nicolaides has argued: 'It is virtually impossible, for example, to transfer enforcement mechanisms that have worked in one country to another. Not only do institutional conditions and policy-making traditions vary significantly from country to country, but ... successful application and enforcement of rules ultimately depend on organisations which are capable of learning and adjusting. Exact recipes or quantitative prescriptions, therefore, are bound to suppress those much needed learning and adjustment processes.' (Nicolaides 1999, p. 2).

These problems can be particularly intractable in the post-communist context, where policy-makers were under great pressure to find models quickly in order to replace discredited communist institutions. Grabher and Stark (1997) have argued that 'limiting the search for effective institutions and organisational forms to the familiar Western quadrant of tried and proven arrangements locks in the post-socialist economies to exploiting known territory at the cost of forgetting (or never learning) the skills of exploring for new solutions.' (pp. 1–2). Grabher (1994a) has argued that this is dangerous from an evolutionary perspective; although institutional homogenisation might foster adaptation in the short run, the consequent loss of institutional diversity will impede adaptability in the long run. This factor is important not only in responding to endogenous processes of change in CEE, but also in globalisation. The EU restricted policy options in responding to international competition, and in the long run the CEE countries may find that they adopted sub-optimal policies and institutions. The question is whether the disadvantages of such choices were outweighed by the advantages of membership.

Agenda-setting

In order to track where exactly in the policy-making process EU influence acted, we can learn from a study of public policy processes by John Kingdon (1997). Kingdon conceives of policy-making as a set of four processes:

1. setting the agenda;
2. specifying alternatives from which a choice is to be made;
3. authoritative choice (vote or decision);
4. implementation of the decision.

In the context of his US cases, Kingdon looks at the first two (agendas and alternatives), whereas the case-studies in this book will examine 1, 2 and 4 in assessing the EU's impact on CEE, because implementation is a key phase in policy transfer between the EU and the applicants. Kingdon's approach was formulated for a single-country study (congressional policy-making in the United States), so it has to be adapted for use in a transnational context

According to Kingdon's conception, the policy 'agenda' is the list of subjects to which government officials are paying serious attention at any given time. The agenda-setting process then narrows this set of conceivable subjects to a focus set; however, Kingdon distinguishes between agenda-setting and alternative-specification, because these can be governed by quite different processes: e.g. presidents can dominate the congressional agenda, but they have less control over the alternatives considered by members.

Kingdon distinguishes between the governmental agenda (the subjects getting attention) and the decision agenda (subjects within the governmental agenda up for an actual decision). Three kinds of process affect the agenda: problems, policies and politics. Each of these three can serve as an impetus or a constraint on items rising on the agenda (e.g. too costly, lack of public acceptance, opposition of powerful interests, more pressing items). A revised version of the Cohen *et al.* (1972) 'garbage can' model of organisational choice can be used to understand agenda-setting and alternative-generation in the framework of these processes.

This overall framework can be used to answer the question 'At what points in the policy-making process was EU influence greatest?'. EU influence was present both at the agenda-setting and alternative-specification stages, but our case-studies suggest that the EU was more important in alternative-specification than agenda-setting, and more important in defining the decision agenda than the government agenda. Many items on the EU's agenda for accession were also relevant to the process of post-communist transition, or such measures were required for joining other international organisations. Political actors may thus have known that a particular issue would emerge at some point. However, the EU could affect the timing of when a decision was taken and the response of domestic policy-makers.

These two concepts of the decision agenda and alternative-specification are very useful in analysing EU influence on CEE:

1. The EU could force some items up the decision agenda by setting timetables and demanding attention at a particular time. The EU singled out particular ideas for attention by CEE policy-makers. The integration process was a perpetual presence on the government agenda and pervaded the other items on it (because checking with EU norms became routinised in the legislative system); however, the EU as an actor was often most important in demanding action on a particular item at a particular time, so its influence was greatest on the decision agenda. Hence the EU had influence because it defined problems for the attention of CEE governments; after all, key EU policy documents like the Accession Partnerships and Regular Reports were lists of problems for attention with timetables for tackling them.

2. We can see Kingdon's 'alternative-specification' at work in some policy areas but not others. The EU supplied policy solutions only in a limited range of fields because of its own patchwork of Europeanised policies. Hence there are two different types of policy area that can be influenced by the accession process. The first type is areas that have to be

adjusted because they have once been an EU problem. These policy areas are already part of the *acquis communautaire*, and the EU may have quite detailed institutional and policy preferences to communicate to the candidates. The second type is areas which the EU defines as a problem for the candidates, but where the Union does not supply a solution in terms of detailed preferences about how to deal with it. The first and second Copenhagen conditions (political and economic) mostly contain this second type of policy area, where the content and extent of political and economic reforms are not specified by the EU. The third condition on the obligations of membership contains more of the first type of policy areas, where there is a clear *acquis*. However, new policy areas like JHA may grow, where the EU took a long time to decide what the *acquis* was and the details of how it should be implemented.

Conclusions

This chapter has set out the key research questions for the case-studies. It has made a *prima facie* case that EU policies penetrate CEE political systems, and that they do so in ways that are similar to the mechanisms operating in the EU, but that the effects are likely to be wider and deeper in scope. This chapter then made a case for using approaches from the Europeanisation literature on the existing EU in the context of CEE, and introduced the key analytical tools to be used, including intervening variables. In this book, the study of Europeanisation is confined to the influence of EU accession policy on public policy-making. It leaves for further research interesting questions that are related but separate, such as the role of bilateral contacts between member-states and candidate countries.

The scope of potential Europeanisation through accession policy is very wide, owing to the breadth of the accession conditions. Europeanisation was able to penetrate deeply in CEE public policy-making because of the fundamental transformations taking place in post-communist polities, and the importance of EU models in CEE political discourse. However, the EU may not have used its rule-setting power effectively when it was sporadic and inconsistent in its attention to particular policy areas, and consequently wasted opportunities to influence CEE policy-making. In other words, the Union may not have used its routes of influence persistently to enforce a consistent policy agenda.

Europeanisation is an area of enquiry as much as a concept. It is a tool to make sense of phenomena in CEE which involved domestic policy processes in a context of international relations. The complexity of the EU's demands for the eastern applicants and the multi-faceted role that the EU played in CEE require deep investigation both of the EU's agenda and domestic policy processes. This means paying greater attention to the details of EU policies than has been paid by comparativist scholars primarily looking at the international relations aspects of EU-CEE relations, such as classifying transition paths (e.g. Vachudová and Snyder 1997, Linz and Stepan 1996). It is also requires more than a simple 'balance of power' research design. Using Europeanisation as the framework enables us to investigate processes at both international and domestic levels without a simplification of them into bargaining games.

Although it is appropriate to use the concept of Europeanisation to study the effects of the EU on CEE, researchers need to go further than just looking for the same effects in CEE as have been observed in the EU. The key question that remains open is the extent of change. How far did the EU change domestic political structures and public policy in CEE? What conditions determined its success in effecting change? Empirical and theoretical work on the EU provides a starting-point, but the approach needs greater refinement to capture the particularities of the Europeanisation process in the context of accession conditionality. In particular, the case of the CEE applicant countries shows the need for bottom-up research design because both EU and CEE policy-makers had an incentive to exaggerate the extent of EU influence. In fact, individual policy choices were affected by multiple variables, including conflicting demands from different parts of the EU. The rhetoric from both candidates and the EU about the influence of enlargement obscured a complex interaction between the processes of Europeanisation, accession and post-communist transition.

4
Routes of Europeanisation and Constraints on EU Influence

This chapter analyses the routes that the accession process provided for the EU to exert influence on CEE, in order to establish a structure for the analysis in the two case-studies that follow. The chapter proceeds as follows: Section 4.1 identifies five mechanisms by which the EU exerted influence through the accession process to cause Europeanisation in CEE. Section 4.2 introduces the main intervening variables on each side – the factors which mediated the EU's impact. Section 4.3 then discusses in detail the two central variables on the EU side – diffuseness and uncertainty – while the following chapter discusses the variables on the CEE side. The intervening variables can mediate the impact of EU policies, so they have the potential to explain the likelihood and direction of Europeanisation in a given policy area. The explanatory power of these intervening variables is tested in the case-studies.

4.1   Europeanisation mechanisms in the accession process

EU accession involves a number of different processes that had the potential to effect some degree of institutional and policy transformation in CEE. This study uses the terms 'mechanism' and 'route' to indicate that these are potential means of influence, without pre-judging the impact each had in practice. The most important mechanism for any would-be member is the EU's gate-keeping role, through which it decides when a country can progress to the next stage towards accession (as discussed below). However, there are many other measures that directly or indirectly shape institutional reform and increase the organisational capacity of the state in the CEE countries. Indirect pressure can be equally effective, but it only works over time and it is not necessarily coordinated at EU level, so it is hard to discern any consistent policy influence. The plethora of contacts between the EU and the candidates undoubtedly had a major impact, but it is hard to gauge which EU policies and institutions were most influential through indirect routes such as example-setting, policy learning, and providing models of best practice.

This section investigates the mechanisms used instrumentally by the EU to effect change through conditionality and the accession process, grouping them into five categories. The effects of EU influence in the area of movement of people are investigated in the case-studies.

- Models: provision of legislative and institutional templates
- Money: aid and technical assistance
- Benchmarking and monitoring
- Advice and twinning
- Gate-keeping: access to negotiations and further stages in the accession process

Two of these processes had long caused Europeanisation effects in the EU-15 countries: the EU produces legislation for implementation in the member-states, along with money from the Community budget which affects many policies. The third mechanism was also used in the EU-15, with benchmarking becoming a more important method through the Lisbon process introduced in 2000. Indeed, some of the benchmarking and monitoring methods developed for accession may have had feed-back effects, as the Commission used its experience in CEE to apply the same methods to existing member-states. The last two mechanisms are primarily reserved for applicant countries, and they had particularly strong Europeanisation effects in CEE.

Models: provision of legislative and institutional templates

The CEE candidate countries had to take on all the EU's existing laws and norms, so they were subject to the same Europeanisation pressures as member-states in the policies and institutional templates that they 'downloaded' from EU level. Legal transposition of the *acquis* and harmonisation with EU laws are essential to becoming a member-state, and they were the central focus of the accession process and preparations by the candidates.

Some of the legal templates were transferred through binding agreements such as the Europe Agreements. Indeed, legislative adaptation to EU norms was initiated by the Europe Agreements, and continued with the Single Market White Paper, and then the Accession Partnerships. Legislative gaps and institutional weaknesses were also identified by the screening process that took place with each applicant prior to negotiations on each of the 31 negotiating 'chapters'. The European Commission used the screening process to identify the main areas where applicants' legislation was not compliant with the *acquis communautaire*, and the results of screening were used to formulate EU negotiating positions and to establish priorities in the Accession Partnerships. There were also particular policy and legislation monitoring programmes for individual policy areas; for example, under the 'MISSOC' programme, CEE countries had to provide the European Commission with information on legislative and regulatory developments and implementation arrangements in the field of social policy.

In addition to imposing its own norms, the EU reinforced other international legal norms by making them part of accession conditionality. In order to join the EU, the applicants had to have ratified various international conventions. In the case of human rights, for example, these included the European Social Charter, the Framework Convention for National Minorities, the Convention on the Elimination of All Forms of Racial Discrimination (CERD), and the Convention on the Elimination of All Forms of Discrimination against Women (CEDAW). EU conditionality also reinforced that of other international agencies such as the World Trade Organisation, the Council of Europe, and the international financial institutions (the International Monetary Fund and the World Bank). Implementation of agreements with the development banks was part of Romania's 1998 Accession Partnership, for example, and the IMF's focus on macroeconomic stability was reinforced by EU priorities for maintaining internal and external balance.

The EU promoted both the strengthening of existing institutions (such as ministries and central banks) and the establishment of new ones (such as competition authorities and regional administrative units). As with the old member-states, the transfer of legislative and institutional models involved both 'vertical harmonisation' and 'horizontal harmonisation' (Radaelli 2003), depending on whether the policy area in question involved positive or negative integration (Knill and Lehmkuhl 1999). However, a critical difference was that the candidates could not 'upload' their own preferences into those European-level policies. They were only consumers, not producers, of the outcomes of the EU's policy-making processes. That meant that they could not object if an EU policy fitted very badly with their domestic structures or policies. Moreover, the candidates had less room for manoeuvre in implementing EU models because they had to prove themselves to be capable of implementing EU law as well as potential member-states were.

The candidates increasingly became affected by the EU's 'framing' mechanisms of Europeanisation as well. This occurred through all three 'soft' Europeanisation mechanisms identified by Radaelli (2003). Candidates were encouraged to comply closely with minimalist directives and non-compulsory directives, in order to convince reluctant member-states that they would be good partners in sensitive policy areas. For example, they were invited to shadow the 'Lisbon process' of economic reform, even though it was not officially part of the accession *acquis*, and the candidates voluntarily signed 'Joint Assessment Papers' with the Commission to guide their labour market policies. Another example of where the candidates were encouraged to do more than strictly required by the *acquis* was social policy, where the Commission presented a maximalist version of a largely non-binding *acquis* to the applicants (Brusis 1998). CEE activity in both of these policy areas also involved cognitive convergence, where the EU did not have a coherent corpus of directives, but the CEE countries nevertheless looked to the EU for guidance on good policy. CEE governments had a double incentive to respond to framing integration: one was to show the EU that they were willing and able to play a full part as member-states and take on the future *acquis* as it developed. The other was to show their domestic electorate that they were taken seriously by the EU as a full partner, and sometimes to legitimate their policy programmes by reference to EU policies.

However, the extent to which references to EU norms actually resulted in changes in policy depended on the domestic political context, on the policy area in question. One of the problems in analysing the EU's impact in CEE lies in distinguishing how far an actual EU model was used, and how much the EU's own diversity provided multiple points of reference in the CEE debates. The EU often lacks a single model to export (as discussed by Mörth 2003), and its own diversity can undermine its efforts to export a single model of governance. For example, an appeal to 'Europe' was a constant feature of the domestic debate about regional policies (see Fowler 2001 on Hungary). All sides and all political parties made this appeal, yet the EU was a confusing model, as CEE actors could point to the very different examples of sub-state governance in EU member-states to support their positions. This provided ammunition for different sides in domestic political battles.

Candidate countries tended to engage in anticipatory adjustment to EU policies as well, adopting EU norms or practices before the EU told them they must do so. In the first years of post-communist economic transition, policy-makers in central Europe frequently made reference to EU economic models and EU regulatory and competition policies to justify their policy choices, even before the EU required conformity. In the last years before membership in 2004, candidates adjusted their domestic policies and institutions in advance of specific EU requirements to do so in the area of justice and home affairs. All of the candidates rapidly adopted the EU's still sketchy *acquis* for border control, police cooperation, asylum, migration and crime prevention. After the terrorist attacks in New York and Washington on 11 September 2001, several leading candidates (e.g. Hungary and the Czech Republic) quickly put forward plans for tighter border controls and cooperation with US and EU intelligence and police forces that went beyond official requirements for accession. They did so because current member-states could veto their membership if their capacity to control cross-border crime and other threats was judged to be inadequate (see Grabbe 2002). Candidates also had to show willing, by proving that they took these issues seriously, because member-states' acceptance of the candidates' readiness for the JHA *acquis* was largely based on degrees of confidence in their border controls and legal systems, rather than formal technical standards.

The most detailed guide to the EU's preferences on institution-building was provided in an informal working document produced by the Commission in May 2000 (and subsequently updated), entitled 'Main administrative structures required for implementing the *acquis*'. This document described the institutions required to implement the various chapters of the *acquis*, their functions, and the characteristics they must have to fulfil those functions. It covered not only the *acquis* itself, but also other institutions which the Commission considered necessary for effective implementation of the *acquis*. For example, the document lists the 'common elements' among member-states' varying labour market institutions. This document's status was indicative of the EU's uncertainty about how far to go in providing detailed institutional preferences. It remained an unofficial paper, labelled 'for information purposes only', and explicitly stated that 'it should not be construed as committing the European Commission'. This reluctance demonstrates the political sensitivity of defining specific administrative models in areas where member-states' administrations remain so diverse. It also reflected the EU's general desire to retain flexibility in deciding when a country was ready to join. The Commission could not pre-judge the Council's view on what might be acceptable or unacceptable in a prospective member-state. However, the Commission's preferences were communicated informally to different parts of the public administration in CEE.

Aid and technical assistance

The EU was the largest external source of aid for CEE after 1989, through the funds administered by the European Commission and also bilateral programmes from individual member-states (the largest from Germany). The Phare aid programme initially covered the ten CEE countries which applied for membership; it was later extended to Turkey and the Balkan countries.

The amounts transferred to CEE were relatively small in comparison with the fiscal transfers to the existing member-states under the structural and cohesion funds. However, they had an important role in reinforcing the transfer of EU models, because the aid helped to pay for implementation and the technical assistance built institutional capacity to take on EU practices. The co-financing requirements forced applicant countries to allocate public resources to particular policy areas too, so EU aid changed the order of priorities on governments' agendas.

Until 1997, EU aid policy was oriented towards a broad range of goals connected with transition towards pluralist democracy and market economics, largely through technical assistance. Phare was demand-driven, allowing CEE governments to formulate their own requests in the fields of institutional reform and infrastructure development. Projects were awarded to consultants under a competitive tendering process, but without a policy framework, so there was little opportunity for consistent and persistent policy influence from the EU.

After the Luxembourg European Council in December 1997, Phare was turned into an explicit instrument of pre-accession policy, with aid focused on preparations for accession. The two main priorities were institution-building, with a stress on training of public servants (30% of funds) and development of infrastructure (70%), concentrating on transport and environmental projects.

Under the Community budget for 2000–2006 (called the 'financial perspective'), Phare was allocated €1.5 billion a year to spend on the ten CEE applicants (eight of which joined the Union in 2004). The core priorities of Phare activities remained similar, with institution-building receiving around 30% of Phare resources and investment

70%. Institution-building was defined as 'strengthening the candidates' capacity to enforce and implement the *acquis*' (CEC 2000b), and it also aimed to prepare candidates for participation in EU policies such as economic and social cohesion. The funds for this area were mainly given through secondment of officials from member-states. Support was also available to public authorities and NGOs to help fulfil the requirements of the first Copenhagen criterion, related to democracy.

Investment support was given to strengthen the regulatory infrastructure needed to comply with the *acquis*, and also for economic and social cohesion measures similar to those supported in the member-states through the European Regional Development Fund and the European Social Fund. These two funds supply finance for a broad range of social and economic measures in the EU, and the projects supported by Phare in CEE range widely. The Commission identified priorities which national governments had to follow in their applications for Phare funds.

Aid money to the candidates was specifically devoted to accession-related tasks and disbursed through an inflexible bureaucratic process. It was thus hard to use it as a carrot to get the countries to move in a particular direction. Moreover, EU aid to CEE was still small compared with FDI inflows for the front-runner candidates, so withdrawal of aid was not a heavy sanction economically. Nevertheless, the political embarrassment a withdrawal caused could be effective. When Poland lost €150 million in Phare funding in 1998, for example, the government's embarrassment was widely reported in both the Polish and international press.

After 2000, the EU also started transferring funds to CEE from its Common Agricultural Policy (CAP) budget (€500 million per year through SAPARD[21]) and Structural Funds (€1 billion annually through ISPA[22]), making a total of €21 billion available in pre-accession aid over the period 2000–2006. After they joined, the new members became eligible for considerable additional funds from the structural funds and agriculture budgets, and these pre-accession funds were designed to develop their institutional capacity to handle such large transfers and increase their familiarity with EU procedures.

ISPA provided structural funds money to contribute to accession preparations specifically in the area of 'economic and social cohesion', which covered environmental measures and transport infrastructure measures. Measures had to comply with EU law and the Accession Partnership objectives. SAPARD funds contributed to the implementation of the *acquis* concerning the common agricultural policy and related policies, and could also be used to solve specific problems in adapting the agricultural sector and rural areas to EU membership.

EU agricultural policies were more controversial than the structural measures because the EU's agricultural policy is based on a system of managed prices and large subsidies to farmers that ran counter to the free-market reforms promoted in post-communist CEE agricultural sectors (Ockenden and Franklin 1995). The applicants were not encouraged by the EU to replicate this system – both for doctrinal and financial motives – but they had to prepare their administrations to deal with CAP funds. Decisions on how to spend the SAPARD money for agricultural development were largely in the hands of national agriculture ministries (subject to broad guidelines set by the EU), whereas ISPA funds were much more closely controlled by the Commission because it approved each individual project proposed by the CEE authorities.

EU aid – both current receipts and the prospect of future transfers – had a direct impact in creating new governance structures in the candidate countries because of the EU's insistence that particular administrative units and procedures be created to receive transfers. For the structural and cohesion funds, the EU required the creation of regional and local institutions to administer funds after accession, although the Union was ambiguous about whether these should be governmental or purely administrative institutions. The EU also advocated greater decentralisation and regional development in what had been strongly centralised states under communism. The combination of these two incentives – including the prospect of large regional transfers after accession – provoked some large-scale decentralising measures across CEE, including the creation of new sub-national units in most countries.

However, the outcomes varied considerably between countries (Hughes *et al.* 2004), particularly because the EU had no clear model of regionalism to present, with diversity marking the arrangements in the member-states. There were questions about the EU's capacity to realise all of its detailed institutional preferences at regional level (Brusis 2001). In the case of Hungary, for example, the FIDESZ-MPP party used EU demands for a 'strong' regional capacity to support a statist conception of regional administration at the expense of a multi-sector 'partnership' model (Fowler 2001). Nevertheless, the prospect of aid after accession certainly had a considerable influence on sub-state reform across the candidate countries.

Benchmarking and monitoring

Progress towards EU accession was a central issue in CEE political debates, so the EU was able to influence policy and institutional development through ranking the applicants, benchmarking in particular policy areas, and providing examples of best practice that the applicants sought to emulate. Monitoring was a key mechanism in the conditionality for membership, through the cycle of 'Accession Partnerships' and 'Regular Reports' published by the European Commission on how prepared each CEE applicant was in different fields (as discussed in Chapter 2). This process provided the EU with a subtle and highly effective route of direct influence on domestic policy-making. Not only did the Regular Reports give an indication of the performance of individual ministers, but they covered implementation of individual policies, so they implicitly judged the performance of lower-level officials within the ministries.

Moreover, the cycle of task-setting and reporting on progress established a public monitoring process that could be used by other actors – both domestic and external – to judge the progress of politicians and officials. The Regular Reports became a focus of interest for both the domestic and international media each year. Both voters and foreign investors paid attention to what the EU said about progress in key areas like privatisation and financial sector regulation.

The Commission's Regular Reports were used by the member-states to decide whether to admit each country to further stages in the accession process, so they could be a powerful tool to force changes in particular policies. However, the language used in the Regular Reports was usually very general – like that in the Accession Partnerships – and the assessments jumped from description to prescription without a detailed analysis of the problems and how to overcome them. The goals set were often vague, for example declaring a need for 'increasing capacity' or 'improving training', rather than stating detailed institutional preferences. For example, on data protection for the internal market *acquis*, Bulgaria was told to 'adopt national legislation and establish a monitoring body' in 1999 – with no indication of what the legislation should contain or what an appropriate monitoring body might look like. Candidates were often asked to 'prepare a national strategy' in a particular area, with no further details on what it should contain or what the features of particular institutions should be. That made it difficult to use the reports as a detailed guide to EU-compatible public policy. Instead, the detailed guidance was provided informally by a range of EU actors – from different parts of the Commission,

Council, Parliament and member-states. Although benchmarking can be used instrumentally, the EU did not necessarily use it effectively where it had no detailed policy or legislative framework that could be used as a template for the candidates. One condition for effective use is thus the existence of an EU norm or template to be transposed.

The experience of setting standards and creating monitoring mechanisms for the applicants was an important learning process for the European Commission – with potential feedback effects on the existing Union. Several key officials used their enlargement experience in planning monitoring processes for the existing member-states. The Commission discovered benchmarking almost by accident (Begg and Peterson 1999), and it was increasingly used as a powerful vector of Europeanisation for both candidates and member-states.

Advice and twinning

The EU provided a wide range of policy advice to CEE through the technical assistance offered by the Phare programme from 1989 to 1997 and through the 'twinning' programme that started in 1999. TAIEX (the Technical Assistance Information Exchange Office) also provided experts to give short-term advice. The EU's efforts were supplemented by SIGMA (Support for Improvement in Governance and Management in Central and Eastern European countries), an OECD body funded by Phare that provided advice on horizontal government functions.

'Twinning' was aimed at helping CEE countries to adapt their administrative and democratic institutions to comply with membership requirements by learning from member-state experiences of framing the legislation, and building the organisational capacity necessary to implement the *acquis*. The programme used Phare funds to pay for the secondment of officials from EU member-states to work in CEE ministries and other parts of the public administration (e.g. institutions, professional organisations, agencies, and European and regional bodies). CEE governments put forward twinning projects – subject to approval by the Commission – and member-states bid for the contracts to supply the officials, either individually or (more commonly) in consortia (see CEC 2000a). Table 4.1 below lists the twinning projects financed under Phare in 1998–2000, when it applied to just a few areas. Twinning was extended to all Accession Partnership priorities after 2000.

Twinning provided the EU with a direct line into policy-making structures in CEE because EU civil servants worked alongside CEE counterparts. It could thus provide a route for cognitive convergence,

Table 4.1　Twinning projects financed under Phare in 1998–2000

Candidate country	Agriculture (incl. veterinary and phytosanitary projects)	Environment	Public Finance (incl. taxation, customs, internal market etc.)	Justice and home affairs	Social policy	Regional development and preparation for structural funds	Others	Total
Bulgaria	7	11	12	6	4	3	2	45
Czech R.	3	5	7	11	9	2	5	42
Estonia	4	2	7	5	3	1	–	22
Hungary	6	5	9	5	4	2	–	31
Latvia	3	2	4	4	1	3	1	18
Lithuania	2	1	6	6	3	1	6	25
Poland	16	5	15	6	4	3	8	57
Romania	7	3	13	8	5	3	3	42
Slovakia	6	6	8	12	6	1	5	44
Slovenia	6	2	7	7	4	2	3	31
Total	60	42	88	70	43	21	33	357

Source: European Commission, *Strategy Paper*, 8 November 2000, Annex 4.

as EU officials taught their CEE colleagues how to 'do things the EU way'. However, the advice and expertise offered by the twinning agents was not controlled centrally by the EU.

The lack of any overall coordination of the advice and expertise offered by the twinning agents suggests that the impact on individual policies was diffuse, rather than reflecting any consistent European model. Indeed, one of the main principles of the programme was that the existing member-states should implement the EU's legislation by different means, and they could help the candidate countries to do the same, but without imposing any particular system.

The quality and consistency of the policy advice provided through twinning in the CEE countries are difficult to assess. Anecdotal evidence from the member-states which sent their own civil servants suggests a success rate of about one in four projects.[23] The 'pre-accession advisors' (the title of the twinning agents) largely set their own agenda in collaboration with the host CEE government. Because twinning projects used civil servants and focused on implementation, most agents were concerned with standards and technical issues rather than overall institutional models or policy direction. Their advice also reflected their own assumptions, national backgrounds, and professional experience in their home EU ministries. Whether an advisor was French, Greek, British or Swedish could make a considerable difference to the policy advice he or she offered, because these countries have different traditions and 'policy styles'.

Gate-keeping: access to negotiations and further stages in the accession process

The EU's most powerful conditionality tool with any candidate is access to different stages in the accession process, particularly achieving candidate status and starting negotiations. Aid, trade and other benefits can also be used to promote domestic policy changes, but they do not have such direct and evident consequences as progress towards membership. It took a decade for the EU to evolve an explicit use of conditionality in a gate-keeping role for the CEE countries, where hurdles in the accession process were related to meeting specific conditions. For several years after the conditions were first set in 1993, it was not clear exactly which elements of the political and economic conditions had to be fulfilled for an applicant to be admitted to which benefits. However, by the time of the Luxembourg 1997 and Helsinki 1999 European Councils, a rough progression had emerged of stages in the accession process:

- Privileged trade access and additional aid.
- Signing and implementing an enhanced form of association agreement (Europe Agreements for the current candidates, Stabilisation and Association Agreements for south-eastern European non-applicants).
- Opening of negotiations (explicitly dependent on meeting the democracy and human rights conditions after 1999).
- Opening and closing of the 31 chapters.
- Signing of an accession treaty.
- Ratification of the accession treaty by national parliaments and the European Parliament.
- Entry as a full member.

The Helsinki European Council (December 1999) made an explicit linkage between access to negotiations and the democracy condition for the first time, stating that to start negotiating, an applicant had to have achieved stability of institutions guaranteeing democracy, the rule of law, human rights, and respect for and protection of minorities. In December 1999, only Turkey was judged not to have met this condition, whereas all the CEE applicants had done so.

This sequence of moving into an ever closer relationship with the EU provides a coercive tool to reinforce other mechanisms of Europeanisation, such as transfer of models and benchmarking. But it also works as a Europeanisation mechanism in its own right, because the EU can attach specific conditions to particular stages in the accession process. At the Helsinki European Council in 1999, the EU explicitly made fulfilment of the democracy and human rights conditions for accession a pre-requisite for starting negotiations – and excluded Turkey from negotiations on these grounds. The Commission also imposed specific tasks for Bulgaria (on nuclear power) and Romania (on economic reform and state orphanages) before they could join negotiations in 2000. This was an innovative move for the EU, in making an explicit linkage between a benefit and specific tasks for applicants, and it heralded the start of more targeted use of conditionality.

However, although access to negotiations and other stages in the accession process is the EU's most powerful political tool for enforcing compliance, it is not a precise instrument that can effect complex changes in institutional frameworks. Rather, it is a blunt weapon that can be used judiciously for priority areas only. Its main value is as a shock tactic, to embarrass applicant countries' governments into making dramatic changes owing to the domestic repercussions of failing to meet a major foreign policy goal. This results in 'shaming' through political contacts and press coverage.

Criticisms made in EU reports can have a powerful impact on domestic debates about public policy and the government's political fortunes. Conversely, gaining international approval was an important way of legitimising political choices in the post-communist context. The EU made exceptional criticisms of undemocratic practices in particular countries in '*démarches*', which are public criticisms that are intended to embarrass CEE governments into making particular institutional or policy changes.[24] *Démarches* are used only for very serious breaches of the conditions, such as human or minority rights abuses. The first explicit use of conditionality to exclude a country occurred in 1997, when Slovakia was not allowed to join the first round of negotiations as the only candidate judged not to meet the democracy criteria. The EU's disapprobation was expressed in several *démarches* which had an impact on the elections in Autumn 1998, when the government of Prime Minister Vladimir Mečiar was voted out (Bútorová 1998). Following the change of government in 1998, Slovakia was allowed into accession negotiations in 2000.

There tends to be strong political opposition in the EU to excluding an applicant once it is part of the process. The Union finds it easier to keep countries from joining the process than to stop their progress once they are a candidate. For example, the EU refused throughout the whole of the 1990s to sign a Europe Agreement with Croatia or the Federal Republic of Yugoslavia on political grounds. However, use of the gate-keeping sanction becomes more controversial as countries get closer to membership. For example, this was evident the second time that the EU stopped a candidate from starting accession negotiations because of non-fulfilment of the political criteria in 2005, when Croatia was told that it could not begin negotiations as planned on 17 March because it had not fully complied with the International Criminal Tribunal on the former Yugoslavia.

Exclusion is a risky tactic, because the EU's own credibility is at stake: it can effect change only if it is credible that the applicant's failure to meet one of the conditions is the reason behind the exclusion from the next stage of the accession process, not any other political or economic motivations. Moreover, it is risky because the CEE government may not respond by complying with EU demands, but instead use the tactic of blaming the EU for unfair discrimination and appealing to national pride – as Mečiar did. As Schimmelfennig (2001) points out, this process of 'socialising' CEE countries into international norms happens through 'reactive reinforcement' rather than active conditionality: 'internalisation is rewarded but a failure to internalise the community rules is not punished beyond withholding the reward.' (p. 2). It works only if governments and political elites as a whole are committed to EU accession.

These factors make it difficult for the EU to use exclusion and gate-keeping to shape institutions, which requires sustained and consistent pressure at a deeper level within national administrations. Moreover, given the risks involved, it is not worth using this major weapon except for high-profile political issues, and governance only becomes one of them when it involves evidently undemocratic practices and abuse of human rights. However, EU actors can use the threat of exclusion or the prospect of slowing progress to encourage particular changes in policies or institutional structures.

4.2   The role of intervening variables

The previous section has set out the mechanisms by which the EU can put different forms of adaptational pressure on candidate countries, and hence cause Europeanisation. But how (and how far) did the routes of influence analysed above actually drive change? The process was dynamic and the potential effects were wide-ranging. The EU had no specific test of institutional change, and its assessments were based on an opaque methodological framework. Moreover, adaptational pressure is not the best predictor of how a country responds to Europeanisation (Radaelli 2003). There can be a number of intervening variables that determine the actual impact in a given policy area and country. It is already clear, for example, that there remained persistent differences between the CEE candidates; for example, there was little evidence of convergence towards a standard model of governance (Goetz and Wollmann 2001). We also know that only limited convergence had happened in the existing 15 EU member-states (Goetz 2000; Risse and Börzel 2003); indeed, it was the continuing diversity of member-states' institutions and policy preferences which inhibited the emergence of a detailed agenda for CEE.

To work towards an explanation of the effects of Europeanisation, this section sets out the chief intervening variables on the EU and CEE sides. The intervening variables are a variety of mechanisms that stand between the EU and CEE, and hence influence the interpretation, implementation and outcomes of the EU's conditions. The variables can work on either or both sides of the relationship, being present in the EU's policy-making structure or content, or in that of CEE. They were present in the EU's overall framework of conditionality for eastern accession, and hence generally intentional, as the EU set the rules of the game. But they were also present in the detailed content of the conditions – i.e. the EU's substantive agenda for CEE. In the latter case, the variables could be either intentional – for example, deliberate prioritisation of a particular issue – or unintentional, in that they were inherent in the structure of its policies developed for the existing EU that were then applied to CEE.

The variables on the EU side can represent significant constraints on the Union's influence in CEE. They are:

- Diffuseness of influence.
- Uncertainty.

On the CEE side are three further intervening variables, whose interaction determines a candidate's response to the structure of incentives and constraints imposed by the EU in a given policy area:

- The country's institutional capacity to achieve its political goals.
- Political salience of the issue.
- The macro-strategy of adaptation to the EU.

The first two variables are discussed in the next section, and the latter three in Chapter 5.

4.3   Constraints on EU influence: Diffuseness and uncertainty

Diffuseness of influence

The diffuseness of EU influence results from the characteristics of the conditionality, as well as the specifics of the accession process presented above. The first cause of diffuseness is the EU's own lack of institutional templates, because of its limited role in the governance of its current member-states. Moreover, it moved into many key areas of governance and policy relatively late. An important example is justice and home affairs, where the European Commission gained the expertise and personnel to promote the development and functioning of political institutions at national level in JHA only in the early 2000s.

Moreover, there were inconsistencies in the EU's advice to applicants. The most obvious example with regard to governance was the
EU's stress on regionalisation and democratisation. This produced tensions: decentralisation versus control and efficiency, and democratic
legitimacy versus fast and full implementation of the *acquis*. Various
EU actors appeared to demand and approve subsidiarity, sub-national
government autonomy, and also pluralistic decision-making. But then
specific EU requirements produced a set of incentives and constraints
that largely excluded both sub-national actors and parliaments from
the accession process and increased the weight of central state bodies
(Hughes *et al.* 2004).

Finally, the actor constellations involved were very complex.
Different parts of the EU – both its institutions and member-states –
gave different advice and signals, and different actors even in the
same institution did so as well. Even within the most centralised
institution – the Commission – numerous directorate-generals were
involved in the enlargement process, and they had particular interests and policy preferences when advising and presenting demands to
the applicants. In particular, markedly different policy paradigms
underlay the interpretation of the accession requirements that were
presented by different parts of the Commission (Sedelmeier 2001).

The Council Secretariat, the European Parliament and individual
member-states all had direct contact with applicants too. Beyond the
institutions, the individuals representing different parts of the EU
who had contact with the applicant countries all took their own pre-
conceptions and assumptions with them. These views varied because
they came from such diverse actors as national civil servants (the
twinning agents), parliamentarians (under the joint committees),
trade union officials and employers' organisations (sent by the
Economic and Social Committee), Commission officials, national
experts from the Council, and politicians from individual member-
states. These actors presented diverse and sometimes contradictory
advice. There was no coordination of the many different missions,
fact-finding groups, task-forces and joint committees travelling
around Central Europe in the name of the enlargement process.

Six dimensions of uncertainty

There are six dimensions of uncertainty built into the accession conditions, each of which acted as an intervening variable in the implementation of policies to meet the conditions. The degrees of uncertainty in

these six dimensions varied considerably between policy areas and they changed across time.

1. There was an uncertain linkage between fulfilling particular tasks and receiving particular benefits. The connection with rewards was much less clear than in other forms of international conditionality – for example, that used by the international financial institutions. The three Copenhagen conditions for accession were themselves very general and vague. The detailed criteria that constituted complying with them were spelled out by the EU incompletely and over a long time-period, from 1993 – when the conditions were set – to the end of negotiations nearly a decade later.

2. Uncertainty about the hierarchy of tasks was a major characteristic of accession policy between 1993 and 1998. CEE policy-makers complained that they did not have sufficient information about the relative importance of different conditions to sequence their preparations for accession. The EU's official position was that all 80,000-plus pages of the *acquis* had to be implemented; yet it was obvious that some pages of the *acquis* were more important than others. Moreover, it was unclear what the EU would judge as an adequate pace of preparations to clear hurdles in the accession process, such as joining negotiations.

Partly in response to such criticism, this uncertainty about sequencing and prioritisation was reduced with the introduction of the Accession Partnerships in 1998. However, this dimension of uncertainty did not entirely disappear, because there were sometimes discrepancies between the formal priorities set out in the published Accession Partnerships and the signals (e.g. policy advice and informal communication) given by different EU actors over the relative importance of the various priorities. Moreover, the shifting political agenda within the EU member-states caused sudden changes in priorities from one year to the next; for example, treatment of the Roma and border controls rose up the agenda in 1999 owing to flows of asylum-seekers to the UK and Finland and the inclusion of a far-right party in Austria's government.

3. There was uncertainty about the policy agenda that should be undertaken by the applicants. In mature policy areas like the single market – where the EU had developed a large *acquis* over many years – the agenda was fairly certain because the requirements had been tried and tested already by the existing member-states. Uncertainty might remain about the timing and standards to be achieved, and how important the area was politically, but the tasks were relatively clear. But in nascent policy areas – such as justice and home affairs, social policy, and direct tax policy co-ordination – the agenda was uncertain because the tasks had not yet been decided for the member-states either. In the case of social policy, the

uncertainty was heightened by the fact that the most common method of integration used is framing integration rather than positive integration, so it contains a much less specific agenda.

4. Timing has been identified as a dynamic factor in Europeanisation by Goetz (2000), who borrows the categories of time, timing and tempo from Schmitter and Santiso (1998). The applicants faced several problems of uncertainty concerned with timing. First, there was the timing of costs and benefits. The ultimate reward of accession was far removed from the moment at which adaptation costs were incurred, so conditionality was a blunt instrument when it came to persuading countries to change particular practices. There were, of course, intermediate rewards, such as aid and trade liberalisation. But in the end, accession was tied to overall readiness, and membership benefits were not disaggregated to reward partial readiness. Since the accession reward came in one big step – and at the end of a very long and highly politicised process – CEE policy-makers could believe there was time to make up deficiencies closer to the accession date. It was difficult to use EU membership conditionality as a precision tool to sculpt institutions and policies during the accession process; rather, it was a mallet that could be used only at certain points in the process to enforce a few conditions at a time.

Then there was the timing issue involved in negotiations. All of the *acquis* had to be implemented eventually. But which areas absolutely had to be fully in place prior to accession and which could be left until afterwards? The CEE countries still had to calculate where the EU was likely to make concessions on transition periods, in order to decide where to invest in full compliance and where to try for a transition period and invest only in partial implementation. Incomplete information thus caused uncertainty about allocation of resources across time.

Timing is often a key area for negotiations, and the EU's position on timing changed according to the politics of enlargement in the EU. For example, the debate about social and environmental 'dumping' was very lively in the early 1990s and led the EU to emphasise implementation of process standards in the Europe Agreements and Single Market White Paper (Sedelmeier 1994). But later this pressure eased, and the candidates faced little opposition to their transition period requests once they had attached financing plans to them in July 2001.

For the CEE countries, the timetable for negotiations and the cycle of priority-setting and annual monitoring reports reduced the scope for stalling, because the timing of tasks was frequently defined to within a year or even a few months. Moreover, there was stronger pressure on the CEE countries to adapt quickly because of the incentive not to fall behind the other candidates. Indeed, the EU had more scope to use tempo as a trade-off to gain concessions in negotiations, because the candidates were keener to get into the EU quickly than were the member-states to accept them. So timing was important, but the ways it was used were different from those for member-states in implementing EU business.

5. The applicants faced uncertainty about whom to satisfy. Who was the veto-player for a given policy area? In the case of single market regulation, it was likely to be the Commission, because of its role as guardian of the treaties and regulator of the internal market. However, in justice and home affairs, the Council tended to predominate both in establishing the *acquis* and judging compliance with it. The member-states paid more attention to some policy areas than others, and only some countries were likely to veto a candidate's progress in a particular area; for example, Germany and Austria might have vetoed an applicant for accession because its borders were not seen as sufficiently secure, whereas Portugal was unlikely to do so. The candidates had to work out whom to satisfy in a given policy area year-on-year, but they also faced longer-term uncertainty about who might emerge as a veto-player over another issue later in the accession process. For example, in 1997 it would have been hard to predict that in 2001 Spain would block closure of the chapter on free movement of persons, or that most of the member-states would restrict admission to their labour markets in 2004.

6. The final dimension is uncertainty about standards and thresholds. What counted as meeting the conditions and complying with the various EU demands? The judgement about whether a country had met the EU's conditions was made by the same actor who set them, and the requirements were generally not amenable to quantitative targets.

The Commission's 1997 Opinions and annual Regular Reports used a variety of sources, but these were not published, and the precise criteria used were never specified. Moreover, member-states and previous applicants had been allowed a considerable degree of slack in implementing the *acquis*. How much slack would be allowed to each applicant in assessing compliance? This was uncertain because the answer depended on which candidate, which policy area and by whom the decision was made.

The effects of uncertainty on Europeanisation

In general, Europeanisation effects depend not only on the individual uncertainties in a given policy area, but also on the interaction between these different dimensions of uncertainty. Where uncertainty about the agenda, timing and standards was high but the political salience was also high (as in the case of justice and home affairs), the EU may have had a large impact despite its uncertain agenda because

CEE policy-makers endeavoured to meet whatever criteria were hinted at. Where uncertainty about the agenda, timing and standards was high but political salience was relatively low (as in the case of social policy), the EU was likely to have a small impact because the incentives to second-guess EU requirements were low and CEE policy-makers were able to use the uncertainty to implement them less strictly.

The explanatory value of uncertainty thus depends on the priority that the EU attached to the policy in question, and the degree of domestic resistance to it in CEE. The explanatory value of uncertainty also depended on the type of policy under consideration. In framing integration, uncertainty about standards and thresholds was much higher because so many of the concrete measures were a matter of national discretion.

Table 4.2 below summarises the dimensions of uncertainty that can operate in a given policy area. It also specifies the questions that should be asked in assessing the types and levels of uncertainty associated with that policy. In Chapter 8, we will be able to fill in this table

Table 4.2   Dimensions of uncertainty

Types of uncertainty	Levels of uncertainty in this policy area	
	Policy A	Policy B
Linkage: Is there a particular benefit closely tied to the costs of adopting this policy?	Low/medium/high	Low/medium/high
Ranking: How important is this policy among the EU's priorities? Is it a veto-point that could prevent accession?		
Agenda: How well-specified are the EU's demands?		
Timing: What has to be done before accession?		
Principal agent: Who has to be satisfied?		
Standards: What counts as compliance?		

on the basis of an assessment of the dimensions of uncertainty surrounding the policies examined in the case-studies (Table 8.2).

Conclusions

The EU had enormous potential influence in CEE: every government in every applicant state claimed that membership was its first foreign policy priority. Beyond its magnetic attraction, the EU had specific routes of influence through which it could shape political choices: models, money, benchmarking, advice and gate-keeping. However, the EU did not necessarily use these tools effectively. This chapter has suggested three main reasons why the EU may not have used its full potential to shape outcomes effectively: the interaction of European-isation with other processes of change; the diffuseness of its influence, partly owing to the diversity of its current member-states; and the dimensions of uncertainty faced by the applicants in trying to meet the EU's accession conditions.

The limits of the EU's influence depended not only on the degree of resistance on the CEE side, but also the Union's own limitations as a political actor. The EU may not use its potential influence to the full extent if it does not have detailed policy preferences to communicate. Although power and conditionality may have created a demand for policy and institutional templates on the part of the candidates – which wanted to fulfil the conditions but did not necessarily know how the EU wanted them to do so – the EU could not necessarily supply these on request. If it has no detailed template, and if different EU actors interpret the conditions differently, the EU's impact will be diffuse. Moreover, uncertainty can affect implementation. The EU may set a particular policy area as a high political priority, but if the Union creates uncertainty about what candidates should do, it will have much less influence over the policy or institutional outcomes.

For this book, we need to consider how such a failure of influence may occur rather than why. This book argues that it did occur, largely through the diffuseness of EU influence and the uncertainty built into the accession conditions. These factors are intervening variables because they reduce the EU's ability to use the conditions as a structure of incentives to encourage institutional and policy change. The degree and kind of intervention vary across different parts of the conditions owing to the interaction between these variables. The extent to which these variables affected outcomes is explored in the case-studies.

5
The Receiving End: Politics in the Candidate Countries

Previous chapters have contained frequent references to the politics of enlargement within the EU. But domestic factors came into both sides of the equation: neither the EU nor an applicant country is a unitary actor, and behaviour in the accession process owed much to changing political incentives at home. This book is about how the EU exercised influence rather than about the CEE countries' transition from communism *per se*, so it does not contain a detailed analysis of their processes of democratisation or economic reform. Bulgaria, Hungary and Poland were selected for the case-studies because of their chosen destination – EU membership – rather than for their starting-points. However, political context determines how influence works, so it affects the changes provoked by EU pressure.

This chapter sets out the framework for the case-studies that follow in Chapters 6 and 7, by discussing the variables at work on the CEE side. Section 5.1 presents the background and political context of how the CEE countries exited from communism. Section 5.2 looks in more detail at a particularly important variable affecting Europeanisation: the institutional legacies of communism. Section 5.3 considers the political salience of EU accession and freedom of movement in domestic debates. Section 5.4 sets out the macro-strategies for EU accession of the three countries in the case-studies. Section 5.5 explains the choice of case-studies, in terms of countries and policy areas.

5.1 Diverse paths from communism

A common insight of the transition literature, and of the Europeanisation literature in its concern with 'goodness of fit', is how imported models interact with domestic institutions. In the case of the candidate countries studied here, the political dynamics of the transition from communism affected how they reacted to EU influence. This section sets out the political and economic context and then analyses three central variables in the CEE countries' responses to EU influence. The first is the institutional legacies of communism, the second is the complex interaction between Europeanisation, democratisation and international pressures, and the third is the countries' different macro-strategies to attain EU membership.

The political and economic context of post-communism

One of the major preoccupations of the comparative literature on post-communist transition is how to account for the major differences in the paths followed by all the formerly communist countries. The countries ranging from Hungary to Tajikistan to Yugoslavia were diverse before 1989, of course, but they shared comparable institutions, economic relationships and foreign policy orientations. They had a common ideology, state-controlled economies and single-party systems, but they produced a range of outcomes.[25] Some subsequently refashioned their state institutions to the point where they joined NATO and the EU, while others did little more than 'exchange the mantras of international socialism for those of nationalist authoritarianism', as Charles King puts it (King 2000, p. 151). Within a decade after 1989, the countries had diverged so much that the CEE countries in this study were much more comparable with West European democracies and market economies than with fellow 'transition countries' like Kazakhstan or Mongolia.

During the late communist period, the ten CEE countries were different in how they balanced domestic and Soviet concerns and how they struggled with the effects of Gorbachev's reform collapse. By the time that they started preparing for EU membership, six of them were new countries, owing to the break-ups of the Soviet Union (which gave independence to Estonia, Latvia and Lithuania), of Czechoslovakia (creating Slovakia and the Czech Republic), and of Yugoslavia (making Slovenia independent). They had different economic starting-points too. Most of the CEE countries had begun to run up debt during the period of slow growth and cheap credit in the 1970s–80s. When real interest rates rose at the end of the 1970s, Czechoslovakia and Romania resolved their international debt problems, resulting in a relatively strong macro-economic position by the start of transition (little foreign debt, nearly balanced budget and low monetary overhang). However, the others left debt to accumulate, resulting in unbalanced economies and inflation because of monetary overhang.

Bulgaria, Hungary and Poland had similar economic problems at the start of transition, but differing orders of severity (see Estrin 1994). Previous attempts at macro-economic reform in Hungary after 1968 and in Poland from the early 1980s had resulted in relatively open economies and some re-orientation of trade away from COMECON markets. By contrast, Bulgaria and Slovakia had industrialised by building huge new factories to serve other communist markets, so they were more exposed to the collapse of the COMECON trading area. Hungary experienced no macro-economic crisis and already had some experience of restructuring. Poland also had some managerial experience, but needed a draconian stabilisation plan for its macro-economy. Czechoslovakia was in the opposite position from Poland, with sound macro fundamentals and effective stabilisation in 1991, but strict controls on firms even after the fall of communism. All of the three Central European countries had a lengthier period in transition and a better position at the outset than Russia, Bulgaria or Romania. Bulgaria began post-communist transition in a very difficult position owing to the collapse of its markets and a subsequent dramatic rise in unemployment in the early 1990s. In Romania, weak government policies made the country's economic position worse.

Some historians of the region predicted a 'return to diversity' in CEE, as Joseph Rothschild puts it (Rothschild and Wingfield 1999). However, many of the variables that were expected to determine outcomes – such as leadership, political culture, civil society, ethnic diversity, economic infrastructure and external support – did not result in the paths predicted by scholars, policy-makers and market analysts.

The quality of state institutions, and how quickly they were transformed after 1989 to deal with new challenges, turned out to be a key factor. Of all the transitions to democracy, the post-communist transitions (in comparison with southern Europe and Latin America) were most likely to expose the state itself to the most profound challenge, because the majority of the countries were new states and so still had to define the political community which the state represented (Batt and Wolczuk 1999). As Claus Offe pointed out in 1991, 'At the most fundamental level a "decision" must be made as to who "we" are, i.e. a decision on identity, citizenship and the territorial as well as social and cultural boundaries of the state.' (Offe 1991, p. 869). Successful state consolidation depended on establishing institutions and structures which provided incentives for political actors to seek compromise and consensus on these issues. However, the extent to which a particular constitutional framework can effectively mediate the tensions in society depends on a wide variety of factors, so each state had to work out its own model (Batt and Wolczuk 1999).

The outcomes of this process of defining identity and reforming economies were surprising, however, and they did not fulfil widespread expectations that the most economically advanced countries – such as Yugoslavia – would do best in transition, while the Baltic states would do badly because of their Soviet heritage. For example, in Estonia, a state-led policy of exclusion of ethnic Russians accelerated radical reforms of state structures and the economy, while Ukraine managed an ethnic 'truce', but suffered protracted economic decline (see Batt and Wolczuk 1999). In Yugoslavia, economic success and relative prosperity did not prevent bloody wars and the break-up of the country. As Batt and Wolczuk (1999) conclude, these outcomes show that '... the whole configuration of pre-existing conditions – inter-ethnic relations, the degree of national consciousness in the native majority, élite alliances, the residual administrative capacity, pre-communist past and aspirations for a return to Europe – all have to be taken into account in explaining the diverging political and economic trajectories of new post-communist states.' (p. 45).

The EU's accession process interacted with this complex mix of variables, making it hard to pinpoint any one condition which determined how easily and quickly a country adapted to the EU. Moreover, the strength and unity of a country's aspirations to 'return to Europe' themselves affected not only its approach to the EU, but also its commitment to other reforms which affected its economy and the success of its state consolidation – both of which in turn determined how quickly it could meet the EU's demands. There was thus a two-way relationship between EU preparations and overall progress in transition, and one cannot be taken as a proxy for the other.

Moreover, 'progress' in transition was very fluid – one year's leader could be overtaken by an economic crisis or political instability the next. For example, in the mid-1990s, the Czech Republic under the government of Václav Klaus was seen as the economic leader in central Europe, only for its government to collapse in 1997 under financial scandals, a banking crisis and the revelation of negligent regulation and superficial privatisation. Conversely, countries could move quickly up the rankings of the EBRD and EU with a change of government and a rapid privatisation programme. For example, international perceptions of Croatia rapidly changed after the death of President Franjo Tudjman in 1999 and the democratic election of a reformist government. Even Serbia rapidly gained credibility in the eyes of the international institutions once Slobodan Milošević was on trial in The Hague. Foreign investors tended to be more wary than international institutions, so FDI receipts were an important gauge of success in transition to a market economy (see Estrin 1994; and Bevan, Estrin and Grabbe 2001).

The great similarity between all these countries was that western recognition and the 'return to Europe' formed a very important part of the legitimation of new democracies in all the Central and East European countries (see Batt 1997). The EU's approbation for reformist governments was a vital support for all of them in the 1990s, when they had to establish institutional arrangements and strike political bargains. These formal institutions and informal political deals were key elements in later trajectories because they set in place the incentives and habits of behaviour which could either further or freeze genuine reform (King 2000). As King points out, a freezing of reform was the most common outcome across the former Soviet Union in the 1990s, so the progress that the CEE candidates made is a remarkable exception. And the EU did play a role in supporting political choices that allowed countries to embed democratic practices in society and establish the infrastructure for a market economy.

However, there is a danger in taking too deterministic a view of CEE political developments and the role of the accession process. Certainly, EU accession was seen throughout the region as a key element in the 'return to Europe', a concept which has historically played an important role in forming a central European identity (see Kumar 1992) and in the Baltic states' desire for re-orientation towards the West and away from Russia. But although EU membership was an important long-term goal in all of the applicant countries, they did not progress uniformly towards EU norms – the most notable exceptions being Bulgaria and Romania, which fell behind the others.

Aspirations to 'return to Europe' were just one element in a configuration of conditions which account for political and economic trajectories in post-communist states (Batt and Wolczuk 1999). Ideas of what constituted this return to Europe were relatively diverse, so the goal of EU membership did not unite all post-communist societies. Slovakia was an extreme case of this disunity under the Mečiar governments in the 1990s, when 'European norms' did not help to resolve ethnic divisions between the Slovak majority and the Hungarian minority. Rather, ideas of European norms themselves became something of a political football, with each side claiming European models in support of its view of how to resolve the problems of national identity and treatment of minorities at national level (Batt 1996).

Too many comparative transitologists have assumed that the EU was a vital support for democratisation in CEE, without looking carefully enough at its specific policies and how far it tried or was able to influence political developments within the region (honourable exceptions are Whitehead 1996a and Pinder 1997). This uncritical assumption about the EU is part of the comparative transitologists' general over-readiness to believe in the benign power of western assistance in building democratic institutions (as pointed out by Wedel 1998 and Carothers 1999). As discussed in Chapter 2, there are very few concrete examples of a direct causal relationship, where the EU imposed a sanction or withdrew a reward to effect a democratic change, and the EU lacked a clearly articulated set of political values (as opposed to policy models) to export to CEE. However, the 'demonstration effect' from West European democracies undoubtedly had an effect, and the attraction of EU membership certainly helped to strengthen the commitment of the candidate countries to the political values articulated by the Council of Europe and other international organisations which promoted democracy and the protection of human rights and minorities (see Grabbe 2001a).

To sum up, aspirations for membership are definitely part of the conditions that affected the transition paths taken by different CEE countries, but EU influence cannot be assumed to be the primary variable that determined the reform trajectory taken by any given country. A host of other variables in the domestic context of that country was operating as well, in addition to the limitations on EU influence that the Union itself introduced through uncertainty and diffuseness. An aspiration for EU membership – however strong – cannot guarantee success in transition if other conditions are not met. The two most important other conditions were the performance of institutions and the importance of EU membership to the political elite. These variables are discussed in the next two sections.

5.2   The institutional legacies of communism

The fluidity of post-communist politics, and the rapidity with which countries can change their position in international rankings, make it difficult to assess which countries 'succeeded' in transition at any given point. Yet the EU took success in transition as a key determinant of whether a country would cope well as a member-state. Recent work on the problem of institutions has illuminated a number of issues that affected both transition paths and how post-communist countries adapted to the EU.

The first question is what kind of institutions were built after communism, because they affected how well imported models worked. The 'transitology' literature – which is concerned with comparing experiences of transition from dictatorship to democracy – has tended to focus on the challenges of institutional design and how to consolidate democracy (e.g. Przeworski 1991, Linz and Stepan 1996, Whitehead 1996b, Lijphart and Waisman 1996, Pridham *et al.* 1997). This literature points out similarities in the problems encountered by countries in different regions. However, its research questions centre around democracy, and so it rarely considers the models exported by the EU, which are mainly concerned with public policy and particularly with regulation of markets.

Regional specialists have also looked at the issue of institutional design, particularly investigating the material legacies, constraints, sets of habits and cognitive frames inherited from the previous regime and its sudden disintegration. For example, Elster *et al.* (1998) argue that Bulgaria and Slovakia had great difficulties in adopting democratic and market institutions because their coercively imposed industrialisation did not favour cultural and political modernisation. The basic concepts and perceptions of an agrarian society survived in the behavioural patterns, values and world-views of the communist era. For this reason, the authors argue that one could not exclude regression to some kind of populist-authoritarian rule. More likely – in their view – was a persistence of unstable governments, erratic coalitions and a low degree of political cooperation among elites. In fact, both Bulgaria and Slovakia proved to be more stable than the authors predicted. But it is true that both countries had a more difficult transition than comparable neighbours such as the Czech Republic, Hungary or Slovenia. Overall, the experience after 1989 showed that institutional legacies mattered in how well countries managed to achieve stability and embed democratic practices in their societies.

A further dimension of this question is the complex interaction between the new, post-communist institutions, and the old communist ones onto which they were grafted. This question has not yet been widely investigated, but it is critical to understanding why countries took such divergent paths, and more particularly why some managed to integrate transplanted institutional models more successfully than others.

The political economy literature picked up this theme in the mid-1990s. An important strand of the literature was concerned with the path-dependency of the outcomes of economic reforms, particularly privatisation (Grabher 1994b, Hausner *et al.* 1995, Bohle 1996, Chavance and Magnin 1997, Comisso 1998, Stark and Bruszt 1998). These authors argue that the different methods used to move firms out of state control played only a secondary role in determining governance structures. They assign a more important role to the complex institutional legacies of partial reforms under socialism. As a result of these legacies, institutional reforms remained much less complete than privatisation programmes did, and micro-economic restructuring was much less than expected. In response to such studies, in the mid-1990s international financial institutions started stressing the need for institutional reform and the continuing importance of the state as a rule-setter (e.g. World Bank 1996, EBRD 1999).

It took a remarkably long time for the issue of institutional legacies to emerge in the democratisation literature, given that institutions are a central concern of the wider political science. In particular, post-communism seems eminently suitable for study from the perspective of historical institutionalism, which focuses on how institutions structure the individual's choices about institutional reform, making them resistant to change (Hall and Taylor 1996). A historical-institutionalist perspective on post-communism would focus on how the institutional organisation of a policy or political economy structured collective behaviour.

Valerie Bunce (1999) was one of the first authors to use such a perspective to consider the whole region. She argues that the design of the communist state provides a key to understanding why authoritarian regimes collapsed in different ways, and whether they destroyed the state in the process. All socialist regimes featured an extraordinarily powerful party-state and a weak and dependent society. However, the long-term impact of socialist institutions was the opposite of what party elites intended, because the system became feudal, even though it was organised as a hierarchy. Central command and control deteriorated as the upper levels of the party bought off lower levels – both the regions of the Soviet Union and the CEE countries – by redistributing economic resources and power to them. Under communism, the institutions became self-subversive because they functioned over time to undermine the economic and political monopoly of the centre – both the party within each state, and the Soviet Union's influence within the eastern bloc – while homogenising and strengthening the peripheries. Bunce concludes that 'By its very design, then, socialism had deregulated itself – over time and by accident.' (p. 131).

In reviewing the literature on communist institutions, King (2000) concludes that 'The communist system was institutionally rich but organizationally weak.' (p. 158). The system created an elaborate network of state institutions that reached down into almost every aspect of society – from trade unions to chess clubs. They were intended to work in one direction, mobilising political, economic, social and cultural resources to achieve the ends of state planning. However, as the system became increasingly feudal, administration of the various levels in the institutional network depended on distribution of power and resources to institutional agents throughout the state (King 2000).

The implications of institutional legacies for Europeanisation

The CEE countries were thus used to creating a plethora of institutions, most of which did not function as intended under communism. This experience had a number of potential implications for Europeanisation.

1. It means that CEE countries could be prone to creating dysfunctional institutions. Such institutions may not work as they should because they are starved of resources, because they do not have adequate leadership, or because they are largely symbolic administrative structures. Dysfunctional institutions may emerge by accident, owing to lack of political leadership, resources or experienced personnel. But they may also emerge by design, because some CEE policy-makers were already used to creating such institutions as a way of avoiding substantive change and protecting the *status quo*.

This last outcome is the most difficult to control for in research. The concept of 'institutional isomorphism' was introduced in Chapter 3 to explain how an institution can grow to resemble another. In the CEE context, this isomorphism can develop into what sociologists call 'functional dualism', where a great deal of ceremonial activity occurs, but not necessarily much substantive change. The CEE countries may thus have set up institutions which looked like those functioning in the EU member-states, but which did not have the same impact on policy as their western counterparts. There is always 'the possibility that national elites will talk the European talk while continuing to walk in a national walk' (Jacoby 1998, p. 12).

The legacy of dysfunctional institutions is a factor that makes it difficult to gauge the depth of Europeanisation in CEE institutions. The parts of a ministry that are in contact with the EU may talk the language of Brussels, but that does not mean that the whole institution has become Europeanised in the sense of taking on the behavioural logic of the EU. Over time, Europeanisation effects may deepen – as happened in the existing EU member-states – but it is difficult to distinguish between paper changes and real effects in the early years of implementing EU models in CEE. The danger is that researchers may assume that formal structures have a substantive impact on policy-making, when in fact their function is largely symbolic.

For example, a group of researchers at Cornell University published a book in 1997 which argued that forms of corporatism were emerging in CEE that were comparable with the German and Austrian models (Katzenstein 1997). However, several of the case-studies focused on typically corporatist structures which certainly existed, but which were essentially formal in nature and did not necessarily influence policy-making. In particular, the case-study on Poland (Aniol *et al.* 1997) and the background work on Bulgaria (published as Iankova 1998) assumed that the elaborate structures for tripartite consultation between the government and social actors (employers' organisations and trade unions) actually affected policy. However, other studies have found that these structures were not influential and were essentially an institutional legacy of communism that subsequently withered (ECOSOC 2001). In particular, organised labour became very weak in the post-communist period because of its loss of class identity, producing 'illusory corporatism' (Ost 1997). It is thus vital to follow the whole chain of policy-making to see how the institutions actually worked.

This tendency to produce formal but dysfunctional institutions emerged in several CEE countries, and it was most marked in the countries that were slowest to respond to the EU's conditionality. Bulgaria and Romania had the most serious problems with inadequate institutional capacity, according to the World Bank (Nunberg *et al.* 1996) and the OECD, as well as the EU's reports.

2. The legacy of communism caused EU influence to work within a landscape of institutional relics. The CEE countries did not start with an institutional *tabula rasa*, but rather with a complex mixture of institutions (see Lijphart and Crawford 1995). Some of them had disappeared (e.g. the party apparatus), some had been partially dismantled (e.g. economics and labour ministries), and some had survived largely intact (e.g. foreign and defence ministries). Other institutions needed for EU membership simply did not exist, because communist systems had not produced policies in areas like financial sector regulation, immigration or protection of minorities.

This background varied between countries, however. Hungary had started re-orienting its markets in the 1970s, and by 1989 the economy had been a mixed system of functioning markets and state ownership (Halpern and Wyplosz 1998). To a small extent, Hungary had started working to establish institutional structures to implement EU norms in a few areas under communism, so many of its economic institutions were already changing. For example, the Prices Office evolved into the competition authority. As the head of that Office recalled with irony, 'In the morning we would fix the prices, and in the afternoon we would liberalise them.'[26] Hungary had a better institutional infrastructure than most post-communist countries at the start of transition, which helped in the painful period of economic reforms. Poland also had relatively sound institutions which were reformed relatively quickly, but Bulgaria's took longer because of the inertia under the Bulgarian Socialist Party (the communist successor party) which was in power until the 1997 parliamentary elections.

3. The EU's policy and institutional models were not designed to tackle the particular problems faced by CEE institutions. The policies and institutional models that the EU seeks to transfer are defined by the *acquis*, not by an assessment of a candidate's institutional needs, and the Council and the Commission were very inflexible in how they defined the *acquis* for candidates (as discussed in Chapter 2). This factor has a direct impact on Europeanisation, because it affects the 'goodness of fit' of EU models.

Moreover, the EU's pre-accession policies were specifically designed to promote particular aspects of institutional functioning, rather than taking a holistic view of how public administrations should develop. For example, the EU did not prescribe particular models of civil service reform. By contrast, the OECD (through its SIGMA programme) and the World Bank were more active in providing specific advice on public administrations. Tensions emerged where different logics underlay the general development of administrative capacity and the specific demands of EU membership (Nunberg *et al.* 1996 and Nunberg 2000). After all, the EU's focus in each area was limited to the functions that needed to be standardised to EU norms; it was not a complete blueprint for the public administration. As a result, the goodness of fit between an EU model and the CEE institutional context depended largely on chance.

5.3   Political salience

Political salience is a complex variable, because an issue's sensitivity in domestic politics is the outcome of a complex interaction of domestic politics and external pressures. But it is an important one, and the Europeanisation literature rarely looks systematically at different external and internal pressures (Goetz 2000).

The two case-studies unpack the reasons why freedom of movement was an important issue for all three countries. The first reason was the desire of people to travel and work in other countries when they were finally free to do so after communism. However, the degree of political unity behind each country's approach in negotiations also depended on how far the general issue of EU accession was contested by politicians at domestic level. A brief analysis of the political salience of the issue of free movement of persons is provided here, centred around two questions about the degree to which it was contested in domestic politics:

- How contested was the goal of EU integration?
- How contested was this particular policy area?

Until the start of negotiations with the EU, there was little opposition to joining from organised interests in any CEE country except the Czech Republic (Grabbe and Hughes 1999). Nearly all political parties represented in the parliaments of the candidate countries were in favour of joining, with only fringe parties opposed (see Hughes *et al.* 1999). However, particular EU demands interacted with domestic debates about the role of different branches of government and the role of sub-national and regional government. The process of 'EU-isation' became an integral part of the domestic political ground, not just another external pressure among many (Grabbe 2001a).

Poland had an overwhelming consensus in favour of accession in the first half of the 1990s, and opinion polls showed it had the highest levels of public support in any applicant country except Romania until 1998 (details in Grabbe and Hughes 1998). This support was not a reflection of widespread public knowledge or discussions, as there was a virtual absence of debate (Millard 1999). When negotiations began in 1998, so did a much more profound discussion about EU membership and its implications. Poland then experienced the most significant growth of party-based Euroscepticism in the region, although it was of a confused nature and it was not a re-aligning issue in Polish politics (Szczerbiak 1999 and 2001) until after accession in 2004. In the September 2001 elections, one-third of the seats in the Sejm (the lower house of the Polish parliament) went to parties whose leaders had taken Eurosceptical stances of various kinds. However, Europe was not a key issue in the election campaign, and many of the votes for the Eurosceptical parties seem to have been protest votes against the political establishment, rather than votes against joining the EU (Roguska and Strzeszewski 2002).

Nevertheless, several issues were extremely important in the Polish domestic debate about Europe, even if the goal of joining was largely supported by the political establishment and a majority of public opinion. The three most sensitive areas were free movement of labour, the sale of land to foreigners (owing to the EU's free movement of capital provisions), and aid to farmers. These were issues that appeared frequently in the Polish press and parliamentary debates from 1998 to the end of 2001.

In Hungary, there was a relatively consistent consensus in favour of accession across the political spectrum. Viktor Orbán, as prime minister from 1998 to 2002 and as the main opposition leader before and after, sometimes criticised the EU's lack of generosity on issues ranging from the Community budget to the transition period on free movement of labour (as discussed in Chapter 6). However, on the whole, the Hungarian debate focused on material gains to be secured in the accession negotiations. As a result, parties with identities that might have conflicted with EU integration – such as Orbán's own FIDESZ-MPP – successfully avoided the sensitive and potentially divisive questions that arose from the country's membership bid. This pre-emptive strategy to a great extent de-coupled the issue of European integration from identity politics, ensuring that the debate focused on economic and technical issues. As a result, European integration did not become a primary point of reference for party differentiation, which in turn caused a relatively lacklustre public debate (Batory 2001). EU policies and models became entwined with domestic debates about particular issues, such as granting greater regional autonomy (Fowler 2001), but the goal of joining the EU was rarely contested openly as it was in Poland.

In Bulgaria, there was also a very high degree of consensus about EU accession, but for a different reason. Between 1989 and 1996, the country's political life was dominated by economic problems under a succession of governments led by the Bulgarian Socialist Party. These problems culminated in huge demonstrations in 1996 owing to bread shortages, a banking crisis, the collapse of the currency, and the revelation of the mafia connections of government leaders (Gallagher 1998). The Bulgarian Socialist Party left office and agreed to early elections, which were won by the centre-right Union of Democratic

Forces in April 1997. This history caused the political class to focus on external ideas and values to legitimate themselves through foreign political models: 'Europe (EU) is the model to be followed [in Bulgaria], undisputed by any influential political power.' (Todorov 1999, p. 9). The debate about Europe focused on which party could make progress towards the EU fastest, rather than on the requirements of membership and their impact on Bulgaria. That is not to say that 'Europe' was an uncontested ideal. But it differentiated the political space through a 'competition of sorts among the parties on the European theme, a kind of rivalry concerning which party most fully, efficiently, and comprehensively embraces the "European idea". This rivalry in itself stimulates differences in pro-Europe argumentation ...' (Todorov 1999, p. 9).

Free movement of persons was politically salient in Bulgaria primarily because of the visa restrictions that the EU maintained on Bulgaria until the end of 2000. Opposition to the visa regime united the political elite, and this issue dominated the political debate about relations with the EU until the visa requirement was lifted. There was much less attention to the issue of labour mobility than movement of persons. The visa requirement made implementation of the Schengen *acquis* less controversial, because there was widespread support for measures that might lead to its abolition (Jileva 2002).

In sum, the goal of EU accession was most contested in Poland, much less in Hungary, and hardly at all in Bulgaria. However, in none of the countries was Euroscepticism a significant determinant of political alignment until the last couple of years before accession, when it rose significantly in Poland. Debates about EU policies tended to focus on only a few issues. In Poland, one of the most controversial of these issues was freedom to work in the EU after accession. In Hungary and Bulgaria, the issue did not have such great salience in domestic politics. However, in Hungary, the freedom of movement of ethnic Hungarians living in surrounding countries was an important issues with regard to the Schengen *acquis*, and in Bulgaria the EU's visa restrictions were much resented until 2000. As we shall see in the case-studies, the political salience of these issues was an important variable that determined the extent of Europeanisation.

5.4   Strategies of adaptation to the EU

The countries' overall approach to EU accession is a 'macro-strategy' of adaptation, distinct from the meso-strategies they used to deal with each policy area and the micro-strategies used for the detailed points in the negotiations.

The macro-strategies of Hungary, Poland and Bulgaria

Hungary consistently pursued a strategy of rapid adaptation, with few attempts to resist EU demands. In negotiations, the Hungarian team generally worked rapidly to find solutions that were acceptable to the EU, and it was usually among the first candidates to close a chapter, even controversial ones such as free movement of persons and justice and home affairs. Its government was able to achieve rapid progress towards accession owing to a high degree of consensus on its strategy to join the EU and a relatively sound institutional legacy in the public administration. This strategy was dubbed by Hungarian journalists and officials as trying to be 'the best pupil in the class'.

By contrast, Poland's macro-strategy of adaptation was much more combative, involving tough negotiating stances and slow implementation of the policies that caused most domestic controversy. This strategy reflected Poland's size and the geo-political importance of its accession to the Union, particularly in the eyes of the EU's largest member-state, Germany. Polish politicians often goaded the negotiating team to take a tough line, and demanded that the EU make concessions. Indeed, the Polish approach led one exasperated EU official to remark in 1998, 'They don't understand that Poland is trying to join the Union, and we're not joining Poland!'. Among the Polish political elite there was a widespread assumption – frequently contested by Commission officials, though not necessarily in the member-states – that the EU had to include Poland in the first group of accessions because it was the largest and hence the most important applicant. German officials sometimes justified this strategy by saying that 'enlargement without Poland is not really enlargement'.

Poland was often slow to implement EU legislation, but that was not always because of a conscious strategy. Rather, it resulted from the political and institutional problems that beset Poland's policy-making apparatus for EU accession issues. A series of fractious coalition governments politicised the EU-related institutions to a very large degree, and resulted in fast turnover of personnel and major problems with coordination between the Committee for European Integration and the various line-ministries. Poland's strategy could be described as 'We're too big to fail'.

The strategy of adaptation adopted by the 1997–2001 Bulgarian government could be described as 'catch-up and imitation'. It resembled the

Hungarian strategy, but Bulgaria had much more difficulty in gaining the confidence of the Union that it would be able to meet the promises it made in negotiations, owing to the weakness of its institutions. It also suffered from a slow start because of the economic crisis in 1996, when the country underwent a very serious banking and monetary policy crisis which resulted in hyper-inflation and a devaluation of the currency. The Bulgarian National Bank had to put nine banks with liquidity problems under special supervision on 23 September 1996. The crisis was only resolved thanks to a bail-out by the IMF and the imposition of a currency board to stabilise the lev (the Bulgarian currency).

A reformist government comprising a coalition of economic liberals took over in 1997 and started a new strategy of strict compliance with the demands of the IMF and the EU. For the incoming Bulgarian government, it was important to catch up quickly, both because of domestic politics and competition with neighbouring countries. The chief negotiator openly acknowledged that his strategy was to get as many chapters open as possible, so that Bulgaria could move ahead of Romania and show its willingness and readiness to join the first group of candidates.[27] The first year of negotiations was critical in domestic political terms as well because parliamentary elections were coming up in June 2001, and the governing coalition led by the Union of Democratic Forces faced a new challenger in addition to the formal opposition of the Bulgarian Socialist Party. The National Movement for Simeon II quickly gathered support in the first half of 2001, and won an overwhelming majority in the June elections, with former King Simeon II taking the role of prime minister.

In the first year of negotiations (2000), the government of Prime Minister Ivan Kostov needed to show rapid progress in approaching accession in order to bolster its domestic credentials as effective reformers. As the government as a whole and Kostov personally were criticised for not responding adequately to problems with corruption and organised crime, progress in EU negotiations became a rare example of good news and international approbation for their efforts. The negotiators thus had every incentive to move as fast as possible, and little incentive to make demands for transition periods that might slow chapters down. The government received criticism for slow progress much more often than for conceding too quickly to the EU's demands.

Bulgarian policy-makers also wanted to put a distance between their country's own position and that of Romania. The two Balkan candidates had been frequently grouped together in press and academic assessments of progress towards membership, and the Bulgarian government wanted to make enough progress that the EU began to consider it part of the second group in negotiations, with Latvia, Lithuania and Slovakia, rather than forming a third group with Romania. The EU began in 2001 to contemplate a 'big bang' first enlargement which would include Latvia, Lithuania and Slovakia, but not Bulgaria and Romania. In addition to the incentive of possibly achieving accession in that first group, Bulgaria faced the negative incentive of fearing that such a large first eastward enlargement would lead to a long wait for a second round. In the area of free movement of persons, the Bulgarian government had an additional incentive to make progress because of the EU's visa requirement.

However, persistent problems with corruption, organised crime and economic under-performance had taken a toll on Bulgaria's public institutions. Bulgaria made much more progress than Romania in both preparations and economic reform, but it was insufficient to pull the country up into the next category of candidates at the critical moment. The EU set 2004 as the target-date for the first eastward enlargement at the Gothenburg European Council in June 2001. In its Regular Report on Bulgaria of November 2001, the Commission judged that Bulgaria was still far from having a functioning market economy or being competitive in the single market, and it excluded Bulgaria from the group of countries presented to the Council as ready for membership. Bulgaria and Romania both concluded negotiations in 2004 and they aim to join the EU in 2007.

5.5   The choice of cases: Countries and policy areas

The cases form a three-by-two matrix, as they include two policy areas and three countries. The purpose of using evidence from three different countries is to check that the findings are not country-specific, or specific to the front-runners in negotiations. More than one policy domain and one country were studied to ensure that generalisations about policy processes and countries were not due to the idiosyncrasies of one case.

The three countries were selected to provide points of similarity and of contrast. Two of the countries – Hungary and Poland – were front-runner candidates which joined in 2004. However, they presented different problems for the EU: Poland has a population of nearly 40 million people, around a fifth of whom live on the land.

Poland's size raised fears that it would affect the institutional balance of the Union, while its large number of farmers would have bankrupted the Common Agricultural Policy if they had received full entitlement to transfers from the EU budget from the start. Hungary has only 10 million people and a relatively small and efficient agricultural sector.

However, Hungary had borders with three other applicant countries (Romania, Slovakia and Slovenia), and three non-applicants (Croatia, Yugoslavia and Ukraine). These countries are home to an estimated three million ethnic Hungarians, and successive Hungarian governments felt a sense of obligation to continue offering them access to Hungary for travel and work. However, such open access ran against the principles of the EU's Schengen area, because so many ethnic Hungarians were citizens of non-applicant countries.

Although they were both front-runners, Hungary and Poland differed somewhat in their macro-strategies to accession and in their approach to negotiations – as discussed above. Bulgaria was very different because it took longer to complete the accession process, and so a comparison between the three candidates offers an opportunity to test whether closeness to accession was a key determinant of Europeanisation effects.

The two policy areas were also chosen for similarity and contrast. They are both concerned with the same substantive issue – regulating movement of persons across the EU – but they have different histories within European integration and developed independently to some extent. Free movement of persons (FMP) was a single market issue, while movement of persons across external frontiers was part of justice and home affairs. This allows the case-studies to examine how the EU takes very different approaches in similar policy areas. Moreover, the EU had a clear set of requirements for FMP, so levels of uncertainty about the EU's agenda were low, whereas they were very high in the case of borders policies.

There are also contrasts on the candidates' side, because one policy – FMP – was relatively easy and cheap to implement, while regulating movement across borders was extremely difficult in both political and practical terms. For the candidates, both policy areas were very controversial in negotiations, which allows us to study the interaction between negotiations and Europeanisation at domestic level in the candidate countries. The outcome of this interaction was seemingly perverse, leaving a puzzle which will be explained in Chapter 8.

Conclusions

Three variables on the candidate countries' side have been explored in this chapter: institutional capacity to achieve political goals; political salience; and strategy of adaptation to the EU. The intervening variables on the EU side were presented in Chapter 4: diffuseness of influence and uncertainty. The two case-studies will explore how these variables interacted in the following two chapters. Chapter 8 compares the case-studies to explain how EU influence worked.

6
Free Movement of Persons in the Single Market

> 'In the 1960s we asked Turkey for workers and we got people.
> Now we open our eastern borders to people and we get workers.'
> German Foreign Ministry official, October 2000.

This case-study concerns the policy area of free movement of persons within the single market *acquis*. The single market chapters were presented early in the accession process, and were relatively low on the political agenda in both the EU and CEE until negotiations reached the FMP chapter. The EU's agenda was clear in terms of legislation and institutional templates, and the standard of implementation to be attained prior to accession was relatively well-defined; hence uncertainty was low in comparison with other policy areas. The front-runner candidates substantially implemented the *acquis* prior to accession, not just because of the accession goal but also because of the FMP provisions in the Europe Agreements, which provided the interim benefit of access to EU markets. Slowness or incompleteness of implementation was mainly the result of limited resources rather than lack of political will for Poland and Hungary; however, for Bulgaria progress was much slower because alignment with the whole single market *acquis* began in earnest only in 1997.

The story of the accession preparations for this policy area is a relatively straightforward one of adaptation to a part of the *acquis* that uses prescriptive and prohibitive policy transfer – in other words, it involved traditional methods of integration and a set of mechanisms for Europeanisation that was well-established in the EU (unlike for Schengen, discussed in the next chapter). However, the story has a sting in its tale because member-state politics intruded into the EU's negotiating position and changed its goal from effective functioning of the single market to protection of labour markets in existing EU member-states. The three countries reacted differently to the EU's negotiating position, and this chapter seeks to explain why.

Free movement of persons was chosen as a case-study with the following aims:

- to show how processes of Europeanisation work in a relatively easy part of the accession *acquis*, in order to provide a baseline for comparison with the more complex case presented in Chapter 7;
- to show how the EU can contradict its own policy paradigms if high politics intrude on a meso-policy area;
- to illustrate the different adaptation strategies of three countries to Europeanisation pressures in a particular policy area;
- to show how the EU exercises power in accession negotiations, and how candidates can respond differently to the same political pressures.

This chapter proceeds as follows: Section 6.1 gives the background to the EU's approach in terms of the existing *acquis*. Section 6.2 sets out the EU's formal agenda for free movement of persons as presented to the candidates. Section 6.3 presents the responses of Bulgaria, Hungary and Poland to the EU's agenda. Section 6.4 discusses the negotiating positions presented by the candidates and the EU. Section 6.5 presents two explanatory variables for the outcome in this policy area: the dynamics of Europeanisation on the candidates' side, and the role of policy paradigms on the EU side.

6.1   Background to the EU's approach

The policy area studied here is the alignment of the candidates with the single market regulations for free movement of persons. It is about the movement of people within the EU, defined as the right of EU citizens to reside and seek work anywhere within the Union. It is related to – but distinct from – the movement of persons across external frontiers, which is the case studied in Chapter 7.

The free movement of persons is a founding principle of the European Union and it has a well-developed legal basis. Its long-standing treaty base, and the accumulation of legal instruments confirming its scope and application, stand in contrast to the recent evolution and uncertain legal status of much of the *acquis* on social policy and on justice and home affairs – which are the other areas related to movement of persons. The free movement of persons is the more straightforward case because it involves traditional mechanisms of integration, based on legal instruments and institutional requirements. The EU therefore had a very clear and detailed agenda to present to candidate countries. Because FMP forms part of the single market, it was also presented early on in the accession process, starting with the Europe Agreements. It was of relatively low political salience on both sides, at least until negotiations on this chapter began. For the candidates, the institutional changes required did not run against domestic interests, so the goodness-of-fit might be described as neutral (it was neither a good fit nor a bad one). Moreover, the additional human and financial resources required for implementation were not large in comparison with other policy areas. Political attention to this area grew only when it became clear that the EU would ask for a transition period of its own – a very rare exception – owing to the domestic politics of enlargement in several of its member-states.

The foundation of EU policies and legislation

Three articles of the Treaty of Rome refer to free movement of persons: an internal market characterised by the abolition, as between member-states, of obstacles to freedom of movement of goods, persons, services and capital (Article 3 EEC);[28] the right of citizens to move and reside freely in the territory of the member-states (Article 8a EEC); and the principle of free movement for workers, subject to some limitations (Article 48 EEC). Free movement of persons evolved from the above articles into a legal framework that now entitles nationals of member-states to practise a trade or profession anywhere in the Union – with some exceptions (see Weatherill and Beaumont 1995).

In the evolution of this policy area, the initial stress was on workers, who are at the centre of legislation intended to give effect to these treaty requirements. In 1968 a regulation and a directive laid down the rights of workers to move and reside freely within the member-states with a view to taking up or seeking employment. The definition of 'worker' was gradually extended, thanks to European Court of Justice rulings and the evolution of the single market in the 1980s, for which an open labour market was seen as an essential component. Legislation to cover students, retired people and nationals of member-states not covered by other provisions was introduced in 1990, when the Council of Ministers adopted three linked directives based on the Palma Document discussed at the Madrid European Council in June 1989. The directives effectively allowed a citizen of the Union to reside anywhere in the member-states, as long as he or she is covered by health insurance and is receiving income or welfare benefits sufficient 'to avoid becoming a burden on the social assistance system of the host member-state'.[29] However, these components primarily refer to the free movement of citizens of the Union, not of 'persons' as the commitment in the Treaty states. An obvious corollary to these single market policies was the removal of frontier controls, which happened later through the Schengen Agreement and justice and home affairs cooperation (as discussed in Chapter 7).

Essentially, there are two different logics governing regulation of the movement of persons in the EU's treaties. Article 7a in Part One of the Maastricht Treaty on 'Principles' mentions the concept in connection with the establishment of the internal market and implies that persons are not to be subject to controls when crossing the internal frontiers between the member-states. On the other hand, Article 8a in Part Two of the Maastricht Treaty on 'Citizenship of the Union' gives every citizen of the Union the individual right to move and reside freely within the territory of the member-states, subject to certain conditions. The abolition of frontier checks must apply to all persons, whatever their nationality, if Article 7a is not to be meaningless. While the rights deriving from Article 8a apply in all member-states, those stemming from Article 7a had not yet been fully applied throughout the Union until the Schengen Agreement was incorporated into the Amsterdam Treaty.

By the time the EU came to define an accession *acquis* for the CEE applicants in the 1990s, FMP had well-established principles, legislation and methods of implementation and enforcement. Its essential components were by then freedom to move around the Union, freedom of establishment and freedom to provide services (the right to practise a trade or profession in either an employed or self-employed capacity), which in turn were facilitated by the mutual recognition of professional qualifications and by coordination of social security systems. The health, architecture and legal professions had specific legislation. The approach to social security is not harmonisation of national systems, but coordination to ensure that people moving across frontiers retain their rights to social security benefits.

Related to the FMP provisions in the single market *acquis* were those in the social and employment policies of the Union. There is a 'nexus between the market and social policy' which was at least partially acknowledged at the outset of European integration, when social policy in the Community was addressed largely in relation to reducing restrictions on labour mobility (Leibfried and Pierson 2000, p. 277). Article 51 (TEU)[30] provides for measures in the field of social security 'as are necessary to provide freedom of movement for workers ...'. There were already bilateral and multilateral social security treaties prior to the Treaty of Paris (1951), standards set by the International Labour Organisation, and a labour mobility regime of 'coordination' restrictions on welfare-state sovereignty. Leibfried and Pierson (2000) demonstrate how creating a free market for labour and services directly intruded on the sovereignty of national welfare states, for example.

Given the spread of a complex patchwork of regulations and court decisions over 40 years, there was little room for member-states to insert their own methods and preferences into this policy area, because the *acquis* was so well-established. Implementation is by 'downloading' policy, with little possibility of 'uploading' domestic policy preferences (to adopt the distinction made by Jordan 2000 in analysing environmental policy). For the applicants, there was still less room for manoeuvre in implementation, because full application of the single market *acquis* was considered by the EU as essential, right from the start of the eastern enlargement process. Both official statements (e.g. European Council 1993) and academic analyses (e.g. Baldwin 1994, Faini and Portes 1995, Smith *et al.* 1996) stressed that strict implementation was essential for the single market to function in an enlarged EU.

Nevertheless, in the development of the single market, mobility of labour remained more limited than mobility of capital and goods. Indeed, Schengen was established in order to facilitate the movement of people in order to ensure the free circulation of labour in the Union. The limitations on labour mobility were partly the result of continuing barriers to persons seeking recognition of their qualifications, which was imperfectly assured across the existing EU-15. The *acquis* provided some room for manoeuvre in implementation, where member-states were able to protect national labour markets, either for political reasons or simply bureaucratic inefficiency. In addition, the *acquis* specified only the broad parameters for the institutional arrangement for mutual recognition, leaving room for national professional bodies to discriminate against foreigners. For the applicants, this meant that the EU's institutional preferences were well-defined in comparison with other accession requirements, such as having a 'functioning market economy', and even other parts of the *acquis*, such as justice and home affairs. But even in this core element of the single market, there was some margin for national differences to persist and there remained some obstacles to free circulation.

6.2   The EU's agenda as presented to the CEE candidates

The formal agenda

1993–94: Europe Agreements. The applicants started formal alignment with the *acquis* on free movement of persons in the early 1990s. Essential measures for movement of workers were included in the Europe Agreements that were concluded with Hungary and Poland on 13 December 1993 and Bulgaria on 19 December 1994. Title IV of the Europe Agreements provided for the non-discriminatory treatment of workers who are legally employed (as well as their families), with regard to working conditions, remuneration and dismissal in candidate countries and member-states. There were also articles covering social security entitlements (including pensions, medical care and family allowances), which extended to Hungary and Poland the basic elements of the single market framework which allowed workers transferable benefits across the Union. These covered the possibility of cumulating or transferring social security rights, and encouraged member-states to conclude bilateral agreements with the candidates on access to labour markets. The Europe Agreements also offered technical assistance and other forms of cooperation to assist in the establishment of a suitable social security system (and a labour services system in Hungary), as well as technical assistance aimed at improving the health and safety of workers.

The structure for monitoring the application of these provisions was the Association Council, but that did not include a formal structure for measuring compliance or assessing the practical effect of these measures. The text of the Europe Agreements did not specify how these legal articles were to be implemented, in terms of legislation, institutions or other measures. It is an example of the regulatory policy of 'market-making' whereby the EU defines conditions for market access and market operation to secure proper functioning (e.g. liberalisation and deregulation). This type of integration is 'prohibitive' in the schema established in Chapter 3.

1995: Single Market White Paper. The Commission spelled out much more detailed requirements in the Single Market White Paper of 1995 (CEC 1995). In an annexe to the paper, the Commission not only set out all the legislative and enforcement measures required, but also described and justified them. As with other parts of the single market *acquis*, the legal and institutional requirements for implementing the measures connected with FMP were specified in detail – very different from the JHA *acquis*. The measures were mainly Council directives, and they were divided into four categories: three stages of implementation and a fourth category of 'non-key measures'. The two main areas for FMP were:

1. *Mutual recognition of professional qualifications* relied on three types of non-discriminatory measure: recognition of professional qualifications; measures relating to proof of good health, good repute and sound financial standing; and membership of professional organisations and compliance with codes of conduct. Alignment with the *acquis* required amendments to national laws in order to introduce machinery for the recognition of qualifications obtained in other member-states. The EU required the introduction of legislation and the establishment of a supervisory body for regulated professions – either a ministry or a professional organisation, or both.

2. *Coordination of social security systems* had to be done in a single step rather than gradually, so the Single Market White Paper recommended that the two relevant regulations should be adopted after accession. However, preparatory work such as technical amendments, exchange of information and training had to be carried out prior to accession. The candidates also had to establish bilateral agreements with each member-state so that workers from each country had rights in the other.

The Europe Agreements were concerned with the legal arrangements to remove barriers to FMP, and the Single Market White Paper with the correct functioning of the single market. However, concerns about potential labour migration from CEE began to emerge in 1996–97 as the Commission prepared its 'Opinions' on each applicant and they began to approach negotiations.

1997: Agenda 2000. In Agenda 2000 (CEC 1997d), the Commission stated its concern that the substantial East-West wage differential served as a strong incentive for CEE citizens to migrate to the EU, but the analysis played down the likelihood of major problems after accession. It noted with approval that wage-driven migration might accelerate the drive towards more flexible labour markets, especially in bordering countries, but also stated that labour market imbalances might increase. The Commission argued that 'the size of these effects is hard to gauge' (p. 107), pointed to the lack of migration from Greece, Portugal and Spain after accession, and noted that expected improvements in CEE economic conditions and uncertain employment opportunities in the West might check migratory movement. When discussing FMP under the Internal Market section, the Commission's view was that 'fears that mass migration would "flood" the labour markets of present States do not seem justified', but that 'Measures to alleviate adjustment strains will evidently be critical in ensuring that this freedom will not be exposed to pressure'.

In Agenda 2000, the Commission stated that it did not expect any major problems from the application of freedom of movement to other categories of persons who were not workers, although it noted that 'in certain health-related professions, safeguard mechanisms against excessive migration exist' (p. 118), and 'Family reunification ... could put some strain on the social security schemes and infrastructure as well as on the labour market'. (p. 118). The Commission referred to the functioning of the single market only once, in reiterating the requirements for strict implementation of company and accounting legislation 'lest the right of establishment of firms (assimilated to physical persons in terms of free movement) results in insecurity for third parties beyond the acceding countries.' (p. 118). There was no discussion of whether labour mobility was needed for the full functioning of the enlarged single market.

In assessing the candidates' readiness in this area, the 1997 Opinions described briefly the current situation in the country and they assessed the scope of what needed to be done. Hungarian legislation already recognised the principle of non-discrimination between nationals and foreigners legally residing in the country, so the application of the principle of equal treatment to those EU workers already legally residing in Hungary was not a problem. Training, where coordinated by directives for seven professions, was broadly in line with the *acquis*, although some adaptation was still necessary. Professional structures (such as professional chambers or associations) were in place for many professions, although these probably needed to be reinforced in the future. Integration with EU professional associations was developing well (for example, engineering diplomas already met the minimum European standards). The Opinion concluded that the necessary structures in this area seemed to be in place, but it was hard to assess their real effect and enforcement.

For Poland, the *acquis* was only partly and formally achieved concerning the mutual recognition of diplomas and qualifications. As with Hungary, ministries and public bodies were in place for many professions, but needed to be reinforced, while integration with EU professional associations was developing well. The Opinion concluded that compliance with mutual recognition should be achievable 'in the medium term' – so Poland was behind Hungary but ahead of Bulgaria. However, the Commission concluded that 'significant efforts' were required to resolve outstanding issues regarding the free movement of persons in the medium term – meaning that administrative capacity was still low in this area.

Bulgaria was much further behind when the Opinions were published in mid-1997. Bulgaria had no specific legal provisions determining the rights of entry and residence enjoyed by a worker's family, securing rights of residence in the case of voluntary or involuntary cessation of work and for the taking up of alternative employment in the case of unemployment (voluntary or otherwise). The grounds cited by the Bulgarian government for the refusal of work permits did not meet EU provisions governing mobility of the work force stemming from Article 48 (EEC). Family employment rights were unduly restrictive; any right of appeal was dealt with at the administrative level and not in a court of law. There were only a few measures seeking to encourage the occupational and social integration of the worker or family; this lack was reflected in the restrictive conditions applying to participation in the country's educational system.

In 1997, there was little cooperation between Bulgaria and the member-states on mutual recognition of diplomas and professional qualifications. For higher education qualifications, a National Accreditation and Assessment Agency had been set up in 1995, preparing the ground for mutual academic recognition, but no similar body for vocational qualifications existed. Bulgaria had not yet even provided relevant information for a systematic analysis of the equivalence between Bulgarian and member-state professional curricula. The Opinion concluded that 'a major effort' would be required to take up the *acquis* in the medium term; enforcement was further in the future. Overall, the transposition and implementation of the *acquis* were very limited, and the Commission judged that 'a major legislative, policy and administrative reform effort' was required (in comparison with 'significant efforts' for Poland).

The second part of the FMP *acquis* considered in the Opinions was the abolition of checks on persons at internal frontiers. The Schengen agreement was already considered to be part of the free movement of persons by 1997, and the applicants had each already stated its intention to become party to Schengen. When the Opinions were written, it was evident that Schengen would in future be incorporated into the first pillar of the Union under the provisions of the Amsterdam Treaty – then in draft, following the conclusion of the Inter-governmental Conference in July 1997.[31] The Opinions acknowledged how fast the *acquis* was moving, and told the candidates that they had to keep up with it, regardless of whether the member-states had achieved the goals as stated in the Treaty. Each Opinion stated that:

> The free movement of persons within the meaning of Article 7a of the EC Treaty, i.e. the abolition of checks on all persons, whatever their nationality, at the internal frontiers has not yet been fully implemented in the Union. Doing away with checks on persons is conditional on the introduction of a large number of accompanying measures, some of which have yet to be approved and implemented by the Member-states (see separate section on Justice and Home Affairs). However, that objective has been achieved by a limited number of Member-states in accordance with the Schengen Convention (seven Member-states already apply it and another six are working towards implementation).
>
> The draft Treaty [of Amsterdam] aims to make that objective easier to achieve within the Union by including a new chapter on an area of Freedom, Security and Justice and incorporating the Schengen *acquis* into the EU. (page 52 of Hungary's Opinion).

However, the new *acquis* had yet to be defined, and little was yet expected of the candidates. As ever, however, Hungary was already ahead in preparations, having already started investing in the physical infrastructure for border controls. The Opinions note that Hungary had called for institutional and technical cooperation, and had already devoted significant financial resources to the upgrading and modernisation of border controls. Poland and Bulgaria had started some preparations and had sought assistance from member-states, notably for strengthening border controls.

1998: Accession Partnerships. The first Accession Partnerships issued in 1998 simply emphasised the need to ensure that 'necessary legislative and enforcement measures' were taken to implement mutual recognition of professional qualifications and coordination of social security schemes. The updated Accession Partnerships in 1999 and 2000 urged the candidates to complete alignment of mutual recognition of diplomas, and also professional qualifications for Hungary.

In 1999, DG Enlargement of the Commission produced an informal working document on 'Main administrative structures required for implementing the *acquis*' (its evolution was discussed in Chapter 4). This document defined compliance in this area as having structures to organise mutual recognition, certify professional qualifications, and handle requests for professional recognition by non-nationals. Bodies ensuring compliance could be either a ministry (or ministries) or a professional organisation or both. The document pointed out that the whole system for mutual recognition relied on trust between national authorities – a reminder of how much FMP still depended on intergovernmental cooperation as well as common frameworks.

Table 6.1 sets out a summary of the tasks that the candidates had to undertake to ensure free movement of persons within the enlarged single market. It also presents the Europeanisation mechanisms that each task involved, which are discussed in the next section.

Table 6.1   Summary of tasks to ensure free movement of persons in the single market

Task to be undertaken	Aim of task	Europeanisation mechanisms	First introduced	Timescale
Equal treatment of CEE and EU workers (and spouses and children) regardless of nationality	Removal of barriers to free movement of workers – extending existing single market *acquis* to the applicants	Legally binding agreement (accompanied by technical assistance)	Europe Agreement 1993	Implementation of the EAs from 1993
Coordination of social security systems	Removal of barriers to free movement of workers – extending existing single market *acquis* to the applicants	Legally binding agreement (accompanied by technical assistance)	Europe Agreement 1993	Implementation of the EAs from 1993
Legislation for mutual recognition of professional qualifications	Removal of barriers to freedom of establishment and freedom to provide services	Provision of legislative and institutional templates	Single Market White Paper 1995	Implementation prior to accession
Efforts to ensure the necessary legislative and enforcement measures for mutual recognition of professional qualifications	Implementation of established *acquis*	Benchmarking and monitoring	Accession Partnership 1998 (annex)	Short term (1999) and medium term (5 years)

Table 6.1   Summary of tasks to ensure free movement of persons in the single market – *continued*

Task to be undertaken	Aim of task	Europeanisation mechanisms	First introduced	Timescale
Further efforts to ensure the necessary legislative and enforcement measures for coordination of social security schemes	Implementation of established *acquis*	Benchmarking and monitoring	Accession Partnership 1998 (annex)	Short term (1999) and medium term (5 years)
Complete alignment of mutual recognition of diplomas (and also professional qualifications for Hungary)	Implementation of established *acquis*	Benchmarking and monitoring	Accession Partnership 1999 (and update 2000)	Medium term (within 5 years)
Assess administrative capacity to implement mutual recognition of professional qualifications	Clarification of institutional requirements by unofficial communication	Advice	'Main administrative structures' document from the European Commission	From 1999 until accession

Mechanisms of Europeanisation in the single market *acquis*

The formal agenda for FMP contained several different routes for Europeanisation, summarised in Table 6.1, including legally binding agreements, legislative and institutional templates, benchmarking and monitoring, and advice on standards of compliance from EU institutions. Two of these mechanisms of Europeanisation – legally binding agreements and the provision of legislative and institutional models – were familiar techniques used during the creation of the single market to ensure harmonisation of regulation among the existing member-states. The tasks included both prescriptive and prohibitive forms of Europeanisation. The EU also provided aid and twinning for implementation of single market regulation – although the number of projects was small because the *acquis* for FMP was relatively uncomplicated. Bulgaria was the main recipient of Phare projects in areas like establishing standards for professions because it still had ground to make up once twinning started – whereas Hungary and Poland had already implemented much of the *acquis* by then.

However, in addition to the traditional methods of Europeanisation, the EU used a novel technique of integration in this area that was only just being established among the existing member-states for policies outside the formal *acquis*. Under the Santer and Prodi Commissions, the EU began to use various forms of peer review and benchmarking in multiple areas of EU policy (Bannerman 2001, Begg and Peterson 1999). New forms of 'framing integration' were thus emerging in the Union itself, and they were quickly applied to the candidates as well. The candidates started to be covered by the Commission's single market 'scorecard' assessment in 2000, and its assessments of progress in the 'Lisbon process' for economic competitiveness in 2002.

The Commission introduced a number of separate schemes for benchmarking and monitoring progress in CEE as well. For example, there was a 'joint assessment programme' in which CEE finance ministry officials worked with Commission representatives to produce common reports on the economic situation in their countries. In May 2000, the Commission announced plans for a 'mini-ECOFIN' to run from 2001, with a 'multilateral surveillance scheme' that required candidate countries to adopt EU methodology for presenting their economic data. Countries were not to be formally tested against pre-determined standards but 'free to benchmark themselves against EU members and each other', in a system of peer review.[32] 'Commission dealings with pre-accession states will therefore become more similar to its dealings with EU states,' declared Pedro Solbes, the then Financial Affairs Commissioner, at the EBRD Annual Meeting in Riga in 2001.[33]

These are interesting examples of the EU extending its new techniques of peer benchmarking in parallel with the asymmetric benchmarking of the accession process. The difference in the latter case is that the EU did the monitoring from a position of power. In the former case of voluntary participation, the benchmarking exercise did not officially affect either the dates of accession or the terms of entry. Rather, it was intended by the EU to encourage the candidates in economic reforms that were not directly connected with accession, and to get the candidates used to the processes in which they would eventually be included as member-states.

These additional mechanisms amounted to a form of 'framing integration' (the third type of integrative measure discussed in Chapter 3). It prepared the ground for subsequent integration policies by changing the domestic political climate, through stimulating and strengthening the overall support for broader European reform objectives. In CEE, compliance with framing integration had the effect of making domestic civil servants – who were not directly involved in the EU accession process – part of EU-wide systems, and putting them in direct contact with their counterparts in the existing member-states. This process bolstered domestic support for reform agendas, and started the Europeanisation of hitherto unaffected parts of the state administration. CEE policy-makers were attracted by the prestige value of being included as full partners in EU policy-making fora.

The main framing integration in the area of FMP came through the provisions for free movement for workers that were part of employment and social policy, rather than from the EU's policy-making for the single market. Under the Lisbon process, Anna Diamantopoulou – the then Employment and Social Affairs Commissioner – signed a 'Joint Assessment Paper' with each candidate in Spring 2001. These papers committed each candidate to a set of agreed employment and labour market objectives, together with a regular assessment of progress until accession. The aim of these papers was to involve the candidates in the Lisbon process, and to put additional pressure on them to move towards the European social model.[34] The Commission's press release on the Polish joint assessment explicitly states that 'this joint assessment process proceeds in parallel to the normal negotiations on implementation of the "hard law" *acquis communautaire* ... it is critical that all candidate countries shadow Community employment policy and are up to speed on the substance of this policy by the time they join the EU'.[35]

In conclusion, this policy area involved several different types of Europeanisation. It does not fit neatly into the scheme of types of policy-making presented by Knill and Lehmkuhl (1999), but it is a kind of 'hybrid constellation' of different Europeanisation mechanisms. There were some prescriptive Europeanisation mechanisms working through concrete institutional requirements, in the form of social policy requirements. Other parts of the EU's formal agenda were concerned with prohibitive integration, in the form of the mutual recognition and social security coordination requirements. But from the late 1990s, the EU started using framing integration as well, applying to the applicants the new methods used by the existing member-states.

Because FMP was governed by a well-established *acquis*, the candidates faced very low levels of uncertainty about what they had to do, and how to do it. The *acquis* was relatively easy and cheap to transpose. The EU generally spoke with one voice, because the Commission was the main actor in charge of ensuring that single market regulation was properly implemented. Therefore neither of the variables on the EU side – diffuseness and uncertainty – intervened to prevent transfer of the FMP policy prior to negotiations. The main intervening variables at work were on the CEE side: the Europeanisation of this policy area was mainly determined by the political context in CEE (including both political will and administrative capacity) and by the individual candidates' macro-strategies of adaptation to the EU. However, when negotiations on this policy area began in 2001, the issue of free movement of workers became much more controversial on both sides – bringing in a new variable. The political salience of the issue rose, and the three candidates reacted differently to the EU's negotiating position. But all three candidates continued implementing the *acquis* in this area, showing that the process of Europeanisation continued even when the negotiations gave the candidates little material incentive to do so.

6.3   The candidates' responses

The political context

There was little political attention paid to the implementation of this policy area in Bulgaria, Hungary or Poland, although party political actors expressed enthusiasm at the prospect of their citizens being able to travel and work freely throughout the EU. Freedom to live and work in the EU was one of the few unambiguous benefits of the transition from communism since 1989 (Batt 2001). Unlike economic transition, which was painful and difficult for most people, the new freedom to travel abroad and new opportunities to study and gain experience outside the former eastern bloc were benefits available to all. Freedom to move around and work in the EU was regularly cited as an important freedom in CEE assessments of the overall benefits of EU membership (e.g. Szemlér 1998, Inotai 1999, Mayhew 2000). The political dynamics were thus about a positive benefit being denied to the candidates by the Union, rather than a negative demand being imposed on them.

Goodness of fit: interaction and institutional capacity

Free movement of persons within the single market was not a policy area that conflicted with significant domestic or other international pressures. It did not present major problems in terms of timing, resources, or conflicting policies. In terms of timing, implementation started early – with the Europe Agreements and Single Market White

Paper – and it was not an expensive policy, so resources were not a significant problem. The adjustment costs were low in comparison with other parts of the single market *acquis* like environmental policy and competition. FMP primarily involved the establishment of co-ordination systems within ministries, both with professional bodies (for mutual recognition of professional qualifications) and with EU member-states (for mutual recognition and coordination of social security). It did not require, for example, laboratories for certification and testing of products, or large investment costs to meet product or process standards, or expensive new physical infrastructure. Political resistance to FMP was therefore unlikely to stem from the magnitude of adjustment costs.

The candidates had an interest in complying with this part of the *acquis* because regulatory harmonisation was a prerequisite for their own citizens to move freely in EU-15 after accession. If there was to be any hope of gaining access to EU labour markets, the candidates had to implement the FMP *acquis*. However, this was evidently not a policy area of high priority for the EU – and many other parts of the single market *acquis* were given much more emphasis, particularly competition (Smith *et al.* 1996). So why did the candidates devote resources to FMP at all? Mainly because the candidates could not pick and choose among single market requirements. They came as a package, and the EU published assessments of overall compliance with the single market *acquis*, so progress was needed in all areas.

Adaptation strategies and interests

None of the countries had major countervailing pressures politically, as this part of the *acquis* did not conflict with strong domestic interests. Trade unions were not generally opposed to EU workers being free to compete in CEE labour markets; indeed, Hungarian trade union officials hoped that more foreign workers would drive wages up. Problems and delays in progress tended to be the result of limited human resources and administrative capacity, rather than any political motivation for delay, according to officials involved.

These high levels of anticipatory adjustment to the single market also show political will to transpose the *acquis* for other reasons. In addition to preparations that followed the pre-accession strategy, policy-makers were motivated by the need for their exporters to have a coherent regulatory framework at home in order to trade with the single market; there was thus business lobbying for a clear plan for transposition. Domestic actors in the foreign and social affairs ministries perceived the FMP *acquis* as consistent with domestic interests in at least two respects:

1. Aligning with single market regulations in order to facilitate economic integration. Indeed, many actors (especially those with an economics background) accepted the policy paradigm underlying FMP of liberalisation and harmonisation as an economic rationale in itself, not just as something necessary for accession – this is clear from interviews (Hungarian economics ministry, Polish Committee for European Integration); for example, Poland's 1997 *National Strategy for Integration* states that 'The aim [of free movement of labour] is to facilitate rational utilisation of labour resources in the EU.'

2. Aligning with this part of the *acquis* is a pre-requisite for free movement of labour, including CEE workers. If there was to be any possibility of free movement on accession, the full set of regulations and institutional requirements had to be in place. The CEE policy-makers did not want to give the EU any excuse for imposing a transition period because of slow implementation of the *acquis* on the candidates' side.

Negotiating positions

In the area of free movement of persons, all three countries followed a strategy of complete adaptation, with little attempt at resistance to the EU's demands or at softening the domestic impact. Differences in the timing and completeness of implementation had more to do with each country's domestic institutional capacity and political will to drive EU adaptation as a whole, than any particular problem with this policy area.

In their written negotiating positions, Bulgaria, Hungary and Poland all stated their willingness to provide freedom of movement for workers who were nationals of the member-states in accordance with the *acquis*, and to adopt the necessary laws, regulations and administrative provisions to this end. The negotiating positions explicitly stated that they accepted the *acquis* in full, raised no negotiating problems and did not request transition periods or derogations in this area. However, the Polish negotiators expressed concern that the newly reformed Polish health care and social security systems might not reach adequate financial stability to be able to participate fully in the Community coordination of social security systems. Poland thus wanted to reserve the right to revise its present position in this regard at a later stage of accession negotiations (Republic of Poland 1999); however, in December 2001 the Polish negotiators stated that their country would participate fully in the coordination of social security systems. Their desire to conclude negotiations quickly overcame the earlier hesitation.

These positions should not be interpreted as arising simply from a general reluctance of the candidates to put forward requests for transition periods and derogations. The candidates were not shy to put forward requests for concessions on the other three freedoms of the single market. Hungary and Poland put forward requests in many other chapters, and other candidates put forward requests for the free movement of persons. Rather, the absence of transition period requests on FMP indicated the lack of serious problems in implementation, and also self-restraint in the hope that the Union would moderate its position.

None of the countries' formal negotiating positions mentioned the likely EU request for a transition period, but they all emphasised the fact that they would accept the whole *acquis* after accession, drawing an implicit comparison with the EU position. None of the three candidates studied here asked for concessions in return for transition periods on the EU side. However, although these original positions reflected the countries' adaptation strategies (and hence rapid Europeanisation), the way that each country behaved once negotiations started showed the influence of domestic politics.

6.4   Negotiations

Over the course of many interviews conducted between 1996 and 2002, the author asked EU and CEE policy-makers to rank the various negotiating chapters in terms of difficulty. They generally saw free movement of workers as relatively unproblematic in comparison with other policy areas like competition, environmental policy and agriculture. However, many of them commented several years in advance that the negotiations in this area would be difficult owing to the Union's reluctance to extend freedom of movement to CEE workers. Academic works on the enlargement process predicted that the Union would ask for a transition period before CEE citizens could work freely anywhere in the Union (e.g. Mayhew 1998, Grabbe and Hughes 1998). The Commission's negotiating teams themselves also forecast that free movement of workers would be one of the most difficult issues in negotiations. By 2000, FMP was appearing in the top five or six topics mentioned in most actors' lists of difficult areas that would involve 'real negotiations' rather than an agreement between technocrats. This change was evident both in off-the-record interviews and in published documents (e.g. Biegaj 2000). From the end of 1997 onwards, when the implications of the Amsterdam Treaty began to be known, the negotiating chapter on justice and home affairs was also mentioned increasingly often as likely to be one of the most difficult areas in both preparations and negotiations.

The difference with the negotiations on FMP was that they were not about the candidates' implementation of the *acquis*, but rather about the existing member-states' desire for a transition period. When asked in interviews what could be negotiated in return for the restrictions on FMP wanted by the EU, CEE policy-makers mentioned several other issues. One was the freedom of EU-15 citizens to buy land in neighbouring CEE countries such as the Czech Republic, Hungary and Poland – an issue which fell in the chapter on free movement of capital. In fact the EU did grant a transition period in this area to several CEE candidates who requested one. The delay in implementing could be up to seven years, in order to match the transition period that the EU demanded for FMP in negotiations in July 2001, and Commission officials in DG Enlargement drew an explicit link between the two chapters. Another issue was border controls, which Hungarian and Polish negotiators thought could be directly linked to the question of FMP – their reasoning was that there should be a trade-off between the freedom of their citizens to move westwards to work and the openness of their own borders to their non-candidate neighbours.

Officials in the Council and Commission also thought that such a trade-off was a possibility. However, it became clear in 2000 that the interior and justice ministers considered full implementation of the Schengen *acquis* should be obligatory prior to accession, regardless of whether there were restrictions on the free movement of workers. This change occurred because the issue of the external borders of the Union had risen up the political agenda extremely rapidly. It was no longer conceivable for the Union to grant a trade-off between these two policy areas, because both were too controversial within the existing member-states.

When it came to negotiations on the free movement of persons, the EU's focus was on only one aspect of the *acquis*: the freedom of CEE citizens to work anywhere in the enlarged Union. In presenting its draft common position, the Commission was careful to note that its position did not pre-judge the question of the free movement of persons who were not intending to work in the EU-15; i.e. it only prevented CEE citizens from taking up legal employment, not from travelling in the existing member-states.

The political context in the member-states

'You say the EU's position on workers is "take it or leave it". Well, the choice is yours. Either you can accept the flexible arrangements we are offering or you can join in 2010.' Commissioner Günter Verheugen, speaking in response to an intervention by Slovenian Prime Minister Janez Drnovšek, Salzburg World Economic Forum, 1 July 2001.

This analysis is concerned with the applicants' responses to the EU's demands, so the EU common positions are taken as an independent variable. The formulation of the EU's policies is thus analysed here only in so far as it might affect the applicants' responses. In this respect, there are three important factors which are brought out in the analysis presented below:

- Uncertainty: The solidity of the Union's position, in terms of clarity of agenda, and the strength of the member-states' support for it;
- Political context: The degree of room for manoeuvre that EU negotiators claimed they had in allowing concessions or trade-offs for this position;
- The macro-strategy of adaptation that each candidate adopted, which was separate from its negotiating position but may have affected it.

The solidity of the EU's position was uncertain. The member-states were not united in demanding a transition period that would prevent the full application of the *acquis* on FMP for the candidate countries after accession. Indeed, a number of national politicians and EU officials claimed that transition periods – particularly long ones – were both unfair and unnecessary. However, although there were many signs of disunity, the member-states who were most vocal in advocating a transition period supported it strongly. It was thus difficult for the candidates to exploit the divisions on the EU side, because they faced a strong preference from a few member-states, and relatively weak opposition to this preference from the other member-states. Moreover, the member-states most in favour of restricting labour mobility were those that also had the strongest positive interests in enlargement as well, so to criticise restrictions risked alienating countries that were advocates of enlargement.

The Commission's draft common position (DCP) was preceded by much debate within the EU institutions as well as member-states about whether the Union should demand a long transition period in this area. There was widespread concern about the potential for many CEE workers to come to Germany and Austria, despite numerous German and Austrian academic studies countering these claims (e.g. Bauer and Zimmerman 1997, Richter 1998). In Germany, the CDU/CSU demanded in 1998 that free movement of people from CEE should not be allowed until 2015 at the earliest.[36] Politicians in the eastern *Länder*, particularly those which border Poland and which have high levels of unemployment, also expressed increasing concern about the potential for CEE workers to disrupt local labour markets. Some of the claims about migration were motivated by a concern about competition from cheap labour from eastern Europe. Ironically, in economic terms Germany in particular would probably have benefited considerably from greater immigration of skilled workers from CEE (Bauer and Zimmerman 1997), and sectors such as construction and domestic services quickly became dependent on using largely illegal east European labour. However, the trade unions objected loudly to further inflows, while the large employers' organisations argued for free movement of labour (BDI and BDA 1997).

Under the Kohl government, the German social affairs ministry considered asking for very long transition periods of up to 18 years. When the Schröder government came to power in 1998, its presentation of the issue to other EU member-states changed the German position from concern about real potential disruption of labour markets to the problem in public perception. This shift meant that German politicians continued advocating transition periods, but the discourse shifted from justifying them in terms of objective economic needs to a justification based on the need to gain public consent for the enlargement process. German politicians – both at regional and federal level – presented transition periods on labour mobility as a potential veto-point in the accession process, even though Germany could not constitutionally hold a referendum on enlargement. Officials in the federal foreign ministry argued that although a transition period was not objectively necessary, it was essential to reassure voters.

By Autumn 2000, when negotiations were in sight, German officials argued that symbolic transition periods had to be imposed, but these could be quietly lifted soon after accession because it would become clear to the public that they were not needed. In the international discourse, Austrian politicians tended to present similar arguments, and followed the German line on the length and scope of necessary transition periods.

Institutional actors were also involved, with several Commissioners and many officials attempting to defend the four freedoms of the single market. The Commission itself tried to counter exaggerated claims about migration potential, by commissioning a very detailed study on the effects of enlargement on EU labour markets from widely respected academic economists (Boeri and Brücker 2000). The study estimated that if all ten central and eastern European applicants joined at the same time, 330,000 people a year would move to the current EU member-states. Only one third – 110,000 people – would be workers, and these numbers were predicted to halve within 10 years. The total number of CEE citizens resident in the EU-15 was predicted to rise slowly over 30 years to an equilibrium of 1.1% of the EU-15 population. Commissioners and Commission officials quoted these estimates widely in speeches, policy documents and public presentations, and they were also used widely in the public debate by journalists, commentators and pressure groups (e.g. ERT 2001).

A prime mover on the Commission side was Günter Verheugen, the Commissioner for enlargement and an SPD politician from Germany. It was largely at his insistence that the Commission adopted only two of five possible options for a negotiating position that were outlined in a Commission working paper of March 2001. Option 2 offered the full, immediate and complete implementation of free movement of persons, attached to safeguard clauses that would allow member-states to limit access for workers in the event of serious distortions. Option 3 foresaw a system of flexible transitional arrangements which would allow gradual introduction of free movement during a limited transition period; under this option, member-states were free to decide, through national law, for a faster opening of their labour markets after enlargement, but they could also keep national restrictions in place. In all the options, the candidates had to offer full right of access to their labour markets for EU-15 workers.

The College of Commissioners gave Verheugen a mandate to propose a negotiating position based on these two options to the Council.[37] Verheugen was criticised within the Commission and outside for insisting on Option 3, the position preferred by his home country. He justified the position on the grounds that it was necessary to get agreement on a common negotiating position from Germany and Austria, and that this position provided maximum flexibility so that other member-states could be more generous to the CEE countries. He stated publicly that his aim was to make it as flexible as possible, while retaining the seven-year period that was symbolically important to Germany and Austria (comments to the press, World Economic Forum, Salzburg, 1 July 2001). 'Flexible' effectively meant allowing the member-states to impose their own arrangements: this allowed room for manoeuvre in domestic politics, but it also ran against the fundamental principle of economic integration in the EU, which requires common standards and procedures in order to ensure open markets and the free circulation of goods, services, capital and people.

Tying hands. As in the comment quoted above, Günter Verheugen tended to present the restrictions as inevitable, portraying a stark choice between either restricting FMP or delaying enlargement significantly. This is clearly an argument known in the international relations literature as 'tying hands' (Haggard *et al.* 1993), whereby the policy advocate claims that his negotiating position cannot change because of the bargain struck in the domestic arena (that is, the bargain struck between the EU-15 countries). Verheugen presented this as the firmly held German position to the other member-states, and as the Union's firmly held position to the applicant countries. He managed to overcome the complexity of actor constellations and make the Union speak with one voice on this issue in negotiations.

Trade-offs between negotiating chapters. In the negotiations themselves, seemingly unrelated issues affected the EU's position. In April 2001, the Spanish government sent a 'memorandum' to the Commission suggesting that initial financial guidelines for regional policy after 2006 should be set in the context of the accession negotiations. The political motivation behind this memorandum was spelled out publicly by Spanish diplomats: the Spaniards wanted a guarantee that their Objective 1 regions would continue to receive regional funds after enlargement. Moreover, the government of Jose María Aznar linked this demand to the Union's negotiating position on free movement of persons, arguing that in the interests of 'solidarity', Germans could not impose a seven-year transition period on CEE workers unless Spain could impose a long transition period on its own receipt of structural funds.

There was then an angry public exchange between Spanish and German politicians and officials. The French government also put down a marker on agriculture, arguing that because the transition periods on the purchase of agricultural land by foreigners would affect the price of land, it should be left until the chapter on agriculture was opened in 2002. Although this argument made no reference to the negotiations on free movement of workers, it was widely interpreted as an attempt by the French to indicate that the EU would have to make concessions on its receipts of agricultural subsidies if it heeded Spain's concerns about regional aid. The French declaration raised the stakes, and started the debate about the budget in earnest. The General Affairs Council of 11 June 2001 finally resolved this issue after a review of accession negotiations in the first half of 2001.

The intrusion of the Spanish memorandum and the French marker did not change the EU's negotiating position on free movement of labour. However, they were an important part of the overall political dynamics of the negotiations: they gave some CEE negotiators hope at first that Spanish opposition and discourse about 'solidarity' might shift the EU's position, which encouraged the Czech and Polish negotiators to hold out for longer. However, such readings of the Spanish position were quickly revised when it became clear that the Spanish government was not going to attempt to alter the EU's position on movement of labour, but was concentrating its efforts exclusively on preserving its regional transfers after accession. There was no scope for an alliance between the candidates and the Spanish, because they were seeking different concessions in negotiating chapter 2. Moreover, the CEE candidates had no incentive to support the Spanish position because it worked against their interests in receiving structural funds, a subject on which negotiations were to begin the following year. The aim of both the Spanish memorandum and the French marker was to set up the politics of a later stage of the negotiations, those on the budget scheduled for 2002 – an example of EU member-states starting 'pre-negotiations' for the next EU game (Friis 1998). The point was to indicate preferences and signal firmly held positions in advance, not to change the negotiations or alter potential transition periods on the free movement of labour or on purchase of agricultural land.

The EU's negotiating position

The Commission submitted its initial DCP on the free movement of persons on 14 April 2000. It was accompanied by a recommendation that member-states should not enter the negotiations with requests for transition periods, but should wait until the end of the negotiations for tactical reasons.[38] The DCP then went for examination in the Council of Ministers' Enlargement Working Group, with a view to adopting a formal common EU negotiating position.

A year later, the Commission formally presented the full DCP in the Council, on 11 April 2001. The Commission's position had moved from a general seven-year ban on free movement of labour to the '2+3+2 formula', whereby member-states could use their own discretion. A general transition period of five years was proposed, with a possible extension by individual member-states for a further two years in the case of serious disturbances of their labour markets. After no more than seven years, free movement of workers would operate fully across all member-states. An automatic review would take place after the first two years, in which the member-states could decide whether to shorten or lift the transition period. However, individual member-states could continue their own national measures and safeguards regardless of the general decision.[39] Cyprus and Malta were excluded from these transition periods, and Malta was offered a transition period on the freedom of EU citizens to work on the island.[40] Malta was the only candidate offered any restrictions on the right of EU-15 citizens to work in a new member-state.

The Spanish memorandum to the Commission followed the presentation of this position, but work on the DCP continued nonetheless. It was approved fairly quickly because of the generosity of the DCP in allowing the symbolically important seven years to be maintained, for which Verheugen was widely criticised. The presidency – held by Sweden at the time – then allowed the following formulation:

1. From the first day after accession, each of the EU-15 countries has the right to apply national measures to limit or wholly ban CEE workers from access to their national labour markets (or a part of their national labour markets, e.g. border regions). These national measures may not be more restrictive than bilateral national measures or agreements applied before enlargement. All member-states have the right to liberalise their systems or totally open their labour markets from the first day after enlargement.
2. Before the end of the second year after enlargement, the current 15 member-states must inform the Commission formally if they want to continue implementing national measures over the following three years, or if they want to implement the *acquis* on free movement of persons.
3. Five years after enlargement, each member-state that wants to keep national measures in place may decide to extend them for a maximum of a further two years if they experience 'serious disturbances' of their labour markets.
4. No general transition period would apply to services, but Germany and Austria would be allowed to limit the free provision of certain services (with the exact list to be defined) for a seven-year period to avoid any serious disturbances of their labour markets.[41]

COREPER agreed the common negotiating positions on free movement of persons and free movement of capital on 31 May 2001. In a nutshell, the EU position allowed the member-states to restrict the freedom of new member-state citizens to work in their countries for five years after accession, and for up to seven years in exceptional circumstances. However, free movement of workers was clearly separated from the issue of free movement of persons. The negotiating position did not in itself prevent CEE citizens from travelling in the EU-15 after accession, just from working there.

Within the negotiations, it was difficult for the candidates to gain concessions for three reasons. One was that although the EU actors were divided, a few prime movers emerged with strongly held preferences. A second factor was the 'tying hands' arguments used by EU negotiators – particularly Commissioner Verheugen – to argue that the EU had little room for manoeuvre in the length of the transition period imposed. Thirdly, the surrounding political dynamics were difficult to read: although Spain objected to the transition period, CEE negotiators did not trust the Spanish government as an ally because its motivation was clearly not accommodating CEE interests. So although some CEE negotiators at first took heart from the rows within the Union, most quickly came round to the view that intra-member-state politics would not help their position.

The reactions of the candidates

The first candidates to agree to the EU's position were Hungary and Cyprus, which provisionally closed the FMP chapter on 12 June 2001, less than two weeks after negotiations had formally been opened. But Hungary negotiated concessions in return: its chief negotiator, Endre Juhasz, had demanded in advance a 'tailor-made solution for Hungary'.[42] Once negotiations began, he agreed quickly to the formula for the Union's transition period, but presented a counter-proposal at the same time. Hungarian Prime Minister Viktor Orbán justified the agreement on Hungarian television on two grounds: that member-states could decide individually to allow Hungarians to work in their country 'even the day after our accession'; and that Hungary had got a success in return in the form of a seven-year ban on foreigners buying arable land in Hungary after accession.[43] The Union agreed because it was keen to close this chapter provisionally with at least one country, in order to set a precedent and put pressure on the others.

Poland did not concede for more than six months after negotiations opened. The reasons for this negotiating strategy lay in domestic politics as well as in Poland's relationship with the EU. The centre-right government of Jerzy Buzek was facing defeat in the September 2001 elections, and could not afford to be seen to give in to the EU on this sensitive issue, so it refused the EU's request for a transition period. However, the elections brought a change of government. The new foreign minister, Włodzimierz Cimoszewicz, was keen to make more rapid progress in negotiations than his predecessor, and instructed the new chief negotiator, Jan Truszczyński, to find a solution to some of the major outstanding problems by the end of the Belgian presidency. Truszczyński did so at the last negotiating session of the year on 21 December 2001.

The net result of Poland's attempt at hard bargaining was a deal that did not differ significantly from that obtained by Hungary six months before. Only Malta and Cyprus managed to avoid the EU's transition period on free movement of workers. To try to mitigate the impact of the transition period, the Polish government ended up seeking bilateral concessions from various member-states, such as the letter that Prime Minister Leszek Miller obtained from British Prime Minister Tony Blair in December 2001 promising that the UK would review the need for the transition period on FMP at the time that Poland joined the Union. Poland did not gain all of its demands on free movement of capital either, where its chief negotiator had tried to gain trade-offs against the EU's transition period on labour mobility. The Polish government agreed to a compromise on 1 March 2002 which included a provision to allow EU citizens who had worked leased land to buy it in some regions after a minimum of three years, not the 18-year ban originally proposed.[44]

Bulgaria tried to follow Hungary's strategy, agreeing to the EU's demands rapidly. The main aim was the fastest possible implementation of the free movement of labour (Bokova and Hubchev 2000). However, Bulgaria could open negotiations on FMP only in the second half of 2001, because it was further behind in the overall timetable for negotiations. By the end of 2001, Bulgaria had been unable to close the chapter because the EU was still citing concerns about its administrative capacity. The Commission's verdict in January 2002 was that 'Preparation is taking place, but legislation needs to be adopted in all areas. The appropriate administrative structures need to be developed and capacity strengthened'.[45] The chapter was provisionally closed in June 2002.

The three countries thus followed different strategies in their negotiations on FMP: Hungary prepared well, and managed to extract some concessions from the EU in return for conceding the EU's transition period request quickly. Poland tried to hold out for a better deal for several months, but failed to gain any further concessions. Bulgaria tried to concede quickly to make fast progress, but the EU refused to close the chapter because it regarded Bulgaria's implementation as inadequate.

On the EU side, the member-states reacted unexpectedly, in not all taking advantage of the transition period. Several member-states immediately stated that they would lift the restrictions immediately on accession. Within two months of the opening of negotiations on this chapter, four member-states had indicated that they would sign bilateral agreements with the candidates to allow full access to their labour market after accession: Denmark, Ireland, the Netherlands, and Sweden. The UK announced in December 2002 that it would follow suit. However, in early 2004, Sweden, Denmark and the Netherlands announced that they would use the transition period after all. After intense domestic debates in the run-up to the enlargement on 1 May 2004, Sweden's parliament forced the government to drop its proposals for restrictions on CEE workers, while Britain and Ireland decided to keep their labour markets open.

In tactical terms, the restrictions imposed on labour mobility had the positive effect of speeding up agreements in other areas, because EU negotiators offered transition periods. What one senior Commission official called the 'seven-year effect' emerged as EU negotiators became more generous, seeking to make concessions elsewhere as a trade-off against the restrictions on central European workers. This happened for environmental standards, where EU negotiators started openly advising the applicants not to reduce their requests for transition periods, but just to accompany them with financing plans. The 'seven-year effect' also emerged in the Union's position on free movement of capital, which offered the applicants their own transition periods before foreigners could buy land or second homes in central Europe. Commission officials commented (off the record) that there was a trade-off between the EU's transition period on free movement of workers and the transition periods granted to the candidates on land and on environmental protection.

Commission officials felt very uncomfortable with a negotiating position that so obviously violated one of the four freedoms of the single market. One of them commented to the author in September 2001, 'Most of us in the Commission are ashamed of the position on free movement of labour, so if candidates are clever they can exploit this to gain concessions'. This trade-off was not needed to gain the agreement of the candidates, but resulted from a sense that the candidates should be given time to deal with their own problem areas, especially when there was a much sounder economic case for transition periods on buying farmland than there was for the EU's restrictions on labour mobility (interviews, European Commission, July and August 2001). Thus the EU's negotiators tried to accommodate CEE interests to some extent, even though their bargaining power was much greater than that of the applicants.

6.5   Explaining outcomes

The outcome for the candidates: the dynamics of Europeanisation

Why did the candidates carry on implementing the FMP *acquis* even though they were aware that the EU would impose a transition period on CEE workers? The outcome can be explained partly by the fact that the candidates knew that they would have to implement the *acquis* to allow free movement of persons across the enlarged single market at some point, even if there were a transition period. But this explanation still leaves a timing puzzle: why devote resources to it at this time if the EU was going to make no reciprocal commitment until many years after accession? Explanation requires several variables, and a consideration of EU-CEE relations and also domestic politics.

On the international level, there was the general incentive faced by candidates for accession to show willing and to demonstrate their ability to be a full partner once they became a member-state. The candidates faced a double hurdle for accession: they had to fulfil the technical requirements, but they also had to inspire confidence among the member-states that they would be good partners in the Union. That made it difficult to pick and choose among the items on the EU's agenda. Evident unwillingness and/or incapacity to implement the *acquis* in full would be bad for the applicant's image in the EU-15. The fact that previous joiners like Greece had been slow to implement parts of the *acquis* set a negative precedent rather than a positive one; 'We don't want any more Greeces coming in', as a senior German foreign ministry official put it in 2000. It was also very risky to gamble that the attractiveness and geo-political importance of an individual candidate would outweigh slow and reluctant implementation, as Poland discovered in 2001.

Secondly, the EU's pre-accession strategy itself created a process of adjustment and implementation that was subject to continuous monitoring by EU institutions. There were considerable disincentives for the candidates to go slowly or stall for political reasons in one area of implementation when they knew that the Commission would criticise their level of preparedness in the annual Regular Reports. They would then have to justify their performance to the EU's institutional actors, to the member-states, and to their domestic public.

At the domestic level, there were significant political costs if the EU criticised progress in preparations. Even if political actors could claim that they were defending national interests, or argue that the EU had an incorrect picture, this message was likely to be lost in the press coverage of the EU's assessment and the comments of political rivals claiming that those in charge of accession preparations were not doing their job well. The effect of EU criticism depended on how close an applicant was to accession (e.g. it mattered more in Bulgaria than Hungary), and on the level of domestic support for accession.

The second issue on the domestic level was that the candidates had already committed their own resources and political capital to the process, so they had sunk costs. Institutions and procedures had been established, people had been appointed to new or upgraded posts and sent on EU training courses, public money had been spent to match EU aid funds. Europeanisation was an incremental and on-going process, so it was difficult to stop and start it again. It also developed its own momentum as officials started to internalise EU norms, instituted EU-compatible procedures on their own initiative, and communicated directly with EU officials. Accession preparations were a multi-faceted process involving contacts at all levels, so top-down control was difficult to maintain. Although priorities were set centrally, departments developed their own relationships with the EU. It became expensive to reverse the process of Europeanisation.

The outcome for the EU: the role of policy paradigms as a mediating factor

The EU's own approach to the free movement of workers was very unusual in the accession process, because it was so high-profile within the member-states and it contradicted the logic of the EU's own policies – the 'policy paradigms' discussed in Chapter 3. The paradigms underlying particular policy areas shape the preferences of public policy-makers, and become embedded by acquiring a dominant position in the policy discourse that characterises a policy area (Sedelmeier 2001).

Several policy paradigms underlie the regulation of free movement of persons in the single market. One is that the four freedoms are all essential for the functioning of the single market, and that they are indivisible. The freedom of workers to move around the Union is closely related in economic terms to free movement of services and freedom of establishment, because the freedom to supply many services depends on a supplying firm being able to use its own workers in the market being supplied (Mayhew 1998). Moreover, all three of these freedoms were dealt with in the same part of the Europe Agreements, in Title IV. Free movement of persons is thus linked to other freedoms, and by implication, limiting FMP limits the value of other freedoms and hence the functioning of the single market.

Some political actors appealed to this policy paradigm explicitly in order to oppose the restrictions that others in the EU were advocating. Frits Bolkestein, then Internal Market Commissioner, argued that 'Free movement of persons is a central pillar of the Internal Market ... In a healthy economy it is better to prepare for competition than to draw up new barriers.' (speech at the Centre for European Policy Studies, Brussels, 21 February 2000). He later commented that 'The four freedoms cannot be divided, we cannot pick and choose between them' (Centre for European Reform seminar, London, 5 February 2001). Anna Diamantopoulou, then Employment and Social Affairs Commissioner, argued that labour mobility was an integral part of the single market and the Lisbon process, and that the candidates should be involved in it too (speech in Warsaw, 29 January 2001).

A second policy paradigm is that freedom to work throughout the Union is a basic right of EU citizens. This right has a firm legal basis of direct effect through a number of cases brought to the European Court of Justice, such as that of *Yvonne van Duyn v Home Office*, Case 41/74. In a ruling following this case in 1975, the Court held that Article 48 conferred a right of free movement directly on individuals, without any need for implementing measures at the national level. Given that this right had direct effect, denying this right to citizens of new members of the Union was tantamount to according them second-class citizenship of the Union while the transition period was in force.

A third policy paradigm is that free movement of people within the Union is separate from migration policy. Until the Amsterdam Treaty, FMP lay in the first pillar of the Union, while migration policy was in the inter-governmental third pillar. As Alan Mayhew points out 'In the context of accession, questions of migration and of labour mobility are treated separately' (Mayhew 1998, p. 333), because free movement of persons was within the treaty while migration concerned the citizens of third countries and remained primarily the preserve of individual member-states. This last policy paradigm was maintained in negotiations, while the first two were overruled by domestic interest groups.

This outcome is an interesting counterpoint to the case-studies presented by Sedelmeier on the early phase of accession policy (2001). Sedelmeier illustrates two ways in which a policy paradigm limited the accommodation of the candidates' preferences. In the first – trade liberalisation in the steel sector under the Europe Agreements – an alternative policy paradigm of open markets emerged that was more compatible with the preferences of the candidates, allowing accommodation of these preferences despite opposition from interest groups. In the second – requirements for regulatory alignment of the CEE candidates with the single market – policy advocates in the Commission successfully challenged the viability of certain elements of the policy paradigm underpinning the single market with reference to the specific situation in the CEE countries, particularly in environmental policy.

In the case of FMP presented here, defenders of the policy paradigms underpinning the single market failed to use them to accommodate CEE interests. This outcome accords with one of the key assumptions of the liberal intergovernmentalism approach to studying the EU (e.g. Moravcsik 1993), which is that the strength of domestic interest groups constrains the autonomy of policy-makers in the member-states. The EU's single market policy paradigms were overruled by domestic political actors in some of the member-states.

However, the policy paradigms were not forgotten, and many EU political actors – especially those from Germany and Austria – felt a need to justify publicly their own position and the EU's stance in negotiations. Both Commissioners and Commission officials expressed their embarrassment not just at the impact on CEE interests, but also because the EU's negotiating position did not respect the principles underlying the single market.

Conclusions

In order to illustrate how different mechanisms of Europeanisation can work, this chapter has explored how the EU presented the formal agenda for accession in this area and how the candidates responded. The Europeanisation mechanisms employed by the EU included aid, advice and benchmarking. The actor constellation on the EU side was relatively simple because the Commission presented the *acquis* and the member-states relied on the Commission to judge compliance. The *acquis* was not in itself controversial on either side, as it was accepted by both the candidates and the Union as part of the single market. This case-study then showed how the EU's straightforward presentation of its agenda was then contradicted by the politics in its own member-states. When it came to negotiations, the free movement of workers was the first chapter where the EU asked for a transition period. Domestic political considerations on the EU side overrode the principles of the single market; that is, high politics overturned policy paradigms that were well-established in the Union. The applicants had to accept the outcome – despite its evident unfairness – because of the asymmetrical power relationship.

However, this outcome cannot be explained solely through a 'power politics' explanation on either side. Although the EU exploited its asymmetrical bargaining power, it went to some lengths to accommodate CEE interests as well. EU actors – in both the institutions and the member-states – debated the negotiating position intensely and felt a strong need to justify their common position in terms of existing paradigms. Moreover, EU actors tried to mitigate the impact in several ways: some of the member-states unilaterally offered the candidates full access to their labour markets, while the Commission granted the candidates additional concessions in other negotiating chapters.

On the applicants' side, all three candidates studied here continued to align with the *acquis* despite their different negotiating strategies. Given the likelihood of a transition period on the EU side – which was well known in advance – they did not have a strong incentive to implement and enforce the FMP *acquis* as an accession veto-point; yet they made a sustained effort over several years to implement it along with the rest of the single market *acquis*. The explanation for this response on the applicants' side lies in three variables: the Europeanisation processes already at work in their domestic contexts; the adaptation strategies that they had adopted long prior to the opening of negotiations on this chapter; and uncertainty: The *acquis* in this policy area was clear, and levels of uncertainty were low about timing, whom to satisfy, and the standards of compliance. However, there was an uncertainty about the linkage between implementation and the benefits associated with it, because the candidates were unsure when they might gain full access to EU labour markets.

Although the candidates adopted similar strategies in their preparations, the reaction of the Bulgarian, Hungarian and Polish negotiators to the EU's position shows three very different strategies. The Hungarians aimed to get a deal rapidly, and succeeded in extracting additional concessions from the EU in return for being the first candidate to close the chapter. The Bulgarians followed a similar strategy, but had less negotiating power than the Hungarian team because they were further behind in both negotiations and preparations. The Poles held out for over six months because of controversy in domestic politics, in the hope that the EU would have to make concessions towards them. But in the end, Poland achieved a similar deal to that agreed by the Hungarians, but at the price of stirring up resentment towards the EU in the domestic population.

The outcome for Poland reveals an important feature of accession negotiations: the EU's negotiators were disinclined to grant a better deal to candidates who closed a chapter later than to those who closed it earlier. If they had made additional concessions to countries closing later, it would have encouraged the candidates that had already closed to re-open the chapter and try for a better deal. Thus the Commission had a strong disincentive to grant more to those candidates who held out for longer, and it had every incentive to give concessions to reward a candidate for being the first to close the chapter.

7
Movement of Persons under Schengen[46]

This case-study concerns the policy area of regulating movement of persons across the external frontiers of the Union, which comprised the Schengen *acquis* contained within negotiating chapter 24 on justice and home affairs. This policy area was presented relatively late in the accession process, but it was high on the political agenda in both the EU and CEE. It did not appear in the first phases of accession policy, and received little attention in the Commission's 1997 Opinions, but it became an increasingly important area from 1998 onwards in the Accession Partnerships and in EU aid policy, including twinning.

Implementation of Schengen controls on the prospective external borders of the enlarged EU became an increasingly important part of the EU's accession strategy towards the end of the 1990s, largely because of the political sensitivity of border issues among current member-states. In the late 1990s, the EU began actively exporting its border control technology (e.g. document-readers and databases) and practices to CEE, and also its emerging common methods for handling asylum claims and refugees. One of the central items on the EU's agenda was export of its visa policies, but these were much more controversial because they inevitably broke socio-economic and political ties across borders between candidates and their non-candidate neighbours. Not only did EU border policies go to the heart of the candidates' new-found sovereignty, but their foreign relations were affected as well.

This chapter uses the same structure and methods as Chapter 6, but to analyse a much more complex and politically difficult policy area. Section 7.1 sets out the background to the EU's approach. The political importance of border policies increased considerably following the integration of the Schengen Accord into the Amsterdam Treaty and the

Tampere European Council in 1999. These changes resulted in a rapidly growing new *acquis* that the candidates had to adopt. Section 7.2 presents the EU's agenda for borders policies, what could be called its *'acquis frontalier'*. Section 7.3 presents the responses of Bulgaria, Hungary and Poland to the EU's agenda. Section 7.4 discusses the negotiating positions presented by the candidates and the EU. Section 7.5 assesses the outcome.

7.1 Background to the EU's approach

After the 1997 Amsterdam Treaty entered into force, the term 'justice and home affairs' covered the regulation of the movement of persons across borders, and this part of the *acquis* was presented to the candidates as compulsory for full implementation prior to accession. Unlike the single market, the JHA *acquis* was new and complex. It had little case law and its development was controversial within the member-states. In the case of FMP, there was a ready-made set of legislative and institutional templates to transfer to the candidates, whereas the very nature and scope of JHA were still being hotly debated in the Union. As in other parts of the accession *acquis*, the candidates faced a moving target, but here it was a particularly speedy and fuzzy target. The candidates faced considerable uncertainty in understanding what constituted compliance with the *acquis*. The question of how to define the accession *acquis* for the CEE candidates itself forced the Union to clarify some grey areas in JHA and to reassess the implications of some of its policies.

The foundation of EU policies and legislation

The origins of EU border policies lay in the aspiration to get rid of obstacles to the free circulation of goods, services and people, rather than regulating frontiers more tightly (Bigo 1998). In the 1980s, immigration and asylum policies were matters for national authorities, with European-level policies confined to partially liberalising movement of persons in the single market. The first moves towards common frontier policies were motivated by frustration with the slow removal of obstacles between countries that had geographically close and tightly integrated economies. This led to an agreement outside the European Community framework signed at Schengen in 1985, which was then elaborated and implemented as the Schengen Convention by five countries (Belgium, France, Germany, Luxembourg and the Netherlands) in 1990. The original aim of Schengen was 'the gradual abolition of controls at common frontiers'. Such controls were finally abolished only after 1995, by which time most other EU members had joined, leaving only Ireland, the United Kingdom and Denmark partially outside Schengen.[47]

The EU's institutional framework for 'justice and home affairs' – a portmanteau term for issues ranging from refugee protection to organised crime to citizens' rights – changed enormously, moving from intergovernmental negotiations in the 1980s to the 'third pillar' plus the extra-EU Schengen area after the 1992 Maastricht Treaty. Internal security started to attract the attention of EU policy-makers only in the early 1990s, but this was largely because of concerns about how the emergence of independent CEE states after the fall of the Berlin Wall might cause new threats (see Monar 1999). JHA therefore developed hand-in-hand with East-West integration, but it did not enter the accession conditions as a major priority until the end of the 1990s.

By the mid-1990s, justice and home affairs was governed by a complex policy network among national enforcement agencies. The Schengen agreements on the abolition of internal border controls were incorporated into a new *acquis*, and a new Title IV on migration and asylum was created in the Amsterdam Treaty in 1999 (see Monar 2000; den Boer and Wallace 2000). The Amsterdam Treaty's aim was to create 'An Area of Freedom, Security and Justice', with all matters relating to movement of persons placed in the first pillar.[48] After 1997, border controls, asylum, visas, immigration and cooperation on civil justice were put partly within the remit of Community institutions (such as the European Commission and Court of Justice), leaving the third pillar containing police cooperation and criminal justice. When the Schengen agreements were incorporated into the Treaty on European Union, the *acquis* was 'riddled with soft law, delicate compromises, and reservations by member governments' (den Boer and Wallace 2000).

The Schengen *acquis* is the body of laws emerging from the incorporation of the Schengen Convention into the EU's treaty structure after the 1997 Amsterdam Treaty came into force: it became fully part of the EU *acquis*, but for clarity it is referred to as the 'Schengen *acquis*' in this chapter. The *acquis* contains special arrangements for three EU member-states (Denmark, Ireland and the UK), while Norway and Iceland are associated despite not being members of the Union. However, candidate states were not offered the opportunity to negotiate similarly flexible arrangements.

Despite the rapid growth of the internal security *acquis*, member-states remained divided over how asylum and immigration policies should develop at EU level. Although the EU made some moves towards a common asylum policy following the Tampere European Council, as well as further cooperation on tackling cross-border crime, there remained fundamental disagreements over the degree of legal harmonisation needed on migration policies, burden-sharing in dealing with refugees, and use of EU trade and development policies to reduce immigration pressures (Monar 1999). In defining the JHA *acquis* for the eastern candidates, the main stress was on the formulation of policies to control migration and fight crime in various forms, and on building the institutional capacity the candidates would need to implement external border controls.

7.2   The EU's agenda as presented to the CEE candidates

The process of 'Europeanising' border policies in the candidate countries involved the transfer of EU legislation, institutional models and working practices. The process was complicated by the fact that the various measures related to borders and internal security were scattered across different parts of the EU's agenda for the candidate countries.

The candidates had to take on the whole of the Schengen *acquis* – which meant harmonising with EU law and undertaking a range of measures to build the institutions and policies to implement it. That included the EU's common visa regime and common regulations for procedures at land and coastal borders and airports; extensive police cooperation; and the 'Schengen Information System' (SIS) database, on which details of persons entering the Schengen area can be logged.

Justice and home affairs came onto the agenda relatively late in the accession process, with its first appearance in the Accession Partnerships of Autumn 1998. It was only after the Amsterdam Treaty was ratified and came into force that the EU could start to define the JHA *acquis*. The general conditions set out by the EU included accession of the candidates to the relevant international treaties, observation of the rule of law, stability of administrative and judicial institutions, and data protection. More specific policy requirements were the establishment of equitable asylum procedures and laws, as well as the adoption of restrictive measures to limit immigration and to ensure stringent border controls. The latter included tightening visa regimes and admissions systems (rules on residence and work permits), strengthening enforcement and deportation procedures, introducing penalties for illegal immigration, concluding bilateral readmission agreements with other countries, and improving control and surveillance of borders. The tasks that the Commission set in its policy documents consisted of specific measures with a clear timetable – for example, establishing a record of persons refused entry and setting up new reception centres for asylum seekers – and also general exhortations to 'improve border management'.

There were additional responsibilities for the countries located on the outer rim of the Schengen zone. The countries whose borders formed the external frontier of the Union faced a greater burden in keeping data on who and what was crossing their borders, and on their legal apparatus to deal with asylum claims and refugees. These countries took on major responsibilities, both economic and legal, as they became part of the EU's front line in dealing with transnational population movement.

1997: Agenda 2000. In 1997, there were few specific measures to recommend to the candidates. The Commission's 'Agenda 2000' document simply put forward general policy aims for JHA, stating that 'The expansion of the Union offers ... an opportunity to tackle common transnational problems in the fields of migration and asylum, policy and customs cooperation, and judicial cooperation' (p. 101).

Although the JHA part of Agenda 2000 was included in 'The effects of the Union's policies of enlargement to the candidate countries of Central and Eastern Europe (Impact Study)', the benefits of justice and home affairs were couched entirely in terms of the interests of the current member-states: 'Just as any weaknesses in the defences of the candidate countries in these areas will represent a threat to the existing EU member-states, so also strong justice and home affairs (JHA) performance in candidate countries will contribute positively to security and freedom of citizens in the present EU' (p. 101). The stress was on applying JHA measures 'according to common and high standards throughout the enlarged Union ....', in order to prevent 'spill-over of crime and fraud into the Union' (p. 102).

The Commission was already signalling to the candidates that they would have to take on whatever measures the EU decided were necessary. The comments in Agenda 2000 suggest a much more outcome-led process than the approach to the single market, where the accession *acquis* was more process-oriented. That is unsurprising, because a well-established, tried and tested *acquis* inspires greater confidence that implementation of the rules will in itself create the desired outcomes. The area of internal security was quite different, because member-states were themselves unsure what measures would be needed, and they were still debating how far such policies should be decided at EU rather than national level. The rules to ensure effective regulation of the movement of persons were not firmly established, either in a legal *acquis* or in the discourse among policy-makers. Many EU policy-makers thus had doubts as to whether the tasks set for the applicants from year to year would be sufficient to gain the desired outcome in terms of adequate border controls.

1998: Accession Partnerships. The Accession Partnerships developed in parallel with the justice and home affairs agenda after the Amsterdam European Council. The first Accession Partnerships introduced the main themes for JHA in 1998, and the tasks were given substantive detail in subsequent annual programmes. In 1998, the candidates were told to make progress in areas like border management and control, and to deal with other areas such as migration policy, asylum systems, fighting against organised crime (in particular money laundering, drugs and trafficking in human beings) and corruption, aligning visa policy with the EU, and joining international conventions. The language used in the 1998 Accession Partnerships was fairly general, not specifying *how* they are to be fulfilled but saying that 'steps must be taken', 'attention paid', 'functioning improved' or 'important work remains to be done'. This very general language featured in other areas of the Accession Partnerships too, but in JHA it was particularly vague. This vagueness reflected the EU's uncertainty about the tasks, as the Schengen *acquis* was still being defined for the member-states in preparation for its partial integration into the first pillar in 1999.[49]

After 1999, the tasks were spelled out in more detail, as methods and standards of border control were more clearly defined following the publication of the Schengen *acquis* (its legal base and the body of law comprising it) in July 1999.[50] However, there were still a large number of general exhortations (e.g. to 'improve coordination') rather than specific policies. The implication of the Accession Partnerships was that the CEE countries should aim for institutional isomorphism – that is, becoming like the EU in their approach to the different JHA policies. There was much less stress on the transfer of specific policies than in the case of FMP, largely because the EU did not have such detailed policies and institutions to transfer.

Table 7.1 below sets out the principal measures presented in the Accession Partnerships. The key areas were border controls, migration, asylum, visas, policing, law enforcement and fighting crime in various

Table 7.1 Overview of principal measures for justice and home affairs presented in the Accession Partnerships[51]

Task to be undertaken	Aim of task	Europeanisation mechanisms	Countries covered	Timescale: short term defined as 1 year, medium term as 5 years
Strengthen border controls and coordinate services to prevent illegal immigration and to enable full participation in Schengen Information System, including data and telecommunication infrastructure	Border controls	Institutional capacity and international cooperation	All	Short
Upgrade border posts and 'green border control'	Border controls	Institutional capacity	Hungary, Latvia	Short
National integrated inter-agency border management strategy with particular attention to the budgetary requirements of the Eastern Border	Border controls	Framing integration	Poland	Short and medium
Adopt new law on National Border Control and complete border demarcation with Belarus; start border demarcation with Kaliningrad	Border controls	Framing integration, including for foreign relations	Lithuania	Short
Implement law on the state frontiers including merger of the border guard and border police	Border controls	Legal and institutional reform	Romania	Short
Adopt, implement and enforce new legislative frameworks on migration, alien and asylum procedures	Migration and asylum	Framing integration: policy development	All	Short

Table 7.1 Overview of principal measures for justice and home affairs presented in the Accession Partnerships[51] – *continued*

Task to be undertaken	Aim of task	Europeanisation mechanisms	Countries covered	Timescale: short term defined as 1 year, medium term as 5 years
Align legislation and improve administrative capacity for implementation of the Asylum and Migration *acquis* and international norms	Migration and asylum	Prescriptive integration and institutional capacity	Latvia, Lithuania, Poland	Medium
Upgrade facilities for asylum seekers and refugees, including reception centres	Asylum	Infrastructure building	Bulgaria, Hungary	Medium
Amend asylum legislation and improve procedures for dealing with asylum applications, including staffing	Asylum	Institutional capacity	Hungary, Lithuania, Romania, Slovakia, Slovenia	Short
Progressive alignment of visa legislation and practice with that of the EU	Visas	Prescriptive integration	All	Medium
Strengthen police cooperation mechanisms with EUROPOL	Police	Institutional capacity and international cooperation	All	Medium
Reinforce police and customs authorities and ensure better coordination between law enforcement and judicial bodies at central, regional and local level	Law enforcement	Institutional capacity	All	Short or medium

Table 7.1 Overview of principal measures for justice and home affairs presented in the Accession Partnerships[51] – *continued*

Task to be undertaken	Aim of task	Europeanisation mechanisms	Countries covered	Timescale: short term defined as 1 year, medium term as 5 years
Upgrade and better coordinate law enforcement bodies	Law enforcement	Institution-building	Bulgaria, Czech Republic, Poland	Medium
Speed up reform of penal law	Law enforcement	Institution-building	Estonia	Short
Speed up the demilitarisation of the bodies subordinated to the Ministry of the Interior	Law enforcement	Institutional reform	Romania	Short
Create an advanced integrated criminal investigation data system and improve forensic research capacity	Crime	Institution-building	Estonia, Hungary	Short or medium
Sign and ratify international criminal conventions (OECD Convention on Bribery, European Convention on Money Laundering, European Criminal Law Convention on Corruption, Council of Europe 1990 Convention on Laundering Search, Seizure and Confiscation of the Proceeds of Crime)	Crime	Harmonisation with international norms	All	Short
Implement policies on organised crime, corruption, drug trafficking (legislation, implementing structures, sufficient qualified staff, better cooperation between institutions, training and equipment), including national strategies to combat economic crime	Crime	Framing integration	All	Short or medium

Table 7.1 Overview of principal measures for justice and home affairs presented in the Accession Partnerships[51] – *continued*

Task to be undertaken	Aim of task	Europeanisation mechanisms	Countries covered	Timescale: short term defined as 1 year, medium term as 5 years
Adopt and apply the international instruments related to the fight against drug trafficking (in particular Agreement on Illicit Traffic by Sea, 1988 UN Convention against Illicit Trafficking in Narcotic Drugs and Psychotropic Substances)	Crime	Harmonisation with international norms	Bulgaria, Estonia	Medium
Strengthen capacity to deal with money laundering	Crime	Institutional capacity	All	Short or medium
Continue fight against trafficking in women and children, drug trafficking, organised crime, and corruption	Crime	Exhortation	All	Medium
Implement anti-corruption strategy	Crime	Framing integration	All	Medium
Further intensify international coordination and cooperation in the field of combating trans-border crime, especially in the field of transiting, producing and selling drugs as well as money laundering	Crime	International cooperation	Bulgaria	Medium

forms. Individual countries were given particular tasks that reflected EU concerns about some aspect of their internal security; for example, in 1999 Poland and Lithuania were given tasks for management of external frontiers, while Bulgaria was given priorities on anti-corruption and organised crime, and Romania had to demilitarise its internal security bodies. However, many of the JHA tasks set out in the 1998 and 1999 Accession Partnerships applied to all the candidates, suggesting that the EU did not see their progress as markedly differentiated in the first couple of years.

These general exhortations amounted to a form of 'framing integration', whereby the EU affected domestic policy-making by providing concepts and legitimacy rather than specific policies to be implemented. However, more specific policy preferences later emerged through the reaction of the Commission to each country's annual 'National Programme for Adoption of the *Acquis*', through informal consultations between Brussels and the national capitals, and through the choice of projects for Phare funding.

Framing integration seems to have had a major impact on how borders are controlled in the candidate countries. Many of the tasks in the Accession Partnerships were general exhortations to develop a policy (e.g. on corruption) or develop institutional capacity (e.g. more cooperation or more resources), without any prescription of what in particular these policies should contain or the institutions should do. However, the candidates responded with detailed plans because it was clear that this issue was of high political salience in the EU – an example of anticipatory adjustment.

Aid policy. The bulk of aid provision – as with the demands in the Accession Partnerships – was concerned with reinforcing border controls. The Phare programme in the area of justice and home affairs added incentives to the conditionality constraints that encouraged the candidates to concentrate their energies on reinforcing border controls. The transfer of the EU's redistributive system for asylum claims was accompanied by considerable funds and technology to combat illegal immigration and to deal with refugees. In addition to EU aid, there were large bilateral assistance programmes from Germany to transfer its border regimes to its eastern neighbours.

Until 1997, Phare did not fund justice and home affairs directly. Some of the allocations to sectors such as infrastructure, administration, public institutions and legislation had some effect on JHA, but border controls were not a priority in their own right. But when Phare became accession-driven after 1997, border controls also moved onto the agenda because of the Amsterdam Treaty, and JHA became a major priority for EU aid funding.

Twinning. Justice and home affairs was one of only four sectors identified as priorities for support under twinning (the others are finance, agriculture and environment). JHA twinning projects were focused on customs and border controls, judicial institutions, asylum and immigration, police training and the fight against organised crime.

In the bidding for projects, there was fierce competition between large member-states to get projects in JHA, largely owing to the political salience of border issues. France and Germany were particularly keen competitors for borders projects, and there were also significant British efforts in areas like organised crime. On the CEE side, there were mixed reactions. Some policy-makers reasoned that it was useful to have German and French pre-accession advisors in order to build confidence, but others saw this strategy as risky, particularly if they thought it would be difficult to create a favourable impression for twinning agents to take home to their member-states. Overall, CEE policy-makers preferred consortia of different partners in order to spread the risk and also to avoid the impression that Germany had a dominant influence over their JHA policies.

Twinning followed a significant amount of bilateral aid to certain countries that was aimed at getting their borders controlled more tightly. Germany provided a major aid programme to increase border policing and upgrade border infrastructure, particularly for Poland and the Czech Republic (the two CEE countries on its own border). There was close cooperation between German and Polish border guards, including joint operations and training. German influence considerably speeded up the process of developing mechanisms for migration control, ensuring that would-be migrants heading for Germany were stopped and held in Poland. Asylum-seekers could not be granted asylum in Germany if they had travelled through Poland first, owing to the 1993 bilateral Readmission Agreement,[52] so the whole migration issue once pertaining to Germany was shifted eastward.

JHA also moved to the centre of the other EU aid programmes. It was one of the three sectors eligible for support from the Catch-Up Facility established in 1998.[53] There was also a horizontal programme on JHA in the multi-beneficiary programmes run by the EU to propose potential projects to be financed by Phare. The programme financed missions to evaluate needs and identify JHA projects in CEE, which resulted in priorities to asylum, immigration, border management and control, policing, and the judiciary. The JHA areas funded by the EU were relatively consistent, covering various aspects of regulating movement of people and combating crime in different forms. The EU money and projects encouraged CEE policy-makers to pay greater attention to JHA issues that worried the EU. The EU money and projects also stimulated allocation of matching funds, so significant CEE human and financial resources were devoted to border control and regulating movement of persons.

Europeanisation pressures beyond conditionality: Extra-EU agreements and bilateral pressure

Owing to the legacies of its inter-governmental origins, the EU had a plethora of policy-making bodies with some responsibility for JHA issues. In addition to the *acquis* and continuing inter-governmental cooperation in the 'third pillar', there were also extra-EU fora, resulting in a complex entanglement of inter-governmental, European and international relations (Lavenex 1999). Implementation of the Amsterdam Treaty had led to some rationalisation of policy-making structures, particularly within the Commission, where a new directorate-general was created with responsibility for 'Freedom, Security and Justice'. But running in parallel with accession negotiations were a 'Pre-Accession Pact against organised crime'[54] and CEE judicial cooperation with Europol.[55] The EU applied further pressure on CEE through the inter-governmental Budapest Process (Lavenex and Uçarer 2002).

The Europeanisation pressures on CEE border policies thus went beyond the formal accession criteria. The candidates were also subject to bilateral pressures owing to the expansion of the Schengen zone across the EU to their western borders. For example, when Austria and Italy began applying Schengen to their borders between October 1997 and April 1998, Hungary, Slovakia and Slovenia were immediately affected. The response of the Slovene authorities was to take pre-emptive action: their government adopted Schengen-type identity and customs checks at their Croatian frontier. The aim was to convince the Italian and Austrian authorities that Schengen had been implemented along Slovenia's non-EU borders, thus allowing a more flexible and open approach by the EU countries to their Slovene borders even after Schengen became fully operational on 1 April 1998 (Bort 1999).

In addition, member-states exerted bilateral pressures on the candidates through the growing EU refugee and asylum regime. This regime to harmonise treatment of refugees throughout Western Europe had slowly emerged through a series of inter-governmental conventions and cooperation between national ministries of the interior that was largely hidden from public scrutiny (Lavenex 1998). It included unilateral and bilateral agreements, and also multilateral activities that EU member-states conducted with other European and non-European countries, international organisations and non-governmental organisations. CEE countries were unilaterally incorporated into this regime when the EU extended its redistributive system for handling asylum claims and export of border control technology and practices to strengthen their eastern frontiers. The system rested on a series of readmission agreements that ensured the return of migrants to their country of nationality or their original country of entry, and on the 'safe third country' doctrine (see Lavenex 1998). The CEE candidates had to sign bilateral readmission agreements with EU members and other central and east European countries.[56]

There was also informal pressure from the member-states. Some national experts in the Council urged the candidates to anticipate further development in their preparations, in order to convince member-states that they were able to play a full part in policy-making. Anticipatory adjustment to emerging policies was thus encouraged by the EU, and became part of the informal accession condition for confidence.

Uncertainty I: What exactly was the *acquis frontalier* for accession?

The influence of EU practices above and beyond the formal accession requirements was partly due to the obscure status of these different EU demands. This legal obscurity long clouded the picture of which conditions had to be fulfilled before accession and which could be left until later, a critical question when considering the impact of the conditions on regional relations.

High levels of uncertainty were a result of the obscure status of the different EU demands and the secrecy surrounding much JHA policy-making in the EU (Lavenex 1999; EastWest Institute 1999). This area of EU policies was particularly confusing, even for member-states, partly because it lacked a treaty structure for so long. The justice and home affairs *acquis* developed out of informal contacts and non-public agreements between the police and relevant ministries in the member-states. Networking and the exchange of information, rather than the making of law, were central. It remained unclear which instruments were legally binding and in what context (i.e. international or Community law), an obscurity that long hampered implementation of third-pillar legislation.

Legal complexity caused high levels of uncertainty about the conditionality for the CEE candidates. Until 1999–2000, policy-makers across the CEE region professed confusion and uncertainty about which conditions must be fulfilled before accession and which could be left until later, even after the Schengen *acquis* was published. As a Polish official in charge of organising implementation of the *acquis* told the author in April 2000, 'The Schengen documents are always talking about standards, but there is no description of these standards. It's not clear whether we have to put a border guard every one kilometre or every 500 metres'.

A further uncertainty was the standards of implementation of Schengen border controls. Officially the EU required total compliance with its border policies and strict adherence to the *acquis* prior to accession. However, it was not clear what this meant in practice – which was why confidence was so important, in the absence of clear criteria for measuring standards. Like other forms of policing, border control is not an exact science for its practitioners, but a complex matter of working with local circumstances and coping with changing priorities. That meant that there was considerable room for manoeuvre for practitioners to interpret their mandate in CEE. Moreover, Schengen borders in the EU were already subject to variation in implementation according to circumstances. For example, the border between Belgium and France was still subject to frontier checks because of French fears of drug trafficking through Belgium from the Netherlands. Similarly, the Nordic countries managed to bring their passport union into the Schengen zone, even though Norway and Iceland remained outside the Union. The principle of acknowledging particular difficulties of individual countries was already established, but the EU's position on the CEE candidates was that they had to comply as much as possible before accession. But inevitably, enlargement was bound to bring further diversity to the whole policy area (Monar 2000).

What would count as meeting the conditions for accession – as opposed to the lifting of internal border controls, which was envisaged for a later stage – was also uncertain. If the EU was not going to allow either the lifting of internal border controls or free movement of workers from the candidate countries immediately on accession, what were acceptable levels of external frontier control for the first day of membership? These standards were mainly a matter of confidence rather than technical or legal compliance, and building confidence among the member-states requires different institutional behaviour from compliance with the Commission's technical demands. In interviews, many Hungarian and Polish policy-makers stated that they tried to build confidence through bilateral contacts with key member-states (the ones to whom border controls are most important) and contacts with the Council, whereas in areas like the single market their contacts were primarily with the Commission. Thus the principal agent on the EU side was different in this policy area from that in the single market.

Some policy-makers saw the twinning programmes as a useful means of reassuring member-states that their borders would be secure. If twinning agents reported back directly to their home ministries about conditions in CEE, their reports would have credibility: 'Twinning builds confidence better than Amnesty reports and Commission delegations because twins get direct contact and report back to the member-states,' said a senior British policy-maker in 2001. This could be a risky strategy, however: if twinning agents were horrified by conditions and sent back negative reports, more harm could be done than good, as many candidate country officials quickly acknowledged. Partly this was a question of the familiarity of working methods, and the reaction of individual twinning agents was not necessarily predictable. A senior Commission official in DG JHA commented in 2000: 'Although the Estonian border police are good, the ordinary police have no idea about organised crime and their methods would seem horrific to the British bobby because they are still Soviet methods. Remember that twins can give bad reports too'.

However, where CEE interior ministries were relatively confident in their preparations, they tried to get twinning agents from the critical member-states that were potential veto-players. In 1999, several key Polish policy-makers favoured consortia for JHA projects that included a German partner for this reason, according to interior ministry officials.

Uncertainty II: When would the candidates get the benefits of Schengen?

Within the EU, Schengen offered a bargain, whereby members gained hard non-EU external borders in return for soft internal ones that allowed free movement across the whole zone. This created a larger zone of free movement, but one with sharper edges that were harder to penetrate from the outside. Once inside the Schengen area, people could move without frontier checks,[57] so entry to the area was strictly controlled. In theory, then, borders with Schengen countries should have become softer and more porous, as CEE countries prepared themselves to join the common frontier zone, but only if they applied harder controls on their borders with non-EU members. The candidates initially expected the same Schengen bargain: freer movement for their citizens westwards at the price of not allowing free movement for people from their non-EU neighbours. However, it soon became clear during the negotiations that this bargain would not apply to the candidates.

Implementation of the Schengen *acquis* occurred in two stages for the current member-states: national authorities began implementing the Schengen agreements (and later the *acquis*), but border controls were not necessarily removed until years later – for example, Austria, Italy and Greece were allowed to lift controls only after the other members owing to concerns about how well their external borders were policed.[58] The criterion for lifting frontier controls was confidence: the other Schengen members had to have confidence in the ability of their neighbours to control external frontiers effectively.

In the 1990s, there were different views in Brussels and across the member-states as to whether accession to Schengen had to be simultaneous with accession to the EU. In areas such as visa policy, the timing of the application of EU policies was vital to whether enlargement created new dividing-lines across post-communist Europe. This uncertainty made JHA issues more difficult to handle in CEE domestic politics, because national politicians could not present matching benefits to justify the measures implemented at the EU's behest.

This uncertainty was resolved only shortly before accession, when the EU put forward its negotiating position. Customs controls on the movement of goods within the enlarged EU were largely removed on 1 May 2004, but those on people were not. The terrorist attacks in Madrid in March 2004, just before the enlargement, made member-states even less willing to relax border checks anywhere in Europe.

Even absenting the politics, the new members could not become full members of Schengen for a minimum of two years after accession for technical reasons. The EU did not plan to upgrade and extend its database for recording travellers, called the Schengen Information System (SIS II), for 25 member-states until at least 2006, and the project was expected to overrun this timetable. But the candidates knew they would not get the benefits of Schengen until many years after they had borne the costs.

7.3   The candidates' responses

The EU had a major impact on border regimes in CEE partly because of the limited development of migration policies prior to 1989. Warsaw

Pact countries did not have immigration policies as such, because there was little pressure from third-country nationals trying to enter in significant numbers. Instead, the focus was on preventing or regulating emigration by their inhabitants. Wholesale transfer of EU border policies thus filled institutional lacunae that had been left by the legacy of communism. Border guards had to adapt to the new priority of keeping foreigners out rather than keeping their countrymen in.

Political context

In the candidate countries, there was a very widespread and intense debate about EU border policies owing to perceptions of discrimination against CEE citizens, and also the impact of tighter regulation of movement of people on relations with neighbouring countries. In most CEE countries there were concerns that erecting Schengen borders would upset delicate relationships with their neighbours – such as Ukraine, Kaliningrad (part of Russia) and Croatia – and stall cross-border economic integration. Adopting the Schengen zone's common visa regime meant having to introduce visas for the nationals of neighbouring countries, with major implications for bilateral and regional relations. CEE political leaders repeatedly expressed their concern that such measures should not introduce new barriers between their populations, often arguing 'We must not put up a new Iron Curtain'. Each country tried to navigate between EU pressures and other policy concerns, both domestic and external.

EU-driven changes to the status and porosity of the countries' non-EU borders re-invigorated unresolved bilateral issues over the borders lying between the candidates (for example, the Czech Republic and Slovakia; Hungary and Romania); between candidates and member-states (Germany and the Czech Republic; Austria and Slovenia); and between candidates and non-candidates (Poland and Ukraine; Romania and Moldova) (see Batt 2001). However, joint approaches to dealing with the regional dilemmas posed by accession were rare. The question of visa regimes was frequently discussed in CEE parliamentary debates and the media, but multilateral cooperation between the candidates was largely informal. For example, both Hungarian and Polish leaders made rhetorical commitments not to introduce visa requirements for Ukrainians before joining the EU, but multilateral cooperation was very limited. The Czech Republic, Hungary, Poland and Slovakia started discussing it under the Visegrád Cooperation, but most negotiation on the issue was bilateral between each country and the EU. A regional initiative was launched at a 1999 summit between the

Visegrád leaders to discuss the impact of Schengen borders; their common concern was relations with Ukraine, and the need to maintain good relations with Kiev while tackling organised crime along the Ukrainian border.[59] However, these discussions did not result in a united position *vis-à-vis* EU demands.

The policies that the EU sought to transfer on borders and visas were the most controversial because they affected political relations and economic integration with neighbouring states. Other aspects of JHA such as fighting crime and improving law enforcement required investment on the CEE side, but they did not have the same scope for disrupting foreign relations. Generally, migration and asylum policies were not resisted by policy-makers, especially when the CEE countries experienced a dramatic rise in applications from asylum-seekers just before accession. In 2003, asylum claims in Slovenia more than doubled, while those in Poland increased by a third, according to the UN High Commissioner for Refugees.[60] Because of these growing challenges, the policy-makers in the new member-states wanted to be part of new asylum and migration initiatives, rather than trying to stay outside them as some of the old members did (see Grabbe 2004a).

However, visa policies were generally unpopular in the region. To the population over the age of 30, restrictions on travel were reminiscent of the Cold War restrictions on personal liberty. Two of the countries considered here – Hungary and Poland – followed a policy of resisting the EU's demands for visa restrictions, and imposing such restrictions on immediate neighbours only shortly before accession. However, other candidates implemented visa requirements for Russia and Ukraine much earlier. The Czech Republic and Slovakia started requiring visas from Russians and Ukrainians from Autumn 2000, even though Slovakia shares a border with Ukraine. Both countries immediately had to upgrade their consulates and increase the number of staff dealing with visa applications.

Adaptation strategies, interests and goodness of fit

None of the candidates was well-adapted to the EU model of regulating movement of persons when adjustment to the EU began. Movement of persons and goods across the Warsaw Pact countries had been tightly controlled before 1989, but the methods used were incompatible with EU procedures. Moreover, a number of visa-free agreements had been concluded between the Warsaw Pact states (Laczko *et al.* 1999). The whole system of regulating movement of persons and goods had to be adapted to EU norms, which included more complex procedures for admission of persons. Customs procedures – for regulating the movement of goods – were important too, because the pre-1989 methods used to search vehicles crossing borders had relied on a heavy-handed approach that discouraged trade and was very prone to corruption.

Bulgaria, Hungary and Poland responded similarly to the Schengen *acquis* requirements at first. All three quickly began to tighten up their border controls, and made rapid progress in the development of infrastructure and procedures, assisted and stimulated by EU and bilateral aid and technical assistance. The EU's rapid expansion of its internal JHA activities in the late 1990s helped to stimulate corresponding activity on CEE borders. The candidates were invited to join new EU initiatives and policies on organised crime, drugs and human trafficking, and illegal migration. They were offered training, aid, political contacts and a role in EU fora on JHA issues.

In the short term, the EU-imposed policies increased confusion on the border and produced long queues at crossing-points and in consulates which could not cope with the increased demand for visas. However, in the longer term, there would be benefits for CEE citizens because the rules about border crossing and visa requirements would become clearer. These rules would be applied more consistently as national legislation was harmonised with EU norms, border guards were trained in new methods, and more border crossing-points were opened with EU assistance.

In all three countries, different policy communities rapidly developed which held different views on the EU's demands. The officials directly responsible for border controls – either in the interior ministries or in law enforcement bodies – were largely in favour of the EU's agenda and keen to use EU help to enforce stricter controls on movement of persons. They frequently quoted EU policy paradigms about border control and policies for migration and tackling cross-border crime. However, their counterparts in the foreign ministries and prime ministers' offices were more concerned about the misfit of EU approaches to border management with their countries' foreign policies. The Hungarian and Polish foreign ministry officials pursued a strategy of not resisting EU pressures to implement the *acquis*, but of developing other policies in parallel to try to soften their impact. Hungary put forward a 'status law' for external minorities, and Poland developed a reinforced eastern policy based on engagement and political dialogue with neighbours, especially Ukraine. Bulgaria tried to meet the EU's demands, but it was hampered by weaknesses in the public administration, especially the judiciary and border guard.

Differences emerged in visa policies, the one part of the *acquis* where the candidates used timing to mitigate EU pressures. All three countries stalled on setting dates for ending visa-free regimes with neighbouring countries, and tried to find ways around the visa requirements such as seeking bilateral readmission treaties with neighbouring countries. Bulgaria and Hungary gave in to EU demands earlier than Poland. Bulgaria used timing the least, primarily because the government was also trying to persuade the EU to lift the visa requirement on its own citizens, as well as gaining accession to the EU. However, all three countries tried to implement the rest of the Schengen *acquis* vigorously, because they knew it was a potential veto-point for accession.

Hungary

Hungarian interests and Schengen. The main concern for the central government in Budapest was the impact of EU visa policies on the access of the three million or so ethnic Hungarians living in surrounding countries. Ethnic Hungarians who were citizens of Romania, Slovakia, Ukraine or one of the former Yugoslav countries were able to travel to and work in Hungary without visas until 2003. Ensuring the welfare of these communities was a main tenet of Hungarian foreign policy – especially under the FIDESZ government from 1998 to 2002 – and it was a central issue in Hungary's bilateral relations with its neighbours. Moreover, much cross-border trade and investment depended on family and cultural ties with diaspora communities, and 'pendulum migration' (short trips back and forth) into Hungary provided jobs that supported many families in poorer neighbouring countries. In addition to the issue of borders, EU-inspired tightening of frontier controls had an impact on cross-border trade and investment. For example, after 1 September 1999, all people crossing borders in either direction (whether Hungarian or foreign) had to be registered, and the new procedures initially caused significant queues at Hungary's border posts.[61]

Romania was home to the largest external minority (more than 1.6 million ethnic Hungarians), and the main solution sought by Budapest was for the EU to abolish visas for Romanians before Hungary joined the EU. This strategy succeeded when the EU lifted visa requirements for Romanians in January 2002. However, visa requirements for Hungary's non-candidate neighbours Ukraine and Yugoslavia (later Serbia and Montenegro) remained in place after the 2004 enlargement.

Imposing a visa regime affected EU-sponsored regional cooperation initiatives as well, highlighting the contradiction between the EU's own policy goal of regional integration and its Schengen policies.

The Carpathian Euro-region (which covers the borders of Hungary, Moldova, Romania, Slovakia and Ukraine) was an example of successful regional cooperation in an area of considerable ethnic diversity and potential tension. It was given substantial financial support and political encouragement by the EU. Nationals of the Euro-region's member countries were initially able to travel within it without passports, but this regime ended when the CEE candidates had to introduce Schengen controls on their borders.

Adaptation strategy. The Hungarian government committed itself to adopting the EU's visa policy and to introducing a Schengen-compatible system of controls at its borders in Autumn 1999.[62] The government long avoided setting a date for imposition of visa requirements on immediate neighbours, stating that visas would start only on the day of accession for Ukraine, Romania and Serbia. However, Hungary required visas of Russians, Belarusians and other CIS citizens from 3 June 2001.[63] Such controls were unlikely because the EU itself had bilateral visa-free travel regimes with these countries, but Hungary had to seek clarification of whether it had to erect fences along its green borders with fellow-candidates Slovakia and Slovenia. Hungarian Chief Negotiator Endre Juhasz asked repeatedly in meetings with Commission and Council officials where the external borders of the Union would lie after enlargement, but there was no answer forthcoming. As a senior Commission official in DG Enlargement commented in 2001, 'It's become known as "the Juhasz question". He kept saying "You tell us what the EU's external borders will be, and we will implement the Schengen *acquis* on those borders". But we can't give a firm answer yet.'

In parallel with the accession strategy, Hungary sought a new national policy to cushion the blow for external minorities. A number of proposals were put forward to deal with the problem of allowing ethnic Hungarians access to Hungary. One was a 'national visa' permitting a stay of over 90 days for citizens of neighbouring countries, but in Hungary alone;[64] however, this would have presupposed a system of checks on Hungary's Austrian border into the long-term, which would have been incompatible with full Schengen membership. Another much-discussed possibility was long-term visas, for 10 years or so, to be given to ethnic Hungarians. The Independent Smallholders' Party – the then government's junior coalition partner – called for ethnic Hungarians to be given dual citizenship, but its larger partner, the FIDESZ-MPP party, rejected that option.[65] The government was concerned that offering statutory dual citizenship to millions of ethnic

Hungarians would cause both legal and political complications – establishing criteria for determining who is an ethnic Hungarian is legally difficult, for example. Morover, they were worried that such favourable treatment would also result in resentment against ethnic Hungarians in Romania.[66]

In the end, the government introduced a new 'status law' in 2001. The aim of the law was to give ethnic Hungarians access to education, medical and other benefits without encouraging them to move from their current residence to Hungary (Fowler 2001). This bill was passed by the Hungarian parliament in Autumn 2001, but it could remain in force only until accession to the EU, because it was incompatible with the EU's anti-discrimination legislation. However, Hungary's predicament was eased at the same time, because in December 2001 the Council of Ministers removed the visa requirement for Romanian citizens to enter Schengen. Because visas were no longer necessary for the Schengen area, Hungary did not have to impose them on the large ethnic Hungarian population in Transylvania, although it did have to do so for those in then-Yugoslavia and Ukraine.

Poland

Polish interests and Schengen. Erecting an external Schengen border presented a major conflict with Poland's eastern policies. Polish leaders consistently presented their country as a bridge to Ukraine, Belarus and Russia after 1989, and Warsaw pursued very active bilateral political engagement with these countries. Policy statements by President Aleksander Kwaúniewski, foreign ministers Bronisław Geremek and Władysław Bartoszewski, and the various ministers for European integration, stressed stabilisation of the states emerging from the former Soviet Union as a key foreign policy goal. In particular, Poland strongly advocated extending links between the EU and Ukraine.[67] Polish policymakers and academics presented integration with these markets and constructive engagement with their political leaders as major contributions to European security, providing both NATO and the EU with a stable link in a troubled region. Poland also provided markets for CIS goods and jobs for migrant workers. Hard estimates of economic dependence were difficult to provide, but many Ukrainian families depended on the earnings of family members working in Poland as their main source of income. For example, the Polish foreign ministry estimated that the EU-driven measures introduced in late 1997 on the border with Ukraine had a dramatic effect on the regional economies on both sides of the border, causing a fall of about 30% in trade.

Concern about the impact of EU border policies was widespread in the Polish political elite. Poland has borders with three countries that were not part of the enlargement process: Belarus, Ukraine and Kaliningrad (part of Russia). The implementation of Schengen-compatible controls along these frontiers was a mammoth task. Much of this long border is 'green', running through open country and mountains; it was evidently going to be difficult and costly to patrol the green borders with Belarus (407 kilometres) and Ukraine (526 km). The question of how to manage Russian military transit to Kaliningrad became an issue for the EU once Lithuania started negotiations as well as Poland, because Kaliningrad was then encircled by future EU members.

Poland had to maintain a very delicate balance between its EU obligations and its relations with its neighbours (Bachmann 1999). There was an active domestic debate about whether Poland had to choose between EU links or eastern links; or whether it would serve both Polish and Ukrainian interests better for Poland to join the EU quickly and to try to change EU eastern policy from the inside (*Unia & Polska*, April and May 2000).

Adaptation strategy. Foreign policy concerns did not stop the Polish authorities from adopting a large number of measures to control cross-border movements, some of which caused tensions with neighbouring countries. Poland came under pressure to tighten its eastern borders from late 1997, when Schengen was being brought into force prior to its full operation from 1 April 1998. New laws on the movement of aliens were introduced in 1998, causing major protests from Russia and the withdrawal of the Belarusian ambassador from Warsaw in 1999. With the help of EU aid through Phare, new border crossings were built along the eastern frontier, the number of border guards was increased, and new equipment to read passports electronically was installed at border checkpoints.

Visa policy was the most difficult area because of clear national interests in maintaining movement of persons across the eastern borders of Poland. President Aleksander Kwaúniewski made promises on several occasions that Poland would not introduce visas for Ukrainians prior to its accession to the EU, and Bronisław Geremek made a similar commitment when he was foreign minister in 1999. However, this stance was not sustainable in the face of pressure from Germany and other member-states. The EU's 1999 Regular Report on Poland was highly critical of Polish visa policy and demanded that a date be set for introducing visas on all of its non-EU frontiers. The government was forced to set some general target-dates in 2000. The 2000 National

Programme of Preparation for Membership committed Poland to the termination of non-visa travel with the remaining CIS countries and Cuba in 2000, with Belarus, Macedonia and Russia in 2001, and with Bulgaria, Romania and Ukraine in 2002. However, precise dates were not set until 2002, following a change of government. The government announced on 12 February 2002 that Poland would introduce visas for the citizens of Russia, Ukraine and Belarus as of 1 July 2003.[68] At the same time, the foreign ministry encouraged people in neighbouring countries to apply quickly for multi-entry visas. Polish Foreign Minister Włodzimierz Cimoszewicz started an information campaign to persuade people to apply, both to soften the impact of the visa requirement on neighbours, but also because of the challenge the new policy posed to Poland's administrative capacity. Cimoszewicz remarked that 'Last year, 29 million people crossed the Polish border and it would be nearly impossible for Polish consulates to issue such a number of visas. We want a multi-entry visa valid for a few years to be the most popular one'.[69]

Multiple routes of Europeanisation. Visa policy is an example of prescriptive integration, where the EU set out detailed policies and methods of implementation for the candidates. Moreover, the EU clearly used its bargaining power to strong-arm reluctant candidates – particularly Poland and Hungary – into applying its visa policies despite the harm to their relations with neighbouring countries. However, the Europeanisation of Polish border policies also included 'anticipatory adjustment', whereby the Polish authorities undertook measures to comply in advance of specific EU requests to do so. This adjustment occurred under conditions of strong normative pressures from EU institutions and particularly the member-states (Germany above all); nevertheless, Poland's policy-makers undertook much of the work on tightening border controls in the absence of a clear and specific EU request for a particular policy solution. For example, the Accession Partnership priorities set out in Table 7.1 above referred to border policy measures, and there was a specific one for Poland on its eastern borders. Nevertheless, the demands were so general as to constitute a form of framing integration, whereby the EU called attention to an issue and applied political pressure, but it did not prescribe specific institutional solutions to the problems identified. In Kingdon's agenda-setting terminology, the EU influenced the 'decision agenda' rather than the 'policy agenda' (Kingdon 1997).

The EU influenced policy content through the informal contacts between Warsaw and the EU institutions and member-state governments (particularly bilateral aid from Germany), rather than directly through the accession conditions. Poland's 'National Programme for Adoption of the *Acquis*' (first published in 1999 and updated annually thereafter) and the more detailed 'National Programme for Border Management' (first published in 2000) included all of these elements: prescriptive policies from the Schengen *acquis*, additional measures set in the Accession Partnerships, measures suggested by DG JHA and individual member-states, and also national measures that anticipated EU requirements.

The view of officials involved in the preparations for Schengen (interviewed in the foreign and interior ministries) was that the most prevalent policy model was German, owing to Germany's provision of aid, technical assistance and training in Polish border management, and the absence of clear EU standards. This German influence had wide implications for other policies related to the movement of persons, such as asylum, residence permits and overall migration policy. Germany had a strong incentive to help Poland to prevent people crossing its territory illegally, as Poland then became an immigration buffer-zone for its EU neighbours. Poland became a country of settlement rather than a country of transit for migrants from the former Soviet Union and from Asia.

Bulgaria

Bulgarian interests and Schengen. Although it was evidently further away from accession than Hungary or Poland, Bulgaria also introduced measures to tighten border controls and impose visa regimes on third countries. The Bulgarian authorities' motivations for adjusting to EU norms so early were rooted in their desire to leave the EU's 'black-list'[70] of countries whose nationals needed a visa to enter the EU. The EU's invitation to Romania and Bulgaria to start negotiations in December 1999 raised hopes that the visa black-list might be revised, and increased the incentive for Bulgaria to prove that it could control the movement of persons over its own frontiers to the EU's satisfaction. Its efforts were rewarded when the European Commission recommended to the Council of Ministers on 26 January 2000 that visa restrictions on Bulgaria and Romania be removed. The member-states accepted that recommendation at the end of 2000 for Bulgaria and lifted the restrictions on 1 January 2001; Romania had to wait until a year later.

Adaptation strategy. Bulgaria introduced visa requirements for Ukraine faster than Hungary or Poland did. By the end of December 2000, Bulgaria had harmonised its visa list with that of the EU apart from five countries, with which it maintained a visa-free regime: Macedonia, Romania, Russia, Ukraine and Yugoslavia. In order to prevent the reversal of the EU's decision to lift the visa restriction, Bulgaria then committed itself to introducing visas for Russians and Ukrainians. The Bulgarian government had tried to avoid visa requirements for Russians by sending a draft readmission agreement to the Russian government in April 1999. However, Russia had no readmission agreement with any country, and Bulgaria was unable to circumvent the problem (Jileva 2002). Bulgaria then introduced visas for Russians and Ukrainians in October 2001 – after Hungary had done so for Russians in June 2001, but several years before either Hungary or Poland applied the requirements to Ukraine. The economic impact was significant for Bulgaria's tourism sector, because it increased the price of tourist services by 25% and because Bulgaria had only two consular offices in the Russian Federation, so the logistical obstacles to the organisation of tourist parties increased considerably (Jileva 2002).

Bulgaria's approach to implementation of the JHA *acquis* as a whole was to be 'more Catholic than the Pope'.[71] The Bulgarian authorities sought to show the EU that they could be rigorous in implementation, in order to build confidence in the member-states that Bulgaria was not a security risk to the EU following the years of widespread corruption and organised crime in the 1990s. Bulgaria therefore needed to do more than Hungary and Poland to convince EU actors that it could be trusted to implement the *acquis*.

It was very difficult to build confidence, however, given the state of the institutions that were needed to implement it. As a Bulgarian MP put it in 2001, 'The clear difference between Bulgaria and the other candidates is the judiciary. It is weak, under-funded and not trained in the EU's ways'.[72] However, the EU was a strong motivation for the government to invest in improving the functioning of the judiciary when it might not otherwise have done so. For example, the Centre for the Study of Democracy – an independent think-tank in Sofia – was approached by the government to work on how to reform the judiciary in 2000. The Centre was told by the foreign ministry and parliament that the project had to be called an 'EU accession programme' in order to gain domestic support. According to the project-manager at the Centre, Boyko Todorov, 'They had to sell the programme in the name of the EU because otherwise it would be too painful and difficult'. The process of Europeanisation thus became bound up with the domestic politics of institutional reform.

7.4   Negotiations

In contrast to the first case-study, negotiations on this chapter were not complicated, because the EU had narrowed down the room for bargaining well before the chapter was opened with the candidates. The main issue was the credibility of the candidates' commitments to implement the *acquis* on JHA in the eyes of the member-states.

The political context in the member-states

JHA in general and border policies in particular were matters of high political salience for the current member-states. The dismantling of frontiers to the East after 1989 was often cited in West European political debates as a key reason for the proliferation of transnational crime, because greater liberty to travel coincided with a breakdown in law and order in some East European countries. Frontier-crossing offered numerous possibilities for hard-pressed populations to earn money through both legal and illegal means. The two main concerns within the EU were migration and cross-border crime, the latter covering a vast range of problems including smuggling, trafficking in human beings, drug-running and terrorism. These issues were often talked about in the same breath in public discourse, although they were not necessarily causally linked.

The state of a candidate's external frontier controls was widely regarded by both EU and CEE policy-makers as a potential veto-point for accession. It was entirely plausible that any one of several member-states would block the accession of a CEE candidate if it were unable to regulate the movement of people across its territory to the EU's satisfaction. Threat perceptions in Western Europe had been affected by exaggerated claims about the risks of migration from CEE, both the issue of free movement of workers and also of illegal migration and rising numbers of asylum claims. Populist politicians in the regions along the EU's eastern frontier were quick to exploit public fears about migration, in turn driving their countries' positions in EU debates towards restricting movement from CEE.

The introduction of the Schengen *acquis* coincided with a worsening of bilateral relations between Germany and Austria and their eastern neighbours in 1999–2002. There was pressure in Bavaria from the Sudeten German lobby to re-open with the Czech Republic the settlements reached at the end of World War II on border changes and settlement rights, and to set additional pre-conditions before the Czech Republic could join the EU (Bazin 1999). There were also calls to restrict the number of ethnic Germans who could exercise their right to come to Germany (Rupnik and Bazin 2001). Furthermore, there was already sensitivity in Germany about what was seen as an unfair share of the refugee burden from south-eastern Europe resulting from the Yugoslav wars of the 1990s. Attitudes towards refugees affected German views on overall levels of migration, although in fact in 1997 (before the Kosovo crisis) more foreigners left Germany than entered it (Bort 2000). In Austria there was considerable public support for Jörg Haider's anti-enlargement stance, as the 1999 election campaign demonstrated. The strong reaction from other EU governments against the entry of Haider's *Freiheitliche Partei Österreichs* into the coalition government in 1999 made it harder for Austria to stall the enlargement process at EU level because other member-states already suspected the government of opposing enlargement. On the other hand, the politics of fear that drove so many Austrians to vote for the FPÖ remained a potent force, pushing governments towards increasingly restrictive border policies in relation to CEE.

One indication of the political sensitivity of this area was the fact that the member-states ensured that they controlled transposition of Schengen border policies to CEE, rather than the Commission. The Council took the lead on the internal security agenda for CEE from 1998, when the Council of Ministers set up a working group in May 1998 to establish the accession *acquis* in the area of justice and home affairs,[73] keeping it out of the Commission's hands. Partly this move was because the Commission had only a small and recently established directorate-general for JHA. But it also illustrated the importance the member-states attached to their deciding the contents of the *acquis* and when the standards in JHA for accession had been met by the candidates. Although the Commission reported on progress in JHA in the Regular Reports, it was Council delegations which inspected CEE borders and advised the Council of Ministers on progress.

The EU's negotiating position

The negotiating chapter on justice and home affairs was widely predicted by EU policy-makers (in interviews) to be one of the most difficult, owing to its political salience in several member-states and the uncertainties in the EU's *acquis*. However, when the negotiations opened in 2000 they proved not to be as difficult as expected, largely because the EU decided that internal frontier controls between new and old member-states would not be lifted immediately after enlargement. The EU's long internal debate about whether the candidates would join Schengen when they joined the EU had been resolved in favour of a multi-stage accession to Schengen. Once the Commission had formulated its negotiating position on this basis, the negotiations became just a matter of planning how the candidates would upgrade their border infrastructure and implement the Schengen controls. Although the candidates had to promise to implement the controls over a specified timetable, the EU did not commit itself to any reciprocal timetable for lifting internal border controls. That stage was subject to a separate decision by the Council of Ministers to be taken some time after accession.

Neither the EU nor any of the candidates requested a transition period on chapter 24 (JHA). Instead, the negotiations centred on the credibility of the candidates' promises to implement the *acquis* effectively. As the Commission stated on its web-page about the JHA chapter: 'Negotiations on the Justice and Home Affairs *acquis* are not about transition periods ... Rather, it has been necessary to find ways to build confidence, among member states, in the candidate countries' capacity to implement the *acquis*'.[74] The negotiations on this chapter thus had a very different quality from those on FMP: instead of being a confrontation between the candidates and the EU, there was more of an air of collusion between the Commission and applicant country negotiators in finding ways to convince the member-states that the chapter could be provisionally closed.

CEE negotiating positions

The main contentious issue for the candidates was the expense of implementing the *acquis*, particularly with regard to border infrastructure, and the imposition of visas on neighbouring countries. All three countries hoped for additional aid from the EU, as well as bilateral help from neighbouring EU member-states. However, they reacted differently to the question of visa requirements. Hungary acquiesced to EU demands for visas for Russians long before Poland did, and several months before Bulgaria. Bulgaria gave in on Ukraine several years before Hungary or Poland, mainly to rid itself of the EU's visa requirement for its own citizens.

The EU provisionally closed the JHA chapter with Hungary first (as with most other chapters), in November 2001. The Commission reported that Hungary had already transposed most of the *acquis* on JHA, and had put in place the necessary administrative structures. The Hungarian JHA experts regarded the fast and relatively easy closure of this chapter as the result of their long preparations. These included a number of long-term plans submitted to the EU for approval, covering issues like border controls and development of border-crossing points. Hungary also impressed the EU with its rapid response to the terrorist attacks of 11 September 2001 in the United States. The Hungarian authorities rapidly implemented additional internal security measures and offered both the EU and the US access to data in pursuing terrorist suspects. These gave evidence of effective implementation to present to the member-states.

Poland opened the JHA chapter at the same time as Hungary, in May 2001, but was unable to close the chapter until after the Polish general elections in September 2001 had brought in a new government. The chapter was provisionally closed in July 2002, eight months after Hungary closed it. During the negotiations, the EU's view was that 'It will take considerable efforts to complete the transition [to the *acquis*] by the end of 2002. Particular attention should be paid to the establishment of the necessary administrative structures'.[75] The main problems were the visa regime and implementation. The Polish government decided in February 2002 to set a date for introducing visas for neighbouring countries.

Bulgaria had more serious problems with implementation, and also with the preceding stage of transposing legislation and institutional arrangements. The JHA negotiating chapter was opened in June 2001, but by January 2002, the Commission considered that 'Bulgaria has started to transpose the EU *acquis* on Justice and Home Affairs. However, transposition is only at the very beginning, and will take considerable additional effort to complete'.[76] Administrative capacity was the main issue. The Bulgarian government exhibited strong political will to do whatever was necessary to conclude negotiations, but its plans for implementation were simply not credible to the EU. The chapter was provisionally closed with Bulgaria in October 2003 (all the chapters were formally closed with Bulgaria in December 2004, two years after Hungary and Poland).

7.5   Explaining outcomes

The outcome for the candidates: the dynamics of Europeanisation

The candidate countries had no choice but to take on EU border policies if their citizens were to gain the full benefits of free movement in the EU in the long run. As with the case of FMP under the single market, the political sensitivity of the issue on the EU side was so high that the candidates had to accept EU demands even if they ran contrary to other policy goals, however important.

However, the countries responded differently in terms of timing and the success of their adaptation strategies. None could avoid imposing visas on its neighbours or allocating resources to strengthening border controls. However, each country used its relative negotiating power to the maximum in order to impose visa requirements as late as possible, to soften the impact on bilateral relations, trade and tourism. The most sensitive area was visas for Ukrainians, because Ukraine is an immediate neighbour of Hungary and Poland, and an important source of tourism for Bulgaria. Bulgaria was forced to concede most rapidly on Ukraine, because of the double incentive of making progress in negotiations and having its own visa regime with the EU removed. Russia was a more difficult issue for Bulgaria than for Hungary, because Bulgaria had more trade with and tourism from Russia. However, Bulgaria's relatively weak bargaining power – owing to the visa regime as well as its laggard status in negotiations – caused it to impose visas for Russians shortly after Hungary introduced them. Poland moved to introduce visas for Russians and Ukrainians later, and managed to avoid them until 2003, the year before accession.

In the case-study on FMP, the outcome we were trying to explain was why the candidates accepted the EU's negotiating position, and why they continued to implement the *acquis* nonetheless. In this case, we are again trying to explain why the candidates accepted EU demands, how the strategies of the three countries differed, and why they implemented the EU's border policies. But the factors explaining the outcome are not precisely the same. In both cases, the power of the EU's accession conditionality provides part of the explanation, and certainly provides a convincing reason why the three countries accepted EU visa policies. However, all three also implemented many other EU-inspired policies on their external borders because of anticipatory adjustment to expected EU demands. Europeanisation processes thus provide an important further dimension to the explanation.

Europeanisation in this policy area happened through the pressures exerted by the negotiating process, but CEE policy-makers started aligning their policies with EU norms before the relevant chapter was opened, and they continued afterwards. In interviews conducted at the time of the negotiations, policy-makers indicated that the greatest influence was above and beyond the formal accession requirements because of the incentive to demonstrate to the EU-15 that they were both willing and able to implement current and future border policies.

Uncertainty. In the case of border policies, uncertainty was a very important intervening variable that was lacking in the case of FMP. JHA was one of the few areas that could have stopped accession.

However, the EU's delay in producing its detailed demands wasted time and resources in CEE, and blunted the EU's impact. CEE policy-makers wanted to comply with most of the JHA *acquis* (with the exceptions discussed above), but for several years they did not know what exactly they had to comply with because the EU had no detailed information on the standards to be achieved prior to accession. Once the EU presented the various micro-policies that were included in JHA, particularly visas and border controls, it had a strong influence on practices, procedures and norms in CEE. However, the EU's impact was also weakened by its lack of a clear distinction between what were pre-requisites for accession and what were pre-requisites for removal of internal border controls in the enlarged Schengen area.

Given that the JHA *acquis* involves a confusing mixture of tasks, could the uncertainty be used by CEE policy-makers to mitigate the impact of the EU's demands? For several years they could satisfy the EU by making good progress overall. However, the candidates could not use the uncertainty connected with timing to avoid giving commitments on difficult tasks to which the EU gave priority. They had to show their willingness and ability to apply EU border control policies because there were doubts on the EU side. For example, when the Commission presented its Regular Reports in November 2001, French Foreign Minister Hubert Védrine commented that no candidate's judiciary could be trusted to enforce the *acquis*. He implied that none of them was ready for EU membership in 2004. Perversely, uncertainty made EU influence stronger in this area. Because the *acquis* was developing rapidly and was therefore uncertain, candidates had to strive to show they could keep up. The uncertainty thus gave the EU more leverage over the candidates rather than less.

Institutional capacity in CEE was an important variable in this case-study because the policy area worked partly through prescriptive integration, providing models for the candidates. For example, the candidates had to show that they could cope with implementing the Schengen Information System (SIS), setting up migrant reception centres, establishing an asylum claims processing system, customs posts, and so on. But the EU's use of prescriptive integration as a Europeanisation mechanism was limited by the obscurity and secrecy surrounding the model. For example, candidates had to set up a parallel system for SIS before they could join it, but they were not given access to the regulation explaining how SIS worked for a long time after that demand was made.

Political context mattered because the degree of politicisation on both sides was high. The candidates had to seek institutional solutions that were acceptable to the EU, but without a clear model to follow. In the EU, we would expect this to give national governments more room for manoeuvre (according to Knill and Lehmkuhl 1999). However, the political sensitivity of this issue on the EU side made JHA a potential veto-point in the accession process. It raised the stakes too high for CEE to play implementation games that might threaten their credibility with potential veto-players on the EU side. CEE policy-makers were not told which EU borders model to follow, but Poland and Hungary knew that the most useful ones to adopt were those of their immediate neighbours, because those countries were the most likely to block their closure of the JHA chapter.

At the same time, domestic sensitivity in CEE meant that Poland and the Czech Republic were keen to avoid their policies being interpreted in the national media as being modelled too closely on Germany. For example, CEE policy-makers preferred to choose consortia of several member-states for their twinning projects, to take the focus away from any one member-state model.

Framing integration: the role of legitimacy and concepts. JHA policies involved framing integration, so they provided legitimacy and concepts as resources for domestic actors, in particular to the CEE interior ministries on borders and visa policies. For example, the Czech interior ministry was publicly criticised by the foreign minister when it announced the introduction of visas for Bulgarians and Romanians in 1999, for example.[77] In Poland and Hungary too, interior ministries differed in their approaches to neighbouring countries from other ministries, and used EU demands to justify unpopular and controversial measures (e.g. visas for Ukrainians in Poland, and for Romanians in Hungary).

But legitimacy and concepts also caused problems in the JHA agenda. Although the EU provided a strong motivation to regulate movement of people much more strictly, its influence on cognitive logic was constrained by the conflicts between the different policy paradigms it presented (see next section).

Time, timing and tempo. The EU had an impact on timing by forcing issues up the decision agenda long before they would otherwise have received attention. In the context of relations between the candidates and their neighbours, there were many other, more pressing issues than regulating movement of persons across borders. The EU forced the candidates to tackle this issue because of its own internal concerns.

However, the candidates tried to use timing to mitigate the impact of the EU's demands. Poland stalled on introducing visas with neighbouring countries, but was eventually forced to set precise dates in February 2002. Hungary successfully stalled on setting a date for Romania until the EU itself removed the Schengen travel visa requirement for Romanian citizens. Hungary managed to avoid visas for Ukrainians until accession, but had to introduce them for Russians beforehand. Bulgaria initially tried to use timing to delay imposition, but gave in to get the restrictions on its own citizens removed.

The outcome for the EU: intervening variables

Ideational factors did not play a strong role in this policy area on the EU side. The norm of accommodating CEE interests was weaker in the case of JHA than the single market. The EU pursued its own interests in turning CEE into a buffer-zone for migration. The EU could also claim some aspects were in line with the candidates' interests, such as more effective regulation of frontiers as part of the fight against cross-border crime. But visa policy was evidently not in CEE interests, and the EU simply claimed that it was non-negotiable.

Policy paradigms. The policy paradigm for regulating movement of people under JHA was in contradiction to the paradigms underlying two other areas of EU policy: the four freedoms of the single market, and the CFSP goal of stabilising the EU's peripheries, which led the EU to support regional integration and cross-border cooperation (for the latter argument, see Grabbe 2000a).

There were also different methods of integration used in regulating movement of persons in the different pillars. Free movement of people in the single market was mainly about negative integration – removing barriers to free movement. By contrast, liberalisation was not the goal in JHA. However, these contradictions were not acknowledged in the way that the accession conditions were presented to the candidates. Moreover, in contrast to the case of FMP, the EU granted no concessions in other policy areas to compensate the CEE candidates for agreeing to its demands in the JHA chapter.

Conclusions

Justice and home affairs arrived relatively late on the EU's agenda for CEE, gaining importance only from 1998 onwards. It then became a central priority in the Accession Partnerships and aid policy (through Phare and twinning, as well as the Catch-Up Facility after 2000). JHA is thus an important case-study of how EU accession conditionality changed over time. The way it rose up the accession agenda so rapidly demonstrated that the Copenhagen conditions just set a general frame for policy, and could accommodate new priorities.

In this case-study, domestic institutions and actors both have some explanatory value because JHA measures worked through several different Europeanisation mechanisms. The huge range of JHA measures gave the EU enormous potential influence in CEE. The EU's impact was visible in changing policies on border management; the structure and role of interior ministries; changing attitudes and approaches to asylum-seekers, refugees and immigrants; and the integration of national policies with EU and international norms.

The Europeanisation mechanisms used instrumentally by the EU in the field of JHA changed from general and unfocused encouragement to build state capacity in the late 1990s, to a much more specific range of tasks connected to borders, migration, asylum, law enforcement, and fighting crime by the end of the negotiations in 2002. However, the EU often set only broad parameters for its agenda, calling CEE policy-makers' attention to particular areas, rather than specifying a policy model or institutional solution to be implemented; it thus stands in contrast to the well-defined FMP *acquis* under the single market.

The force of the EU's impact can be felt in CEE approaches to regulating movement of persons across borders, all of which became much more restrictive. However, the EU's overall impact was to force the question of border control up the political agenda in the candidate countries rather than setting precise policy prescriptions. Until the end of the 1990s, its direct influence in shaping the detailed management of border policies in CEE was constrained by its lack of clear policy models for the candidates to follow. The candidates would almost certainly have been willing to follow an EU model for border control more closely if there had been less secrecy and obscurity surrounding the JHA *acquis*. There was considerable demand on the CEE side for more detailed requirements and standards so that the candidates could interpret the accession requirements more precisely. In the absence of EU standards, some member-states filled the vacuum; Germany actively exported its border control techniques to Poland, for example. In failing to provide more detailed preferences on border policies, the EU can be said to have squandered some of its opportunities to influence the candidates.

8
Explaining how EU Influence Worked

This chapter draws together the conclusions of the two case-studies, and links them back to the variables presented in Chapters 3 and 4. Section 8.1 presents the findings of the case-studies in terms of policy transfer. Section 8.2 then considers the roles of the intervening variables, and their power in explaining the outcomes. Section 8.3 seeks to explain why the candidates continued with processes of Europeanisation despite sub-optimal outcomes in negotiations, and traces how Europeanisation became institutionalised.

8.1   The findings of the case-studies

The cases were concerned with how particular EU policies were transferred to the applicant countries. Following Dolowitz and Marsh (1996 and 2000, discussed in Chapter 3), the analysis of policy transfer can be organised around the following series of questions: Who transfers policy? What is transferred? Why is policy transferred? From where? With what success? Dolowitz and Marsh also consider degrees of transfer, constraints on transfer, and how transfer can lead to policy failure. Table 8.1 summarises the answers to these questions for the two case-studies.

In the case of policy transfer through the accession process, the first question is relatively straightforward: the EU as a whole transferred policy through the accession *acquis*, although different actors within the EU had an impact on how different parts of that *acquis* were defined. The other questions are more complex because the EU's agenda contains both explicit and implicit demands. The case-studies looked specifically at the mechanics of policy and institutional transfer, answering the questions 'what?', 'how?' and 'from where?'. At a

Table 8.1   **EU-CEE transfer of policies related to regulating movement of persons**

Policy area	Who	What	Why	How	From where
Single market regulations for free movement of persons	Commission (DG single market)	Removing obstacles to free movement of workers	Four freedoms of the single market	Negative integration for FMP (SMWP, APs), although positive integration also used in other areas	Single market regulation in the first pillar
Regulation of the movement of persons across external frontiers	Commission (DG JHA), Council (JHA working group)	Frontier controls, norms for asylum and immigration policies	Internal security concerns (desire to avoid transit migration, concern to limit movement related to crime)	Prescriptive integration (APs), framing integration (bilateral example-setting)	JHA and Schengen rules and norms in the first and third pillars

general level, the answer to the question 'why?' is about why the EU and CEE engaged in policy transfer at all, and the answers lie in path-dependency: policies were transferred because previous enlargements had always involved the transfer of the *acquis* to new members. However, there are also more specific questions of why particular policies were transferred in a particular way, the answers to which lie on the EU side.

The case-studies looked at the transfer of two policies from different parts of the *acquis*, but all related to the same goal: regulating the movement of persons. Although they all had the same aim, the policies were transferred from different parts of the EU's treaty structure and its body of law, and these different starting-points had implications for how and why they were transferred. In particular, they had different underlying policy paradigms. Both involved multiple mechanisms of Europeanisation – different routes of influence, and also different forms of integration (prescriptive, prohibitive and framing).

8.2　The roles of the intervening variables

In the first case-study on FMP, only a few intervening variables affected the transposition of EU policies, and both lay in the candidate countries: they were political salience in CEE and the macrostrategy of adaptation to the EU. The other variables (diffuseness, uncertainty and goodness-of-fit) were not significant. There was a relatively homogeneous outcome in terms of Europeanisation, with only Bulgaria exhibiting slightly slower implementation owing to problems with administrative capacity. In negotiations, the main difference between the countries was Poland's attempt to gain additional concessions from the EU. In the second case-study on Schengen, by contrast, there was a much greater interaction of intervening variables, resulting in diverse outcomes. The speed of Europeanisation varied a little between Hungary and Poland, but it worked much more slowly in Bulgaria – again because of institutional capacity. In negotiations, all three countries tried tactics of delay on visa policies, with varying degrees of success.

The role of diffuseness

Diffuseness played a role in the case-study on Schengen, but not the one on free movement of persons. The potential kinds of diffuseness identified in Chapter 4 were lack of institutional templates, inconsistencies in the EU's advice to applicants, and complexity of actor constellations.

In FMP, these variables were largely absent, because it was a well-defined policy area from the start, and the political salience of the candidates' implementation of that *acquis* was not high among the member-states. However, in the case of Schengen, all three kinds of diffuseness were very evident. The EU's own *acquis* was in a state of rapid development during the pre-accession period, and it became part of the treaty base of the Union only in 1998, the same year as Hungary and Poland started negotiations. The Council of Ministers and the European Commission lacked the expertise and personnel to promote the development and functioning of political institutions at national level in detail for JHA. As a result, the EU had few well-defined templates to transfer to CEE, and its member-states exhibited considerable diversity in their own policies and institutions. The EU's advice changed over time owing to the developing politics of Schengen and internal security cooperation within the Union. Finally, there were different Commission, Council and member-state actors involved.

The role of uncertainty

The applicants had to play the EU's game under conditions of uncertainty about many aspects of the accession process. Chapter 4 identified the central dimensions of uncertainty: candidates faced uncertainty about the rules in different policy areas, in terms of the hierarchy of different demands (on which CEE countries had to base their allocation of domestic resources); they faced uncertainty about the timing of compliance (before or after accession); there was uncertainty about which part of the EU they had to satisfy in some policy areas (the Commission or particular member-states); and they faced uncertainty about the standards that had to be met – what would count as satisfying the conditions. These dimensions of uncertainty played differently across policy areas, so they are a variable that can partly explain differences in outcomes between policy areas.

The FMP *acquis* was more certain and changed much less, so it was implemented earlier and more completely than the Schengen border *acquis*. It was fairly clear that the single market as a whole might be a veto-point for accession, but that an individual area like FMP would not, especially as the EU itself asked for a transition period on it. But a failure to implement Schengen-compatible border controls almost certainly would have been a veto-point, and if that failure caused more migration to the EU, it could even have led to the re-imposition of visa requirements. The political stakes were thus much higher in the second case than the first.

Uncertainty about standards also differed between the cases. FMP under the single market required functioning institutions that could remove barriers to free movement; once those were in place, the *acquis* had been implemented. By contrast, Schengen involved a large, obscure, rapidly changing and often ambiguous *acquis* whose standards of implementation varied across the existing member-states. Moreover, decisions about whether standards of border control were adequate for accession depended as much on a general feeling of confidence among the main policy actors as on any technical measures of compliance.

The EU used uncertainty instrumentally, but mainly to manage its own internal politics rather than to make gains at the expense of CEE interests. For example, the EU used uncertainty instrumentally to avoid making a commitment to accession that was based on only a few criteria. That allowed its member-states to postpone decisions about when the first accessions would occur and which countries would be involved. Uncertainty about ranking could also be used to force the applicants to make efforts to comply with all of the agenda, rather than just a few key elements, but this was not a major motivation for creating or maintaining high levels of uncertainty. However, uncertainty was sometimes just the unintended consequence of inter-state bargaining and complex actor constellations.

One source of uncertainty is the EU's general tendency to avoid strategic decision-making (Richardson 1999). This tendency, in turn, results from a range of systemic characteristics, particularly transgovernmental coalition formation (Risse-Kappen 1995). These characteristics of the EU might be expected to result in a higher degree of unpredictability in its policy preferences than is the case for a single state's political system. Uncertainty can be the result of the EU's failure (as a system) to make strategic decisions about its policy preferences in the detailed conditions, particularly the trade-offs between them. In the case of eastward enlargement, however, the EU was not forced to make trade-offs because it did not have to decide the allocation of resources to different priorities; rather, this decision was left to each applicant. The EU was free to set as many conditions as its member-states could agree on.

The meso and micro policies that formed the overall composite policy for eastern accession were largely decided at technical level in the Commission (just as for the association policy that preceded accession conditionality – Sedelmeier 1998). However, there was variation across policy areas in which policy-makers decided the meso policies. In the case of JHA, the member-states took a much greater interest in the formation of meso policy and had much greater involvement in decision-making than in the case of single market regulation, where the Commission took the lead.

Uncertainty was a key intervening variable in the Europeanisation of different policy areas because the dimensions of uncertainty varied considerably across policies, affecting how the CEE candidates responded to the EU's demands in different areas. Table 8.2 gives a rough indication of this variation across the policy area of movement of persons in three different parts of the EU's policy-making structures (it fills in the cells in the structure established in Table 4.2). Chapter 4 predicted that where uncertainty across all the dimensions is high, the likelihood of Europeanisation will be low because it would be difficult for CEE policy-makers to justify allocating resources to this area and to make decisions about the sequencing of priorities. Where ranking is more certain (in the cases of FMP and Schengen), the other dimensions of uncertainty should matter to the direction of Europeanisation. Schengen was clearly a priority and the member-states were the main agent to satisfy, so many resources were allocated to this area and Europeanisation was extensive.

Table 8.2 Dimensions of uncertainty in regulating movement of persons

Types of uncertainty	Levels of uncertainty	
	Free movement of persons in the single market	Regulating movement of persons in the Schengen area
Linkage: Is there a particular benefit closely tied to the costs of adopting this policy?	Medium: candidates had to implement the single market *acquis*, but would not get the benefits of free movement for their citizens until a <u>specified</u> number of years after accession	High: Candidates had to adopt the Schengen *acquis*, but would not get the benefits of eliminating border controls for an <u>unspecified</u> number of years after accession
Ranking: How important is this policy among the EU's priorities? Is it a veto-point that could prevent accession?	Medium: part of the single market, with low political significance for member-states in accession policy, although they were expected to introduce transition periods in the final phase of negotiations	Low: clear priority overall, and ranking of tasks given in Accession Partnerships
Agenda: How well-specified are the EU's demands?	Low: established and mature policy area	High: new and fast-developing policy area
Timing: What has to be done before accession?	Low: all measures had to be implemented before accession, but the *acquis* was small	High: large *acquis* and it was unclear what had to be done before and after accession to the Union and to Schengen
Principal agent: Who has to be satisfied?	Low: certainly the Commission	Medium: both the member-states and the Commission
Standards: What counts as compliance?	Low: the test is removal of legal barriers to movement of persons	High: assessment is a matter of confidence among member-states

However, the uncertainty over timing and standards meant that the precise direction of Europeanisation resulting in any given area was hard to predict because CEE policy-makers often did not know how to allocate their resources in implementing Schengen.

In the case of FMP, uncertainty was low across all dimensions, so it was easy to see how to allocate resources, so the direction of Europeanisation was predictable. Likelihood of Europeanisation was reduced by the fact that it was a relatively low priority for the EU, but there were also low levels of resistance to it in CEE because of poor goodness-of-fit ('technical resistance') or opposition from domestic political actors ('political resistance').

Overall, Europeanisation effects are a function of the combination of these different dimensions of uncertainty. Where uncertainty about the agenda, timing and standards was high but the political salience was certainly also high (as in the case of JHA), the EU had a large impact despite its uncertain agenda because the candidates endeavoured to meet whatever criteria were hinted at. Where uncertainty about the agenda, timing and standards was high but political salience was relatively low (as in the case of FMP in the single market), the EU had a small impact because the incentives for CEE to second-guess what the EU might want were low and policy-makers could use the uncertainty to give themselves more room for manoeuvre.

Uncertainty can also interact with other variables. For candidate country policy-makers, it was difficult to use uncertainty to give them more room for manoeuvre in how and how quickly they implemented the *acquis*. Where a policy area was politically important to the EU – such as Schengen – then the two variables (political salience and uncertainty) interacted.

The role of institutional capacity to achieve political goals

This variable was significant for Bulgaria in both case-studies. Bulgaria's weak institutional capacity made it impossible for the country to catch up with the first group of candidates and join in 2004. Even when it did not object to the EU's demands and agreed immediately to its negotiating position, the Union would not allow Bulgaria to close chapters quickly because its institutional capacity to implement the measures agreed in the negotiations was in doubt.

The role of political salience

In the case of FMP, the political salience was not high until just before accession, and the costs of implementing the policy were low so the degree of fit was not a significant factor. The main issue was negotiations, not implementation. In the case of external border policies, however, the political salience was high several years before the negotiations began, and there was a clear misfit with the Schengen *acquis* because it directly contradicted the foreign policies of the candidates. We might have expected that the Schengen *acquis* would be more slowly and incompletely implemented by the candidates than the FMP *acquis* as a result.

But the outcome did not match expectations. All three candidates altered their border policies to fit EU norms, radically reformed the institutions policing the borders (e.g. demilitarisation of the border guard), and devoted resources to putting Schengen-compatible border controls in place. Even distance from accession and a later start to implementation did not prevent Bulgaria from trying to take on the Schengen *acquis* rapidly.

The role of the macro-strategy of adaptation

The three countries' approach to negotiations on FMP and borders policies followed their overall negotiating strategies. Hungary asked for little in both cases, and closed both chapters quickly. Poland held out for a better deal on FMP, in accordance with its overall approach to negotiations. Poland also tried to hold out in the JHA chapter by delaying setting dates for the imposition of visas on neighbouring countries. Bulgaria tried to adjust quickly and asked for little in either chapter, but its credibility was too low to achieve rapid closure of either chapter.

8.3   Explanation

Throughout the development of the accession process, CEE preferences were marginalised: starting with the Europe Agreements, CEE preferences influenced the content of EU policy instruments for enlargement only to a limited extent (Sedelmeier 1994). Conditionality was developed largely in isolation from their interests, with the emphasis on making the new members acceptable to the EU, not reciprocal commitments. As discussed in Chapter 4, the Accession Partnerships extended the range of EU influence in CEE still further, and reduced the scope of negotiations down to transition periods.

Why did the candidates so rarely challenge EU demands? The outcome can be explained partly by the realist approach of power politics: the EU had the benefits to offer, and so it shaped the rules of the game. Although political elites in Poland, conscious of their country's geo-political importance, tended to stress what they could offer the EU, most political actors in the candidate countries were painfully aware of the fact that their desire to join was not matched by an equal willingness on the EU side to take them in. Only the most confident applicant felt it could afford to demand better terms. The EU's own reluctance to enlarge gave it enormous power to set ever higher hurdles for the applicants to meet.

However, this is not the whole story; this approach does not explain why CEE governments did not use their bargaining power more effectively. It also leaves out the interaction between domestic politics and relations with the EU: Why did CEE domestic interests not press their governments to resist EU demands more? It is surprising how little debate there was about the details of EU demands in CEE parliaments or the media until after the accession negotiations had finished. Poland became increasingly assertive in its dealings with the EU, but most other applicants largely accepted EU terms as presented in policy documents. Several levels of explanation are explored below.

Levels of explanation

The first level of explanation lies in domestic politics in CEE since 1989. There remained a wide gap between foreign and domestic policy debates in most post-communist countries, with very few interest groups connecting the EU's demands with controversial reforms (Taggart and Szczerbiak 2001). Even anticipatory adjustment by CEE policy-makers to conform with EU norms only rarely caused interest groups to blame the EU publicly for the policy outcomes. Instead, national governments tended to take the blame.

The reasons for this passivity lie in a second explanation: the low level of knowledge in CEE of what the EU's demands were during the negotiations. In the 1990s, most political actors often exhibited only limited awareness of how wide-ranging the accession requirements were, and the implications of documents like the Accession Partnerships for negotiations. There was little debate about EU demands because they were understood only by a small group of policy-makers. Further, the technical nature of many of the activities needed obscured the extent to which the EU was influencing policy. Moreover, potential losers remained passive about accession and its effects on them (see Gould 1999).

The third level of explanation lies in the nature of the agenda presented. Because the EU presented a largely neo-liberal agenda that accorded with the general international consensus about transition economics, there were few dissenting voices to criticise the policy prescriptions on offer. There were some tensions with the demands of other international bodies; for example, World Bank staff criticised EU agricultural, environmental and social policies as inappropriate for most transition economies. But officials on all sides were unwilling to discuss their disagreements publicly, for fear of disrupting the enlargement process, and so these remained behind-the-scenes discussions within ministries and in Brussels.

The fourth explanation lies in the 'moving target' problem of the conditionality. Rather than resisting EU demands, applicants often asked for more detailed policies and clearer targets from the EU in order to pin down the conditions. They wanted to know where the hurdles were set.

The fifth level of explanation lies in the juxtaposition of Europeanisation and post-communist transition. Throughout the process of post-1989 transformation, there was a tendency to look for models of democracy and economic order; the EU provided an obvious one, and the desire to join added a further incentive to take on what were seen as successful EU political and economic norms. Particularly in the early years of transition, there was a vacuum of credible alternatives to EU policies. Although CEE policy-makers were certainly influenced by US models and IFI policy advice too, the EU had a very large role owing to its political, economic and civil society ties with the region next door.

The desire to take on EU models was compounded by the weak nature of the state in post-communist CEE. The inability to define for themselves what had to be done for transition made many post-communist states very open to external influences; taking on EU policies was an example of the strategy of 'tying hands' that enabled policy-makers to overcome domestic opposition (Moravcsik 1993). In the case of CEE, external relations not only constricted domestic choices, but provided a model when few other credible policy options were on offer. In the aftermath of the fall of communism, states were often content with losing sovereignty in the face of EU demands, because they were looking for outsiders to tell them what to do.

The candidates thus pulled the EU into increasingly detailed conditions, in addition to the push-factors at work in the EU. The EU's agenda was welcomed for many reasons: the fragility of the state in CEE; the lack of experience on the part of policy-makers (especially in newly independent countries); the instability of some of the political institutions; and the unprecedented burdens of simultaneous transformation of the state, the economy and society. The behaviour of Romania and Bulgaria showed the extent to which the EU was helpful to policy-makers seeking to legitimate and substantiate their reform efforts. It might seem puzzling that the countries furthest from membership should continue to accept EU demands, even though they were unlikely to join for many years. But they had an even greater need than the front-runners for a sense of direction. They were the least successful of the candidates at meeting EU conditions, yet accession demands were still felt to be needed as a prop for reform efforts.

A sixth explanation lies in an unwitting collusion between two forms of elitist technocratism that favoured a dictation of terms by the EU.[78] On the CEE side, there were elitist and technocratic elements deeply embedded in communist and post-communist culture that saw policy-making as best left to the experts. This tendency not to debate policy options fell neatly in line with the EU's inclination to leave it to the Commission to work out the details following a decision at political level, owing to member-states' unwillingness to take responsibility for much of enlargement policy (discussed in Chapter 2). These characteristics were different in origin, but they both lie in a deep-rooted assumption that details can be left to the experts: leaders decide that a country should join the EU, and the technocrats can sort out the technicalities. The problem with treating the accession conditions as just a set of technical issues is that it runs against the idea that politics is about choosing between policy options that are alternative solutions to problems.

This technocratic approach to integration implies a democratic deficit in the whole eastern accession process. Accountability was lacking on the EU side owing to the Commission's control of much of accession policy, but there was also little democratic participation on the CEE side. Because of the lack of debate about accession requirements, CEE policy-makers were often constrained more by EU conditions than by their domestic polities. To the extent that there was a 'two-level game' at work in bargaining with the EU, the domestic level played only a very limited role on the CEE side.

The most important explanation lies in the Europeanisation process that worked in parallel with the negotiations. Even when the candidate country negotiators wanted to bargain in Brussels, at home their state administrations were already deeply engaged at many levels in a process of transferring EU legislation, procedures and templates. This process is explored below.

How Europeanisation became institutionalised

By the time the negotiations began, the candidates had devoted considerable resources of their own to a long-term strategy of aligning with EU policies and norms. CEE policy-makers had sunk costs in domestic preparations and their staff was being socialised into EU procedures, so the incentives to keep moving towards the EU grew. By the time that the negotiations reached very controversial items on the EU's agenda, the applicants had devoted considerable financial resources to the accession process, and they had a strong political commitment to seeing it through. The distinct nature of the implementation and negotiation processes is neatly captured by a comment in 1999 from the civil servant in charge of writing Hungary's NPAAs: 'The tasks in the Accession Partnerships and NPAAs are not the subject of negotiations. With law harmonisation and institution-building, there are no real alternatives in how to do it and whether to do it. The real subjects of the negotiations are transition periods.'

It was expensive in both material and political terms to think of withdrawing, or even just slowing the accession process down, because of the following factors:

- Sunk costs. CEE financial resources had gone into implementing their 'National Programmes for Adoption of the *Acquis*', because the candidates had supplied matching funds to complement EU aid. The candidates' public administrations had already started appointing and training staff in EU procedures.
- Institutionalisation of EU priorities. Institutional frameworks had been established to implement the *acquis* whose purpose and functioning were determined by the EU's agenda. The transaction cost of moving to other policy frameworks rose. Although continuing with the EU framework might be expensive, calculating the cost-benefit ratio became more complicated, making it easier to continue with the same policy. According to the Hungarian official in charge of coordinating the preparations in 1999, 'Gradually, EU aspects have been built into policies themselves and into our policy formation process. Now there are no specific EU policies, but the EU-related tasks are built into all our policies'.
- Socialisation of actors. The political institutions were staffed by people who were increasingly socialised into EU procedures and who had absorbed the EU's policy paradigms. Policy-makers had begun to adopt the discourse of the EU, particularly in policy areas where there was little previous policy; for example, officials working

on immigration policy increasingly quoted EU documents when asked to justify the government's policy towards migrants and asylum-seekers. The number of Europeanised staff in the ministries was initially small, but EU policies and methods slowly penetrated deeper as the accession requirements affected more and more areas of public policy.

- Mobilisation of interest groups. Outside the public administration, interest groups had begun to cluster around EU preparations. Business groups, trade associations, employers' organisations, trade unions and non-governmental organisations had begun to adapt to EU policies, take part in EU programmes and operate within EU networks of interest groups. Even if they did not like the EU's demands on the applicant countries, they began to appreciate the continuity and stability of policy that EU requirements brought, particularly in contexts of rapidly changing governments and officials (see Fink-Hafner 1998 and chapters in Schimmelfennig and Sedelmeier 2005).

- Domestic politics. In terms of political costs, it became very expensive for those in charge of EU policy within the candidate countries to show any signs of slowing down, because that gave an opportunity to opposition politicians to claim that government officials were incompetent. The politics of accession played differently in the three countries studied here. Polish negotiators could be criticised for not making progress, but also for not being tough in defending national interests; they thus had a complicated game to play domestically. For both the Hungarian and Bulgarian negotiators, the incentives were simpler. In both countries, there was a stronger political consensus in favour of rapid accession and less interest from the press in the terms of accession than in Poland. However, Bulgarian negotiators were under greater pressure to move ahead in opening and closing chapters because of the strong incentives to narrow the gap with other candidates.

- The relationship with the EU-15. In deciding their adaptation strategies, the goal of the CEE policy-makers was not only to convince the EU that they met the accession requirements, but also to show that they would be good future partners. As the member-states devoted more attention to enlargement once negotiations began, the issue of confidence became more important on the EU side. That increased the incentives for CEE actors to show goodwill; to demonstrate their capacity to participate in future integration, for example by joining in framing integration projects; and to do more than the minimum necessary to join in areas particularly sensitive to certain member-states, such as border control.

These factors created a growing incentive to continue Europeanising, because it made no sense to stop a process that had already become institutionalised. The Europeanisation process had a logic and momentum of its own. The author's interviews with the main actors in the 1990s and early 2000s suggested that policy-makers involved in implementation in other ministries followed the negotiating process carefully, and there was an iterative process of priority-setting throughout this period; thus it was not just a matter of 'blind' or unconscious rule-following in implementing the *acquis* regardless of what happened in the negotiations. However, the candidates had already established policy-making systems that existed primarily to implement EU requirements. Compliance with the *acquis* had become a policy goal in its own right.

Conclusions

The definition of 'Europeanisation' presented in Chapter 2 emphasises changes in the logic of behaviour as the central, defining feature of Europeanisation in the existing member-states. All three candidate countries studied here instituted policy-making systems which operated according to a logic of Europeanisation. At macro-level, these new systems (which themselves involved both old and new institutional components and actors) were designed to fit into a multilateral and extra-territorial governance system. The institutions become Europeanised at micro-level: they develop a logic of behaviour based on complying with EU requirements that operated to some extent independently of the terms negotiated for joining the EU.

Intervening variables affected the extent of Europeanisation. In particular, goodness-of-fit partly determined the extent to which domestic institutions were changed by the EU. Likewise, this process could be disrupted or changed by other political processes, both domestic and external – and accession negotiations were one of these processes. However, the case-studies have shown that the logic of behaviour changed in the CEE countries prior to accession, and the processes at work were a form of Europeanisation. Moreover, the overall Europeanisation process developed a momentum and logic of its own, which was to some extent distinct from the process of negotiations.

9
Conclusion

This book has examined EU influence in the CEE candidate countries, focusing on what the EU actively sought to change and the routes of Europeanisation that were established by the accession process. The EU had an enormous potential influence on public policy in CEE because between 1989 and 2004 every government in every applicant country claimed that EU membership was its first foreign policy priority. Moreover, beyond the attraction of membership, the EU had specific routes of influence through which it could shape political choices, in particular gate-keeping, benchmarking, models, money and advice.

However, the EU did not use its full potential to shape public policy because of the diffuseness of its influence – partly owing to the diversity of its current member-states – and the uncertainties of the accession process. Moreover, the EU's influence interacted with other processes of change in CEE, including the political salience of European issues and the institutional capacity of the country to respond to EU demands.

The EU's power in negotiations and its influence through Europeanisation had different effects in the candidate countries. In the CEE candidate countries, Europeanisation was a process that began prior to the accession negotiations and was distinct from them. Negotiations were an important way of exerting influence, and the outcome of negotiations – the accession treaty – was one of the few legally binding parts of the accession process. However, they were only one part of the accession process (as shown in Chapter 2), and they provided only one of the EU's many routes of influence in CEE (as shown in Chapter 3). Negotiations and Europeanisation were parallel and interactive, but they were distinct processes. For this reason, a framework of analysis based on international bargaining would be inadequate to study the

EU's influence in CEE. The power that the EU was able to exert in negotiations was different from the way it influenced the candidates through Europeanisation. The outcome of negotiations had a direct and targeted effect on a given policy area, but that impact was not necessarily long-lasting if the candidate country lacked the political will or administrative capacity to implement what its negotiators had agreed with the EU. By contrast, Europeanisation had more diffuse and patchy effects, but these were long-lasting where the EU maintained consistent pressure.

The relationship between the EU and the CEE countries as applicants for membership can be and has been characterised in several different theoretical frameworks (Schimmelfennig 1998, Fierke and Wiener 1999). The negotiating process could be researched as a form of 'two-level game' (Putnam 1988) played between the EU and CEE, given the evident interaction between the domestic and international levels. There is clearly room for more empirical work on the negotiations themselves (as shown by Friis 1997 and 1998). However, this book concludes that the negotiations are just part of the story.

The case-studies result in the following broad conclusions:

1. The EU's influence is potentially colossal, but it was not used to the full in Central and Eastern Europe. Through the accession process, the EU can directly affect policy, institutional development, and the capacity of the state. The EU's influence is most readily identifiable where it advocates particular policy and institutional preferences. However, it can also stimulate far-reaching changes simply by moving an issue up the government's decision-agenda, that is, by attracting more political attention to it.

   The EU's influence is constrained, however, by diffuseness and uncertainty. These two constraints are largely the result of the structure of the EU's accession policies and its own nature as a multilateral body that has to achieve complex bargains among its constituent members. When the EU's agenda is ambiguous and/or incomplete, it cannot make full use of its potential influence. However, individual EU actors can take advantage of this absence of clearly specified criteria to advance policy solutions of their own.

   The case-studies have shown how the EU used its routes of influence in CEE to promote the Europeanisation of public policy. It had multiple points of contact with the candidate countries and its approbation or disapprobation played a key role in CEE domestic politics. However, the complexity of actor constellations within the EU made its influence diffuse. The Union as a whole coordinated its accession policy to shape public policy effectively only where it already had a clear set of rules or an institutional model. Where it did not, the diversity of the EU itself undermined the export of models to CEE. The EU's aggregate impact on CEE public policy was great, but it was blunt rather than precise. That diffuseness was increased where the policy paradigms underlying the EU's legislative and institutional models were different or even competing, as was the case in regulating the movement of persons.

2. Negotiating power matters. There is a strongly asymmetrical interdependence between the EU and candidate countries while they remain outside the EU. That power relationship has strong explanatory value for the CEE candidates' strategies in adaptation to the EU and also for the outcome of the accession negotiations.

In the case of free movement of persons, the EU managed to achieve its central goals despite having to override strongly principled objections from the candidates and contradictions with its own policy paradigms. In the Schengen case, the EU managed to effect dramatic changes in the candidates' border and visa policies despite a serious misfit with other important policy objectives. The attraction of accession proved to be more powerful than other goals.

Even when the EU is divided internally, it can still have strong negotiating power. In the case of FMP, many member-states had misgivings about the transition period on labour mobility. However, the strong preference of a few member-states for the transition period allowed the negotiators to tell the candidates that some member-states would not allow them to join without a transition period on labour mobility. However, the lack of consensus between member-states did lead to trade-offs that accommodated the candidates' interests in other areas.

3. Europeanisation can explain seemingly perverse political outcomes. The power relationship is, however, inadequate to explain all the outcomes in these policy areas. The two case-studies presented here show that the candidates did not just respond to the material incentives provided by the EU's exercise of power. They did not follow wholly rational strategies, and their adaptational strategies were distinct from their negotiating strategies.

Even though the candidates were explicitly denied the benefits of free movement of labour and the lifting of internal border controls immediately on accession, they continued implementation at domestic level. Partly this was the outcome of a fear that otherwise their accession might be vetoed, but this threat was less credible once the deal on both negotiating chapters had been agreed. Interview evidence suggested that a parallel process was at work: CEE policy-makers had bought into the logic of Europeanisation, and were using EU policies and standards as their primary reference-point in framing domestic policies. The outcome of negotiations might have had some effect where policies were very controversial or expensive to implement, but on the whole Europeanisation continued regardless of the negotiations.

There are other variables determining the impact of EU requirements on public policy as well. The most important identified in the case-studies are the domestic political setting, the structure and consistency of the EU's agenda in a given policy area, goodness-of-fit and uncertainty.

4. Europeanisation becomes embedded in domestic policies and institutions long before accession. The EU's influence became embedded in CEE through processes of Europeanisation akin to those observed in the existing member-states. These processes can explain why the outcomes of negotiations did not cause expected changes in accession preparations. Indeed, the case of FMP reveals a disjuncture between the candidates' expectations of accession terms and the approach they took to implementation of the *acquis*.

Priority-setting at domestic level involves some strategic choice, but processes of Europeanisation tend to develop a logic and momentum of their own which do not depend wholly on top-down direction from government. Instead, EU tasks are written into the work-programmes of national ministries and a layer of officials becomes 'Europeanised' through contact with the EU and through training courses and participation in EU programmes. The routinisation of EU practices has a long-term effect.

In most CEE countries and in many policy areas, Europeanisation began several years before negotiations began, through adaptation guided by EU legislative and institutional templates. In the cases presented here, the extremes are Hungary and Bulgaria. For Hungary, some regulatory alignment started even under communism in the 1980s, but Bulgaria started alignment in earnest only around 1997. We can thus expect Europeanisation to have been more rapid and to have gone further in Hungary, and this is evident in both of the case-studies. However, although the *acquis* for the first case on FMP was presented much earlier than for the second on JHA, both were implemented quickly in the CEE countries, for different reasons. Negotiating strategies were thus separate from – although parallel with – Europeanisation processes.

5. Credibility is a key intervening variable, one which was not expected at the start of the study. All three candidates studied here promised to implement the JHA *acquis* vigorously, because their officials knew it was a potential veto-point in negotiations. However, their commitments carried different levels of credibility. Hungary had both the capacity and the political will to meet its promises, because of its relatively sound public administration and high degree of political consensus on EU accession. Poland mostly had the capacity to implement the *acquis* – although the EU was unconvinced about some of its border protection infrastructure – but its political class was less united about EU accession preparations, so its promises had less credibility than Hungary's. Bulgaria had strong political will, but lacked the capacity for enforcement of the *acquis* and had not transposed legislation quickly, so its promises had low credibility with the EU.

6. Domestic politics matter. Poland embarked on negotiating strategy that was unlikely to bring gains owing to domestic political pressures. However, in the longer term, the EU's victory in negotiations may prove to be Pyrrhic if the treatment of the candidates in negotiations has a long-term effect on their future behaviour as member-states. Poland's negotiations resulted in deals that fuelled anti-EU movements in its domestic politics. In its first set of EU negotiations as a full partner, Poland took a hardline stance which resulted in the stalling of the EU's Inter-governmental Conference on the draft constitutional treaty in December 2003 (see Grabbe 2004b). That could be a sign of Poland's future behaviour as a member-state.

9.1   Implications for the study of Europeanisation

'Europeanisation' was defined in Chapter 3 as a set of processes whereby rules and procedures are constructed and defined in the EU policy process and then incorporated into the logic of domestic discourse, identities, political structures and public policies. Europeanisation in the CEE countries involved many other processes, such as policy transfer, regime transfer and institutional isomorphism (or mimicry). The specificity of Europeanisation lies in the fact that the processes all involved the influence of European integration, and the interaction between nation-states and EU institutions. In the case of applicant countries, there was an additional dimension to Europeanisation because the conditionality for membership gave the Union significant leverage in transferring its principles, norms and rules, as well as in shaping institutional and administrative structures. This conditionality had two distinctive features which proved to be important to understanding the way the EU influenced policy-making in the CEE candidate countries: power and uncertainty. These two variables resulted from the nature of the EU and its policies, so they may be useful concepts for the study of Europeanisation within the Union, not just in candidate countries.

The study of Europeanisation is post-ontological, investigating not the nature of the beast but the beast's effects on others in its environment. It is obvious that the EU mattered in CEE; the question is how, that is, where exactly in CEE structures and policy processes and with what effects? Processes of Europeanisation were at work in CEE well before accession, and the EU's influence was wider in terms of the policy areas covered than in the current member-states, despite the much shorter timescale. However, it is important not to pre-judge how deeply it has penetrated the applicants' political institutions now, just after they have joined the Union. Europeanisation of public administration and governance structures may have been shallow because direct contact with the EU was confined to a small elite during the accession process. Ministries of foreign affairs might have spoken the language of the EU and had regular contact with officials in Brussels and the member-states. However, in other ministries, these contacts were often limited to a small administrative unit that was specialised in EU issues.

But even political actors who had little direct contact with the EU themselves may nonetheless have implemented EU-inspired policies, because these were written into national work-programmes without necessarily being identified as 'EU policies'. Indeed, one of the most important aspects of Europeanisation is the way in which EU policies, procedures and norms become embedded in national policy frameworks, policy-making structures and discourse. It is when people stop referring to 'EU policies' that they have become truly Europeanised.

This study has not sought to measure the extent of Europeanisation systematically in the CEE countries. There are general methodological problems in finding an appropriate scale for studying Europeanisation (first discussed in Goetz 2000), and this study offers some insights into the analytical difficulties of investigating mechanisms of Europeanisation in would-be members of the EU. First, it is vital to distinguish between mechanisms that are used instrumentally by EU actors to effect change and the processes that are largely spontaneous or are initiated by candidate-country actors in the name of the EU. For example, anticipatory adjustment may occur, whereby actors make changes in the expectation that these adjustments will be needed at some point in the accession process or after accession, even though they are not formally required by the EU until a later stage or at all. Similarly, candidate country actors may use supposed EU models as a justification for institutional or policy choices even though the EU does not explicitly state they are needed for accession.

Secondly, indirect influence and pressure from EU institutions and member-states (for example, bilateral contacts) undoubtedly have a variety of effects, but such mechanisms work over time and are not necessarily coordinated at EU level – so they are very difficult to track systematically. In the case of the CEE countries, the EU's geographical proximity and plethora of contacts, along with policy learning and the provision of models, undoubtedly had a major impact. It is difficult to separate analytically the effects of the mechanisms that the EU sought to use actively, and those which happened unintentionally. However, this book has presented two case-studies in which the processes of Europeanisation have been traced closely, providing the basis for conclusions about the conditions under which EU influence is most effective.

Conditions which affect the extent of Europeanisation

The scope of the Europeanisation effects in would-be members is determined by two conditions:

- The precision and certitude of EU demands. The EU has its greatest influence where it has a detailed policy to be transferred, it gives consistent advice, its actors speak with one voice, and it sets clear and certain requirements. It has its least impact where a policy area lacks these elements, and tends towards diffuseness and uncertainty.
- The degree of political will and institutional capacity to implement a given policy in CEE. Europeanisation effects go furthest where would-be members have strong political will to implement a policy owing to domestic consensus about the goal of implementation, and where they have the institutional capacity required to achieve that goal.

In the case-studies presented here, single market requirements were transferred most easily and completely because there was an established *acquis* ready to be transferred, and its requirements were accepted by most EU actors. By contrast, the Schengen requirements for external border control were poorly articulated, kept changing, and were subject to widely varying interpretation by EU actors for several years. The main reason why they were implemented by the candidates was the high political priority attached to them by the EU. However, the extent and direction of Europeanisation varied across the two policy areas studied, because strong political will could not overcome a diffuse and uncertain *acquis*, and lack of institutional capacity to implement it in the candidate countries. The impact of the EU's conditionality was thus blunted by the uncertainties involved in determining the tasks to be undertaken, the standards to be met, and the administrative structures required.

9.2 What implications for democracy?

The first group of CEE countries joined the EU only in 2004, so it is still too early to see how far the Union has affected their long-term political development, in comparison with other exogenous and endogenous influences. However, this study has revealed that the EU's efforts to promote democratic development were at odds with the incentives created by the accession process, where the EU gave priority to efficiency over legitimacy.

The stability of democratic institutions is one of the three general conditions for accession, and the EU promoted the involvement of political institutions beyond the executive to implement and enforce the *acquis*. Yet, at the same time, the incentives and constraints created by the accession process supported the emergence of a core national executive at the expense of other branches and levels of government – including the legislature and regional actors. The accession process encouraged the emergence of a strong, central team to manage the accession process, reinforcing the tendency towards a 'core executive'. The conditionality was based on implementing a vast array of legislation and procedural rules in order to comply with EU standards, which in turn depended on reporting from the centre of government to Brussels. In addition, although the EU constantly promoted the strengthening of administrative capacity for implementation and enforcement, it rarely prescribed how to do this in terms of precise institutional solutions.

The case-studies have highlighted an 'executive bias' inherent in the whole accession process, because of the structure of negotiations and the fact that EU actors mostly saw the process of adopting EU norms as an administrative exercise. This view exacerbated statist tendencies in CEE, which were already evident owing to the previous decades of state socialism. Negotiations between bureaucracies do not necessarily contribute to the development of shared values as a basis for new governance structures.[79] Europeanisation was frequently used as a means of legitimising institutional frameworks in CEE, but the administrative bias of the accession process impeded the development of a wide debate on governance in applicant countries. EU approbation was used to legitimate political choices between models of governance, but that did not necessarily encourage the development of democratic pluralism in CEE.

Looking into the longer term, the shortcomings of the accession process could affect debates about democratic accountability in the enlarged Union. The danger for democracy is that only the top layer of central state officials in CEE becomes 'Europeanised', while the public remains largely distant from European integration – reducing the prospects for a pan-European *demos* to emerge and exacerbating the Union's democratic deficit.

Notes

1 This chapter builds on research undertaken at the European University Institute in 1998 and published as Grabbe 1999.

2 Meaning 'lighthouse' in French, the acronym stands for 'Poland and Hungary Assistance for the Reconstruction of the Economy', but the programme was later extended beyond these two countries.

3 For analyses of the EU's association policy towards CEE up to 1993, see Sedelmeier 1994 and Torreblanca 1997.

4 This summary is based on Sedelmeier and Wallace 1996.

5 For an account of how policy developed through different EC/EU enlargements, see Preston 1997.

6 *'Acquis communautaire'* is the term used by the EU to refer to all the real and potential rights and obligations of the EU system and its institutional framework. The accession *acquis* is the whole body of EU law and practice, and its definition is discussed in Section 2.6.

7 Council Regulation 622/98, article 4.

8 Much more detail on the content of the Accession Partnerships is provided in the case-studies. This table is intended just to illustrate the wide range of tasks they contained.

9 To use a characterisation of capitalist systems in Western Europe developed in Rhodes and van Apeldoorn 1998 from Albert 1991.

10 However, the Amsterdam Treaty resulted in an extension of Community competence in justice and home affairs, and a slight increase in the European Parliament's role in decision-making: see Manin (1998).

11 *Uniting Europe* 9, 1/6/98.

12 *Financial Times*, 16/6/97.

13 'The EU ... will not grant 17 years as it did for Spain ... but at the very most five years ... in well-defined sectors' and for this reason 'the applicants must make the necessary effort during the pre-accession period ...', Assemblée Nationale (1998), pp. 36–37.

14 Corfu European Council 1994, O.J. 1994, C 241/381.

15 *Uniting Europe* 2, 13/4/98.

16 *Uniting Europe* 9, 1/6/98.

17 N.B. Greater policy convergence is not necessarily the same thing as higher levels of compliance with different parts of the EU's *acquis*. The CEE applicants were working from a much lower starting-point than member-states in terms of institutional development, human and financial resources, and economic capacity, so their capacity to adopt the *acquis* fully was much less than that of a West European state. However, the EU's impact on their political economies is likely to have been much greater precisely because these starting conditions meant that EU policies met with less resistance (in terms of existing policies and institutions) than would have been the case in the EU-15.

18 As termed by Wallace and Wallace (2000).

19   As Klaus Knorr puts it, 'Power arises from an asymmetrical interdependence.' (Knorr 1977, p. 102).

20   Radaelli 2000, p. 26.

21   SAPARD = Special Accession Programme for Agriculture and Rural Development.

22   ISPA = Instrument for Structural Policies for Pre-Accession.

23   Author's interviews with the Spanish coordinators of twinning programmes and British twinning agents, 2001.

24   *Démarches* are issued as part of EU foreign policy by unanimous intergovernmental agreement between the member-states.

25   The most extensive overview of all the transition countries is the four volumes edited by Karen Dawisha and Bruce Parrott for Cambridge University Press; the volume on CEE is Dawisha and Parrott 1997.

26   Ferenc Vissi, interview, Budapest, April 1999.

27   Interview with Vladimir Kissiov, Bulgaria's chief negotiator, January 2001.

28   EEC = Treaty establishing the European Economic Community, signed in Rome on 25 March 1957.

29   Article 1 of Directive 90/364.

30   TEU = Treaty on European Union, signed in Maastricht on 7 February 1992.

31   The 1992 Maastricht Treaty had established a structure of three 'pillars' for the Union. The first pillar comprised the single market, the second was the common foreign and security policy, while the third comprised justice and home affairs. The significance of the pillars was that the first was in the jurisdiction of the EU's institutions (the European Parliament, Commission, Council and Court of Justice), while the second and third were reserved to inter-governmental cooperation between the member-states. The 1997 Amsterdam Treaty then moved most of justice and home affairs into the first pillar (and hence under the remit of the EU's institutions), leaving just police and judicial cooperation in the third pillar. The formal pillar structure was removed in the Constitutional Treaty produced in 2004.

32   *Financial Times* 22/5/00.

33   Quoted in *Financial Times* 22/5/00.

34   Interview, Diamantopoulou cabinet, CEC, Brussels, February 2001.

35   CEC press release, 29 January 2001, IP/01/127.

36   Proposal reported in *Die Welt*, 8/7/98.

37   *Agence Europe*, 21/3/01. This was one of only two DCPs where the full College of Commissioners was involved. Normally, the Enlargement Commissioner alone approved the DCPs, but the transitional period on FMP was so politically sensitive that Verheugen needed the explicit support of his Commission colleagues.

38   *Uniting Europe* 96, 24/4/00.

39   Commission press release IP/01/561, Brussels, 11/04/01.

40   *Financial Times*, 12/4/01.

41   Commission negotiating position quoted in *Agence Europe*, 15/5/01.

42   *Agence Europe* 30/3/01.

43   Duna TV Satellite, 1600 GMT, 12/6/01, reported by BBC Monitoring.

44   *Financial Times*, 4/3/02.

45 Update on the Commission's enlargement website, January 2002: http://europa.eu.int/comm/enlargement/negotiations/chapters/chap2/index.htm
46 Research for this chapter began during the author's visiting fellowship at the Western European Union Institute for Security Studies in 1999. Initial findings were published in Grabbe 2000a and 2000b.
47 The UK and Ireland have opt-outs from Schengen that include a 'selective opt-in', whereby they do not normally participate in migration policy measures. Denmark is a member of Schengen, but until March 2001 it had a special arrangement whereby it had opted out of the third pillar: see Monar 1999. Denmark then exercised its opt-in right in March 2001.
48 For details of the Amsterdam negotiations, see Petite 1998.
49 This process is referred to as the Schengen 'ventilation' exercise: see Adrian Fortescue's evidence in House of Lords 1999.
50 'Council Decision of 20 May 1999 concerning the definition of the Schengen acquis', *Official Journal of the European Communities*, L 176/1, 1999/435/EC, 10/7/99.
51 Note: the wording for the tasks given in the first column reflects the wording in the individual Accession Partnerships, but it is not necessarily a direct quotation because this table presents a shortened summary of the tasks.
52 In addition to the bilateral agreements, there was a prior multilateral readmission agreement between Poland and the Schengen countries (including Germany) signed in March 1991: see Pastore 1998 on the development of the readmission treaty system.
53 The Catch-Up Facility was established following criticism of the financial support offered to the five candidates not starting negotiations in the first round (Bulgaria, Latvia, Lithuania, Romania and Slovakia). The Luxembourg European Council in December 1997 decided to provide additional support to them in areas identified as deficient in the Commission's Opinions, including justice and home affairs.
54 *Uniting Europe* 4, 27/4/98.
55 *Uniting Europe* 2, 13/4/98.
56 This status is conferred bilaterally and is not harmonised across the EU.
57 However, they were still subject to checks by police within each country, and police have additional powers in border areas: see Bort 2000.
58 Border controls were abolished in 1995 between seven Schengen countries; Austria and Italy were able to lift border controls in 1998, while Greece was allowed to do so in 2000.
59 *Neue Zürcher Zeitung*, 18/10/99.
60 United Nations High Commissioner for Refugees 2004.
61 Reported in the Hungarian economics weekly *HVG*, 4/9/99, no. 99/35.
62 Commitment made in the Hungarian position paper for the last five chapters of negotiations submitted to the EU on 29 November 1999, reported in *HVG*, 6/12/99, no. 99/42.
63 János Martonyi, Hungarian Foreign Minister, press conference in Budapest, 26/11/99, reported by *Bridge News*, same date.
64 Proposal made by Zsolt Németh, Political State Secretary, Hungarian Foreign Ministry, reported on Hungarian radio, 3/6/99 (BBC Monitoring Service).

65 Hungarian radio report, 20/2/99 (BBC Monitoring Service).
66 János Martonyi, then Hungarian Foreign Minister, interviewed on Hungarian radio, 5/1/99 (BBC Monitoring Service).
67 Relations with Ukraine feature as a central priority in successive annual 'exposés' of Polish foreign policy and other documents: 'Priorytety polskiej polityki zagranicznej' (Priorities of Polish foreign policy), published on www.msz.gov.pl.
68 *Polish Daily News Bulletin* (government briefing service), 12 February 2002.
69 Foreign Minister Wlodzimierz Cimoszewicz quoted in *Polish Daily News Bulletin*, 11 February 2002.
70 Council Regulation 2317/95.
71 According to Bulgaria's chief negotiator, Vladimir Kissiov, in January 2001.
72 Nickolay Mladenov, Member of the Bulgarian Parliament, Sofia, January 2001.
73 *Agence Europe* 7232, 30/5/98.
74 'Negotiations: Chapter 24 – Justice and Home Affairs', summary on the Commission's website, January 2002: www.europa.eu.int/comm/enlargement/negotiations/chapters/chap24/index.htm.
75 'Negotiations: Chapter 24 – Justice and Home Affairs', summary on the Commission's website, January 2002: www.europa.eu.int/comm/enlargement/negotiations/chapters/chap24/index.htm.
76 'Negotiations: Chapter 24 – Justice and Home Affairs', summary on the Commission's website, January 2002: www.europa.eu.int/comm/enlargement/negotiations/chapters/chap24/index.htm.
77 Reported in the Czech daily *Hospodarske Noviny*, 1/6/99.
78 The author is grateful to Judy Batt for this point.
79 The author is grateful to Boyko Todorov for this formulation.

Bibliography

Principal EU documents

Commission of the European Communities (1992) 'Europe and the Challenge of Enlargement', *Bulletin of the European Communities* Supplement 3/92, 1–24.

—— (1994a), 'The Economic Interpenetration between the European Union and Eastern Europe', *European Economy, Reports and Studies* 6.

—— (1994b), 'The Europe Agreements and Beyond: A Strategy to Prepare the Countries of Central and Eastern Europe for Accession', Communication from the Commission to the Council.

—— (1994c), 'Trade Liberalisation with Central and Eastern Europe', *European Economy* Supplement A, 1–20.

—— (1995), *Preparation of the Associated Countries of Central and Eastern Europe for Integration into the Internal Market of the Union*, COM(95)163 final/2 ed., Luxembourg: OOPEC (known as the Single Market White Paper).

—— (1996a), 'Economic Situation and Economic Reform in Central and Eastern Europe', *European Economy* Supplement C, 1–20.

—— (1996b), *Reinforcing Political Union and Preparing for Enlargement*, Luxembourg: OOPEC.

—— (1997a), *Agenda 2000 – Commission Opinion on Bulgaria's application for membership of the European Union*, DOC/97/11 Brussels, 15th July, Luxembourg: OOPEC.

—— (1997b), *Agenda 2000 – Commission Opinion on Hungary's application for membership of the European Union*, DOC/97/13 Brussels, 15th July, Luxembourg: OOPEC.

—— (1997c), *Agenda 2000 – Commission Opinion on Poland's application for membership of the European Union*, DOC/97/16 Brussels, 15th July, Luxembourg: OOPEC.

—— (1997d), *Agenda 2000: For a Stronger and Wider Union*, Luxembourg: OOPEC.

—— (1997e), *The Phare Programme: An Interim Evaluation*, Brussels: European Commission.

—— (1998a), *Composite Paper: Reports on Progress towards Accession by each of the Candidate Countries*, Brussels: OOPEC.

—— (1998b), *Enlargement 98 Commission Report: Hungary*, Brussels: European Commission, DG1A.

—— (1999), *Composite Paper: Regular Report from the Commission on Progress towards Accession by each of the Candidate Countries, October 13, 1999*, http://www.europa.eu.int/comm/enlargement, Brussels: OOPEC.

—— (2000a), 'Preparing Candidate Countries for Accession to the EU: Phare Institution Building: A Reference Manual on "Twinning" Projects', Revised version, 15 February 2000.

—— (2000b), *Strategy Paper: Regular Report from the Commission on Progress towards Accession by each of the Candidate Countries*, Brussels: OOPEC.

European Council (1993), 'European Council in Copenhagen: Presidency Conclusions', 21–22 June.

—— (1999), 'European Council in Tampere: Presidency Conclusions', 15–16 October.

Official Journal of the European Communities (1993), 'Europe Agreement establishing an association between the European Communities and their Member States, of the one part, and the Republic of Poland, of the other part', L 348/36, published 31/12/93.

—— (1993), 'Europe Agreement establishing an association between the European Communities and their Member States, of the one part, and the Republic of Hungary, of the other part', L 347/36, published 31/12/93.

—— (1994), 'Europe Agreement establishing an association between the European Communities and their Member States, of the one part, and the Republic of Bulgaria, of the other part', L 348/37, published 31/12/94.

References

Albert, Michel (1991), *Capitalisme contre capitalisme*, Paris: Le Seuil.

Amato, Giuliano (1996), 'The Impact of Europe on National Policies: Italian Anti-Trust Policy' in *Adjusting to Europe: The Impact of the European Union on National Institutions and Policies*, (eds) Yves Mény, Pierre Muller, and Jean-Louis Quermonne, London: Routledge, 157–174.

Andersen, Svein S. and Eliassen, Kjell A. (eds) (1993), *Making Policy in Europe: The Europeification of National Policy-making*, London: Sage Publications.

Aniol, Wlodek, Byrnes, Timothy A., and Iankova, Elena A. (1997), 'Poland: Returning to Europe' in *Mitteleuropa: Between Europe and Germany*, ed. Peter J. Katzenstein, Providence and Oxford: Berghahn Books, 39–100.

Assemblée Nationale (1998), 'Rapport d'information déposé par la délégation de l'assemblée nationale pour l'Union Européenne (1), sur les partenariats pour l'adhésion', No. 769, 6 mars, Paris.

Bachmann, Klaus (1999), *Polska kaczka – europejski staw: szanse i pulapki polskiej polityki europejskiej*, Warsaw: Centrum Stosunków Międzynarodowych.

Baldwin, Richard E. (1994), *Towards an Integrated Europe*, London: Centre for Economic Policy Research.

Bannerman, Edward (2001), *The Lisbon scorecard: the status of economic reform in Europe*, London: Centre for European Reform.

Batory, Agnes (2001), *Hungarian party identities and the question of European integration*, SEI Working Paper No. 49, Brighton: Sussex European Institute.

Batt, Judy (1996), *The New Slovakia: National Identity, Political Integration and the Return to Europe*, London: The Royal Institute of International Affairs.

—— (1997), 'The international dimension of democratisation in Hungary, Slovakia and the Czech Republic' in *Building Democracy? The International Dimension of Democratisation in Eastern Europe*, (eds) Geoffrey Pridham, Eric Herring, and George Sanford, London: Cassell, 154–169.

—— (2001), 'Between a rock and a hard place: multi-ethnic regions on the EU's new eastern frontier', Paper for the Political Studies Association Annual Conference, University of Manchester, 10–12 April.

Batt, Judy and Wolczuk, Kataryna (1999), 'The Political Context: Building New States' in *Reconstituting the Market: The Political Economy of Microeconomic*

Transformation, (eds) Paul Hare, Judy Batt, and Saul Estrin, Amsterdam: Harwood, 33–48.

Bauer, Thomas and Zimmerman, Klaus F. (1997), 'Integrating the East: the labor market effects of immigration' in *Europe's Economy Looks East: Implications for Germany and the European Union*, ed. Stanley W. Black, Cambridge: Cambridge University Press, 269–314.

Bazin, Anne (1999), *Germany and the Enlargement of the European Union to the Czech Republic*, EUI Working Paper RSC No. 99/21, San Domenico di Fiesole (FI): European University Institute.

BDI and BDA (1997), 'Stellungnahme zur Agenda 2000/Osterweiterung der EU', Köln: Bundesverband der Deutschen Industrie e.V. and Bundesvereinigung der Deutschen Arbeitgeberverbände.

Begg, Iain and Peterson, John (1999), 'Editorial Statement', *Journal of Common Market Studies* 37, 1–12.

Berger, S. and Dore, R. (1996), *National Diversity and Global Capitalism*, Ithaca: Cornell University Press.

Bevan, Alan, Estrin, Saul and Grabbe, Heather (2001), 'The impact of EU accession prospects on FDI inflows to central and eastern Europe', ESRC 'One Europe or Several?' Programme Policy Paper 06/01, Sussex European Institute.

Biegaj, Agnieszka (ed.) (2000) *Accession negotiations: Poland on the road to the European Union*, Warsaw: Government Plenipotentiary for Poland's Accession Negotiations to the European Union, Chancellery of the Prime Minister, Republic of Poland.

Bigo, Didier (1998), 'Frontiers and security in the European Union: the illusion of migration control' in *The Frontiers of Europe*, (eds) Malcolm Anderson and Eberhard Bort, London: Pinter, 148–164.

Boeri, Tito and Brücker, Herbert (2000), *The Impact of Eastern Enlargement on Employment and Labour Markets in the EU Member States*, Berlin and Milan: European Integration Consortium.

Börzel, Tanja A. (1999), 'Towards Convergence in Europe? Institutional Adaptation to Europeanisation in Germany and Spain', *Journal of Common Market Studies* 37, 573–596.

Bohle, Dorothee (1996), *Governance im Spätsozialismus. Die Herausbildung hybrider Vernetzungen in Ungarn und Polen in den achtziger Jahren*, WZB Working Paper 96–102, Berlin: Wissenschaftszentrum.

Bokova, Irina and Hubchev, Pencho (eds) (2000), *Monitoring of Bulgaria's Accession to the European Union*, Sofia: Friedrich Ebert Stiftung.

Bomberg, E. and Peterson, J. (2000), 'Policy transfer and Europeanisation: Passing the Heineken test?' Queen's Papers on Europeanisation, (2/2000), http://netec.mcc.ac.uk/WoPEc/data/erpqueens.html.

Bort, Eberhard (1999), 'Under the Shadow of Schengen: The Borders of Central and Eastern Europe', Conference paper, Maastricht, February.

—— (2000), 'The Frontiers of Mitteleuropa: Problems and Opportunities at the Eastern Frontier of the European Union' in *Schengen Still Going Strong: Evaluation and Update*, ed. Monika den Boer, Maastricht: EIPA.

Brusis, Martin (1998), 'Residual or European welfare model? Central and Eastern Europe at the crossroads' in *Central and Eastern Europe on the Way into the European Union: Welfare State Reforms in the Czech Republic, Hungary, Poland and Slovakia*, ed. Martin Brusis, München: Centrum für Angewandte Politikforschung, 1–19.

—— (2001), 'Between EU eligibility requirements, competitive politics and national traditions: re-creating regions in the accession countries of central and eastern Europe', Paper for the European Community Studies Association Biennial Conference, Madison WA, 30 May – 2 June.

Bulmer, Simon, Jeffery, Charlie, and Paterson, William E. (2000), *Germany's European Diplomacy: Shaping the Regional Milieu*, Manchester: Manchester University Press.

Bulmer, Simon and Lequesne, Christian (2002), *New Perspectives on EU-Member State Relationships*, Questions de Recherche No. 4, Paris: Centre d'Etudes de Recherches Internationales, Sciences-Po.

Bulmer, Simon and Padgett, Stephen (2005), 'Policy transfer in the European Union: an institutionalist perspective', *British Journal of Political Science*, Vol. 35, No. 1, pp. 103–26.

Bulmer, Simon and Radaelli, Claudio (2004), 'The Europeanisation of National Policy?', Queen's University, Belfast, on-line paper on Europeanisation No. 1/2004, http://www.qub.ac.uk/ies/onlinepapers/poe.html.

Bunce, Valerie (1999), *Subversive institutions: the design and the destruction of socialism and the state*, Cambridge: Cambridge University Press.

Bútorová, Zora (ed.) (1998), *Democracy and Discontent in Slovakia: a Public Opinion Profile of a Country in Transition*, Bratislava: Institute for Public Affairs.

Caporaso, James (1996), 'The European Union and forms of state: Westphalian, regulatory or post-modern?', *Journal of Common Market Studies* 34, 29–52.

Carlin, Wendy, Estrin, Saul, and Schaffer, Mark (1999), *Measuring Progress in Transition and Towards EU Accession: A Comparison of Manufacturing Firms in Poland, Romania and Spain*, CERT Discussion Paper 99/02, Edinburgh: CERT.

Carothers, Thomas (1999), *Aiding democracy abroad: the learning curve*, Washington DC: Carnegie Endowment for International Peace.

Chavance, Bernard and Magnin, Eric (1997), 'Emergence of path-dependent mixed economies in Central Europe' in *Beyond Market and Hierarchy: Interactive Governance and Social Complexity*, (eds) Ash Amin and Jerzy Hausner, Cheltenham: Edward Elgar, 196–232.

Cohen, Michael, March, James, and Olsen, Johan (1972), 'A Garbage Can Model of Organisational Choice', *Administrative Science Quarterly* 17 (March), 1–25.

Coleman, W. (1994), 'Policy convergence in banking: a comparative study', *Political Studies* XLII, 274–292.

Comisso, Ellen (1998), 'Implicit Development Strategies in Central East Europe and Cross-National Production Networks' in *Enlarging Europe: The Industrial Foundations of a New Political Reality*, (eds) John Zysman and Andrew Schwartz, Berkeley: University of California Press, 380–423.

Cowles, Maria Green, Caporaso, James A., and Risse, Thomas (eds) (2001), *Transforming Europe: Europeanisation and Domestic Change*, Ithaca, NY: Cornell University Press.

Crouch, Colin and Streeck, Wolfgang (eds) (1997), *Political Economy of Modern Capitalism: Mapping Convergence and Diversity*, London: Sage.

Dawisha, Karen and Parrott, Bruce (eds) (1997), *The consolidation of democracy in East-Central Europe*, Authoritarianism and Democratisation in Postcommunist Societies Vol. 1, Cambridge: Cambridge University Press.

den Boer, Monika and Wallace, William (2000), 'Justice and home affairs' in *Policy-making in the European Union*, (eds) Helen Wallace and William Wallace, Fourth edition, Oxford: Oxford University Press, 493–522.

DiMaggio, P. and Powell, W.W. (1991), 'The iron cage revisited: institutional isomorphism and collective rationality in organisational fields' in *The New Institutionalism in Organisational Analysis*, (eds) W.W. Powell and P. DiMaggio, Chicago: University of Chicago Press, 63–82.

Dolowitz, David and Marsh, David (1996), 'Who learns what from whom: a review of the policy transfer literature', *Political Studies* XLIV, 343–357.

—— (2000), 'Learning from abroad: the role of policy transfer in contemporary policy-making', *Governance* 13, 5–24.

EastWest Institute (1999), 'Adapting Governments to Integration', Report of a meeting held in Vilnius, Lithuania, 25–26 March 1999 by the EWI Strategy Group for Strengthening Cooperation in Central and Eastern Europe.

EBRD (1997), *Transition Report*, London: European Bank for Reconstruction and Development.

—— (1999), *Transition Report*, London: European Bank for Reconstruction and Development.

ECOSOC (2001), *Bulgaria on the road to accession*, Own-Initiative Opinion of the Section for External Relations, REX/047, Brussels: Economic and Social Committee.

Elster, Jon, Offe, Claus, and Preuss, Ulrich K. (1998), *Institutional Design in Post-communist Societies: Rebuilding the Ship at Sea*, Cambridge: Cambridge University Press.

ERT (2001), *Opening up the business opportunities of EU enlargement: ERT position paper and analysis of the economic costs and benefits of EU enlargement*, Brussels: European Round Table of Industrialists.

Estrin, Saul (ed.) (1994), *Privatisation in Central and Eastern Europe*, London: Longman.

Evans, Mark and Davies, Jonathan (1999), 'Understanding policy transfer: a multi-level, multi-disciplinary perspective', *Public Administration* 77 (2), 361–385.

Evans, Peter B., Jacobson, Harold K., and Putnam, Robert D. (1993), *Double-Edged Diplomacy: International Bargaining and Domestic Politics*, Berkeley: University of California Press.

Faini, Riccardo and Portes, Richard (eds) (1995), *European Union Trade with Eastern Europe: Adjustment and Opportunities*, London: Centre for Economic Policy Research.

Featherstone, Kevin (1998), '"Europeanisation" and the Centre Periphery: The Case of Greece in the 1990s', *South European Society & Politics* 3, 23–39.

Fierke, Karin and Wiener, Antje (1999), 'Constructing Institutional Interests: EU and NATO Enlargement', *Journal of European Public Policy* 6 (5), 721–742.

Fink-Hafner, Danica (1998), 'Organised interests in the policy-making process in Slovenia', *Journal of European Public Policy* 5 (2), 285–302.

Fligstein, Neil (1996), 'Markets as Politics: A Political-Cultural Approach to Market Institutions', *American Sociological Review* 61 (August), 656–673.

Forder, James and Menon, Anand (eds) (1998), *The European Union and National Macroeconomic Policy*, London and New York: Routledge.

Fowler, Brigid (2001), 'Debating sub-state reform on Hungary's "road to Europe"', ESRC 'One Europe or Several?' Programme Working Paper 21/01, Sussex: Sussex European Institute.

Francioni, Francesco (ed.) (1992), *Italy and EC Membership Evaluated*, London: Pinter.

Friis, Lykke (1997), *When Europe negotiates: from Europe Agreements to eastern enlargement?*, Copenhagen: Institute of Political Science.
—— (1998), 'Approaching the "third half" of EU grand bargaining – the post-negotiation phase of the "Europe Agreement game"', *Journal of European Public Policy* 5 (2), 322–338.
Gallagher, Tom (1998), 'The Balkans: Bulgaria, Romania, Albania and the Former Yugoslavia' in *Developments in Central and East European Politics*, (eds) Stephen White, Judy Batt, and Paul G. Lewis, Basingstoke: Macmillan, 43–56.
Gialdino, Carlo Curti (1995), 'Some Reflections on the Acquis Communautaire', *Common Market Law Review* 32, 1089–1121.
Goetz, Klaus (2000), 'Europeanising the national executive? Western and eastern style', Paper prepared for the UACES 30th annual conference, Budapest, 6–8 April.
Goetz, Klaus and Wollmann, Hellmut (2001), 'Governmentalising central executives in post-communist Europe: a four-country comparison', *Journal of European Public Policy* 8 (6), 864–887.
Gould, John (1999), *Winners, Losers and the Institutional Effects of Privatisation in the Czech and Slovak Republics*, EUI Working Paper RSC No. 99/11, San Domenico di Fiesole (FI): European University Institute.
Gourevitch, Peter (1978), 'The second image reversed: the international sources of domestic politics', *International Organisation* 32, 881–912.
Grabbe, Heather (1999), *A Partnership for Accession? The Implications of EU Conditionality for the Central and East European Applicants*, EUI Working Paper RSC No. 99/12, San Domenico di Fiesole (FI): European University Institute.
—— (2000a), 'The Sharp Edges of Europe: Extending Schengen Eastwards', *International Affairs* 76, 497–514.
—— (2000b), *The Sharp Edges of Europe: Security Implications of Extending EU Border Policies Eastwards*, Occasional Paper, Paris: Western European Union Institute for Security Studies.
—— (2001a), 'How does Europeanisation affect CEE governance? Conditionality, diffusion and diversity', *Journal of European Public Policy* 8 (6), 1013–1031.
—— (2001b), *Profiting from EU Enlargement*, London: Centre for European Reform.
—— (2002), 'Stabilizing the East while keeping out the easterners: internal and external security logics in conflict' in *Externalities of Integration: The Wider Impact of Europe's Immigration and Asylum Policies*, (eds) Sandra Lavenex and Emek Uçarer, Lanham MD: Lexington Books, 91–104.
—— (2004a), *The Constellations of Europe: How Enlargement will Transform the EU*, London: Centre for European Reform.
—— (2004b), 'Poland: The EU's New Awkward Partner', CER Bulletin Issue 34, February/March (http://www.cer.org.uk/articles/34_grabbe.html).
—— (2005), 'Regulating the Flow of People across Europe' in *The Europeanisation of Central and Eastern Europe*, (eds) Frank Schimmelfennig and Uli Sedelmeier, Ithaca: Cornell University Press (112–134).
Grabbe, Heather and Hughes, Kirsty (1998), *Enlarging the EU Eastwards*, London: Cassell/The Royal Institute of International Affairs.

—— (1999), 'Central and East European views on EU enlargement: political debates and public opinion' in *Back to Europe: Central and Eastern Europe and the European Union* (ed.) Karen Henderson, London: UCL Press, 185–202.

Grabher, Gernot (1994a), *Lob der Verschwendung. Redundanz in der Regionalentwicklung*, Berlin: Edition Sigma.

—— (1994b), *The Elegance of Incoherence: Institutional Legacies, Privatisation and Regional Development in East Germany and Hungary*, WZB Working Paper 94–103, Berlin: Wissenschaftszentrum.

Grabher, Gernot and Stark, David (eds) (1997), *Restructuring Networks in Post-Socialism: Legacies, Linkages and Localities*, Oxford: Oxford University Press.

Haas, Ernest (1990), *When Knowledge is Power: Three Models of Change in International Organisations*, Berkeley: University of California Press.

Haas, Peter (1992), 'Epistemic communities and international policy coordination', *International Organisation* 46, 1–36.

Haggard, Stephan and Moravcsik, Andrew (1993), 'The Political Economy of Financial Assistance to Eastern Europe, 1989–91' in *After the Cold War: International Institutions and State Strategies in Europe, 1989–91*, (eds) Robert O. Keohane, Joseph S. Nye, and Stanley Hoffman, Cambridge: Harvard University Press, 150–172.

Haggard, Stephan, Levy, Marc A., Moravcsik, Andrew, and Nicolaïdis, Kalypso (1993), 'Integrating the Two Halves of Europe: Theories of Interests, Bargaining, and Institutions' in *After the Cold War: International Institutions and State Strategies in Europe, 1989–91*, (eds) Robert O. Keohane, Joseph S. Nye, and Stanley Hoffman, Cambridge: Harvard University Press, 173–195.

Hall, Peter (1993), 'Policy paradigms, social learning and the state', *Comparative Politics* 25, 275–296.

Hall, Peter and Taylor, Rosemary (1996), 'Political Science and the Three New Institutionalisms', *Political Studies* XLIV, 936–957.

Halpern, László and Wyplosz, Charles (eds) (1998), *Hungary: Towards a Market Economy*, Cambridge: Cambridge University Press.

Harcourt, Alison (2002), 'Engineering Europeanisation: the role of the European institutions in shaping national broadcasting regulation', *Journal of European Public Policy* 9 (5), 736–755.

Hare, Paul, Batt, Judy, and Estrin, Saul (eds) (1999), *Reconstituting the Market: The Political Economy of Microeconomic Transformation*, Amsterdam: Harwood.

Hausner, Jerzy, Jessop, Bob, and Nielsen, Klaus (1995), 'Institutional Change in Post-Socialism' in *Strategic Choice and Path-Dependency in Post-Socialism: Institutional Dynamics in the Transformation Process*, (eds) Klaus Nielsen, Bob Jessop, and Jerzy Hausner, Aldershot: Edward Elgar, 3–46.

Héritier, Adrienne (1996), 'The accommodation of diversity in European policy-making and its outcomes: regulatory policy as a patchwork', *Journal of European Public Policy* 3 (2), 149–167.

—— (1998), 'Differential Europe: administrative responses to Community policy', Paper for the conference 'Europeanisation and Domestic Change', European University Institute, Florence, 19–20 June.

Héritier, Adrienne and Knill, Christoph (2000), 'Differential responses to European policies: a comparison', Max Planck Projektgruppe Recht der Gemeinschaftsgüter, Preprint, Bonn.

Héritier, A., Knill, C., and Mingers, S. (1996), *Ringing the Changes in Europe: Regulatory Competition and the Redefinition of the State*, Berlin: Walter de Gruyter.

Héritier, Adrienne, Kerwer, Dieter, Knill, Christoph, Lehmkuhl, Dirk, and Teutsch, Michael (2001), *Differential Europe – new opportunities and restrictions for policy-making in member states*, Lanham, MD: Rowan & Littlefield.

Hillion, Christophe (1998) 'Accession partnerships with the CEECs: an EU instrument for its enlargement,' *EU Focus* 9, May.

Hine, David and Kassim, Hussein (eds) (1998), *Beyond the Market: The EU and National Social Policy*, London: Routledge.

Hix, Simon (1998), 'The study of the European Union II: the "new governance" agenda and its rival', *Journal of European Public Policy* 5 (1), 38–65.

House of Lords, Select Committee on the European Communities (1999), *Schengen and the United Kingdom's Border Controls*, Seventh Report, HL 37, London: HMSO.

Hughes, Kirsty, Grabbe, Heather, and Smith, Edward (1999), 'Lassen sich die MOE-Staaten einbinden? Integrationspositionen der EU-Anwärter', *Internationale Politik* 54 (4), 63–69.

Hughes, James, Sasse, Gwendolyn and Gordon, Claire (2004), *Europeanisation and Regionalisation in the EU's Enlargement to Central and Eastern Europe*, Basingstoke: Palgrave Macmillan.

Iankova, Elena A. (1998), 'The Transformative Corporatism of Eastern Europe', *East European Politics and Society* 12 (2), 222–264.

Inotai, Andras (1999), *Political, Economic and Social Arguments for and against EU Enlargement: a Survey of the Influence of Pressure Groups*, Budapest: Institute for World Economics.

Jacoby, Wade (1998), 'Talking the Talk: The Cultural and Institutional Effects of Western Models', Paper for the conference 'Post-communist Transformation and the Social Sciences: Cross-Disciplinary Approaches', Berlin 30–31 October.

—— (1999), 'Tutors and Pupils: International Organisations, Central European Elites, and Western Models', *International Studies Quarterly*.

Jileva, Elena (2002), 'Larger than the European Union: the Emerging EU Migration Regime and Enlargement' in *Externalities of integration: the wider impact of Europe's immigration and asylum policies*, (eds) Sandra Lavenex and Emek Uçarer, Lanham MD: Lexington Books, 75–85.

Jordan, Andrew (2000), *The Europeanisation of UK environmental policy, 1970–2000: A departmental perspective*, 'One Europe or Several?' Working Paper 11/00, Brighton: Sussex European Institute.

Kassim, Hussein and Menon, Anand (eds) (1996), *The European Union and National Industrial Policy*, London and New York: Routledge.

Katzenstein, Peter (ed.) (1997), *Mitteleuropa: Between Europe and Germany*, Providence and Oxford: Berghahn Books.

King, Charles (2000), 'Post-postcommunism: transition, comparison and the end of "Eastern Europe"', *World Politics* 53, 143–172.

Kingdon, John W. (1997), *Agendas, Alternatives and Public Policies*, Baltimore: HarperCollins.

Knill, Christoph (2001), *The Europeanisation of national administrations: patterns of institutional change and persistence*, Cambridge: Cambridge University Press.

Knill, Christoph and Lehmkuhl, Dirk (1999), 'How Europe matters: different mechanisms of Europeanisation', *European Integration online Papers* 3, http://eiop.or.at/eiop/texte/1999-07a.htm.

Knorr, Klaus (1977), 'International economic leverage and its uses' in *Economic Issues and National Security*, (eds) Klaus Knorr and Frank Trager, Lawrence: University Press of Kansas, 102.

Kohler-Koch, Beate (1996), 'Catching up with change: the transformation of governance in the European Union', *Journal of European Public Policy* 3 (3), 359–380.

—— (1999), 'The evolution and transformation of European governance' in *The Transformation of Governance in the European Union*, (eds) Beate Kohler-Koch and Rainer Eising, London: Routledge, 20–39.

—— (2000), 'Europeanisation: concepts and empirical evidence', Paper prepared for the international workshop 'Europeanisation: Concept and Reality', Bradford University, 5–6 May.

Kohler-Koch, Beate and Eising, Rainer (eds) (1999), *The Transformation of Governance in the European Union*, London: Routledge.

Kopecký, Petr and Mudde, Cas (2000), 'What has Eastern Europe taught us about the democratisation literature (and *vice versa*)?', *European Journal of Political Research* 37, 517–539.

Kumar, Krishan (1992), 'The 1989 Revolutions and the Idea of Europe', *Political Studies* XL, 439–461.

Laczko, Frank, Stacher, Irene, and Graf, Jessica (eds) (1999), *Migration in Central and Eastern Europe: 1999 Review*, Geneva: International Organisation for Migration.

Ladrech, Robert (1994), 'Europeanisation of domestic politics and institutions: the case of France', *Journal of Common Market Studies* 32, 69–88.

Lavenex, Sandra (1998), 'Transgressing borders: the emergent European refugee regime and 'Safe Third Countries''' in *The Union and the World: The Political Economy of EU Foreign Policy*, (eds) A. Cafruny and P. Peters, Amsterdam: Kluwer, 113–132.

—— (1999), *Safe Third Countries: Extending the EU Asylum and Immigration Policies to Central and Eastern Europe*, Budapest: Central European University Press.

Lavenex, Sandra and Uçarer, Emek (eds) (2002), *Externalities of Integration: The Wider Impact of Europe's Immigration and Asylum Policies*, Lanham MD: Lexington Books.

Leibfried, Stephan and Pierson, Paul (2000), 'Social policy: left to courts and markets?' in *Policy-making in the European Union*, (eds) Helen Wallace and William Wallace, Oxford: Oxford University Press, 267–292.

Lijphart, Arend and Crawford, Beverly (1995), 'Explaining Political and Economic Change in Post-Communist Eastern Europe: Old Legacies, New Institutions, Hegemonic Norms and International Pressure', *Comparative Political Studies* 28, 171–199.

Lijphart, Arend and Waisman, Carlos H. (eds) (1996), *Institutional design in new democracies: Eastern Europe and Latin America*, Westview Press: Boulder.

Linz, Juan J. and Stepan, Alfred (1996), *Problems of Democratic Transition and Consolidation: Southern Europe, South America and Post-Communist Europe*, Baltimore and London: The Johns Hopkins University Press.

Ludlow, Peter (1997), 'Institutional Balance' in *Making sense of the Amsterdam Treaty*, ed. European Policy Centre, Brussels: The European Policy Centre.

Majone, Giandomenico (1991), 'Cross-national sources of regulatory policy-making in Europe and the United States', *Journal of Public Policy* 11, 79–106.

—— (1992), 'Regulatory Federalism in the European Community', *Environment and Planning C: Government and Policy* 10, 299–316.

Manin, Philippe (1998), 'The Treaty of Amsterdam', *Columbia Journal of European Law* 4, 1–68.

Mayhew, Alan (1998), *Recreating Europe: The European Union's Policy towards Central and Eastern Europe*, Cambridge: Cambridge University Press.

—— (2000), *Enlargement of the European Union: an analysis of the negotiations with the central and eastern European candidate countries*, SEI Working Paper No. 39, Brighton: Sussex European Institute.

Mayhew, Alan and Orlowski, Witold (1998), 'The Impact of EU Accession on Enterprise Adaptation and Institutional Development in the EU-Associated Countries in Central and Eastern Europe', Study prepared for the EBRD.

McGowan, Francis and Wallace, Helen (1996), 'Towards a European Regulatory State', *Journal of European Public Policy* 3 (4), 560–576.

Mény, Yves, Muller, Pierre, and Quermonne, Jean-Louis (eds) (1996), *Adjusting to Europe: the Impact of the European Union on National Institutions and Policies*, London: Routledge.

Michalski, Anna and Wallace, Helen (1992), *The European Community: The Challenge of Enlargement*, London: Royal Institute for International Affairs.

Millard, Frances (1999), 'Polish domestic politics and accession to the European Union' in *Back to Europe: Central and Eastern Europe and the European Union*, ed. Karen Henderson, London: UCL Press, 203–220.

Milward, Alan (1992), *The European Rescue of the Nation-State*. Berkeley: University of California Press.

Mörth, Ulrika (2003), 'Europeanisation as interpretation, translation and editing of public policies' in *The Politics of Europeanisation*, (eds) Kevin Featherstone and Claudio Radaelli, Oxford: Oxford University Press, 2003.

Monar, Jörg (1999), *Flexibility and closer cooperation in an emerging European migration policy: opportunities and risks*, Laboratorio CeSPI, n.01, Rome: Centro Studi Politica Internazionali.

—— (2000), *Enlargement-related diversity in EU justice and home affairs: challenges, dimensions and management instruments*, Working Document W112, December, The Hague: WRR Scientific Council for Government Policy.

Moravcsik, Andrew (1993), 'Preferences and Power in the European Community: A Liberal Intergovernmentalist Approach', *Journal of Common Market Studies* 31, 473–524.

Mosley, Paul, Harrigan, Jane, and Toye, John (1991), *Aid and Power: The World Bank and Policy-based Lending*, London and New York: Routledge.

Nicolaides, Phedon (1999), 'Enlargement of the EU and Effective Implementation of Community Rules: An Integration-Based Approach', Maastricht: European Institute for Public Administration Working Paper, 3 December.

Nicolaides, Phedon and Boean, Sylvia Raja (1997), *A guide to the enlargement of the European Union: determinants, process, timing, negotiations*, Maastricht: European Institute of Public Administration.

Nunberg, Barbara (2000), *Ready for Europe: public administration reform and European Union accession in central and eastern Europe*, Washington DC: The World Bank.

Nunberg, Barbara, Barbone, Luca, and Derlien, Hans-Ulrich (1996), *The state after communism: administrative traditions in central and eastern Europe*, Washington DC: World Bank.

Ockenden, Jonathan and Franklin, Michael (1995), *European Agriculture: Making the CAP Fit the Future*, London: The Royal Institute of International Affairs and Pinter.

Offe, Claus (1991), 'Capitalism by Democratic Design? Democratic Theory Facing the Triple Transition in East Central Europe', *Social Research* 58, 865–892.

Olsen, Johan P. (2003), 'Towards a European administrative space?', *Journal of European Public Policy* 10(4), 506–531.

Ost, David (1997), 'Illusory corporatism in Eastern Europe: Tripartism in the service of neo-liberalism', Paper presented at conference on 'Institution Building in the Transformaton of Central and Eastern European Societies', Central European University, Budapest, 5–7 December.

Pastore, Ferruccio (1998), 'L'obbligo di riammissione in diritto internazionale: sviluppi recenti', *Rivista di Diritto Internazionale* Anno LXXXI (Fasc. 4), 968–1021.

Pennock, J. Roland (1966), 'Political development, political systems, and political goods', *World Politics* 18, 421.

Petite, Michel (1998), 'The Treaty of Amsterdam', Jean Monnet Paper 98-2-03, Harvard Law School.

Pinder, John (1997), 'The European Community and democracy in Central and Eastern Europe' in *Building Democracy? The International Dimension of Democratisation in Eastern Europe*, (eds) Geoffrey Pridham, Eric Herring, and George Sanford, London: Cassell, 110–132.

Preston, Christopher (1997), *Enlargement and Integration in the European Union*, London: Routledge.

Pridham, Geoffrey, Herring, Eric, and Sanford, George (eds) (1997), *Building Democracy? The International Dimension of Democratisation in Eastern Europe*, London: Cassell.

Przeworski, Adam (1991), *Democracy and the market: political and economic reforms in Eastern Europe and Latin America*, Cambridge: Cambridge University Press.

Putnam, Robert (1988), 'Diplomacy and domestic politics: the logic of two-level games', *International Organisation* 42, 427–460.

—— Putnam, Robert *et al.* (1993), *Making Democracy Work: Civic Traditions in Modern Italy*, Princeton, N.J.: Princeton University Press.

Radaelli, Claudio (1997), 'How does Europeanisation produce policy change? Corporate tax policy in Italy and the UK', *Comparative Political Studies* 30, 553–575.

—— (1999), *Technocracy in the European Union*, London: Longman.

—— (2000a), 'Whither Europeanisation? Concept Stretching and Substantive Change', Paper prepared for the international workshop 'Europeanisation: Concept and Reality', Bradford University, 5–6 May.

—— (2000b), 'Policy transfer in the European Union: institutional isomorphism as a source of legitimacy', *Governance* 13, 25–43.

—— (2003), 'The Europeanisation of Public Policy' in *The Politics of Europeanisation*, (eds) Kevin Featherstone and Claudio Radaelli, Oxford: Oxford University Press.

Redmond John and Glenda G. Rosenthal (eds) (1998), *The Expanding European Union: Past, Present and Future*, Boulder and London: Lynne Rienner.

Republic of Poland (1999), 'Negotiating position of the government on Chapter 2: free movement of persons', adopted 27 July by the Council of Ministers.

Rhodes, Martin and van Apeldoorn, Bastiaan (1998), 'Capitalism Unbound? The Transformation of European Corporate Governance', *Journal of European Public Policy* 5 (3), 406–427.

Richardson, Jeremy (1999), 'Interest Groups, Multi-Arena Politics and Policy Change', in *The Policy Process*, (ed.) Nagel, Stuart S., New York: Nova Science Publishers.

Richter, Sándor (1998), *EU Eastern Enlargement: Challenge and Opportunity*, Research Report No. 249, July, Vienna: WIIW.

Risse, Thomas and Börzel, Tanja (2003), 'When Europe Hits Home: Europeanisation and Domestic Change' in *The Politics of Europeanisation*, (eds) Kevin Featherstone and Claudio Radaelli, Oxford: Oxford University Press.

Risse-Kappen, Thomas (1996), 'Exploring the nature of the beast: international relations theory and comparative policy analysis meet the European Union', *Journal of Common Market Studies* 34, 53–80.

Robertson, David (1991), 'Political conflict and lesson drawing', *Journal of Public Policy* 11, 3–30.

Roguska, Beata and Strzeszewski, Michal (2002), *Zainteresowanie spoleczne, wiedza i poinformowanie o integracji Polski z Unia Europejska*, Warsaw: Instytut Spraw Publicznych.

Rose, Richard (1991), 'What is lesson drawing?', *Journal of Public Policy* 11, 3–30.

Rothschild, Joseph and Wingfield, Nancy M. (1999), *Return to diversity: a political history of East Central Europe since World War II*, Oxford: Oxford University Press.

Rupnik, Jacques and Bazin, Anne (2001), 'La difficile réconciliation tchéco-allemande', *Politique Etrangère* 2, 353–370.

Sabatier, P.A. (1998), 'The Advocacy Coalition Framework: Revisions and Relevance for Europe', *Journal of European Public Policy* 5 (1), 98–130.

Sartori, Giovanni (1991), 'Comparing and miscomparing', *Journal of Theoretical Politics* 3, 243–257.

Sbragia, Alberta M. (ed.) (1992), *Euro-Politics. Institutions and Policymaking in the 'New' European Community*, Washington DC: Brookings.

Schimmelfennig, Frank (1998), 'NATO, the EU, and Central and Eastern Europe: Theoretical Perspectives and Empirical Findings on Eastern Enlargement', Paper presented at the 3rd Pan-European International Relations/International Studies Association Conference, Vienna.

—— (1999), *The Double Puzzle of EU Enlargement – Liberal Norms, Rhetorical Action and Expansion to the East*, ARENA Working Papers WP 99/15, Oslo: ARENA.

—— (2001), 'The Community Trap: Liberal Norms, Rhetorical Action, and the Eastern Enlargement of the European Union', *International Organisation* 55.

Schimmelfennig, Frank and Sedelmeier, Uli (eds) (2005), *The Europeanisation of Central and Eastern Europe*, Ithaca: Cornell University Press.

Schmidt, Vivien (1997), 'A new Europe for the old?', *Daedalus* 124, 75–106.

Schmitter, P. and Santiso, J. (1998), 'Three temporal dimensions to the consolidation of democracy', *International Political Science Review* 19, 69–92.

Sedelmeier, Ulrich (1994), *The European Union's Association Policy towards Central and Eastern Europe: Political and Economic Rationales in Conflict*, SEI Working Paper No. 7, Brighton: Sussex European Institute.

—— (1998), 'The European Union's Association Policy towards the Countries of Central and Eastern Europe: Collective EU Identity and Policy Paradigms in a Composite Policy', Unpublished DPhil book, University of Sussex.

—— (2000), 'Eastern enlargement: risk, rationality, and role-compliance' in *The state of the European Union: risks, reform, resistance, and revival.* (eds) Maria Green Cowles and Michael Smith, Oxford: Oxford University Press, 164–185.

—— (2001), 'Sectoral Dynamics of the EU's Accession Requirements: the Role of Policy Paradigms', Paper for the ECSA 7th Biennial International Conference; Madison, Wisconsin, 31 May – 2 June.

Sedelmeier, Ulrich and Wallace, Helen (1996), 'Policies toward central and eastern Europe' in *Policy-making in the European Union.* (eds) Helen Wallace and William Wallace, Third edition. Oxford: Oxford University Press, 353–387.

—— (2000), 'Eastern enlargement' in *Policy-making in the European Union*, (eds) Helen Wallace and William Wallace, Fourth edition. Oxford: Oxford University Press, 427–460.

Smith, Alasdair, Holmes, Peter, Sedelmeier, Ulrich, Smith, Edward, Wallace, Helen, and Young, Alasdair (1996), *The European Union and Central and Eastern Europe: Pre-Accession Strategies*, Brighton: Sussex European Institute.

Stark, David and Bruszt, László (1998), *Postsocialist Pathways: Transforming Politics and Property in East Central Europe*, Cambridge: Cambridge University Press.

Stone Sweet, Alec and Wayne Sandholtz (1997), 'European Integration and Supranational Governance', *Journal of European Public Policy* 4(3), 297–317.

Szczerbiak, Aleks (1999), 'Prospects for the Emergence of a Polish Eurosceptic Lobby', Paper presented at Sussex European Institute Workshop, University of Sussex, 12 March.

—— (2001), 'Europe as a re-aligning issue in Polish politics? Evidence from the October 2000 presidential election', Paper for the Political Studies Association Annual Conference, University of Manchester, 10–12 April.

Szemlér, Tamás (1998), *The economic benefits for Hungary of EU accession*, Working Paper No. 98, Budapest: Institute for World Economics.

Taggart, Paul and Szczerbiak, Aleks (2001), *Parties, Positions and Europe: Euroscepticism in the EU Candidate States of Central and Eastern Europe*, SEI Working Paper No 46, Opposing Europe Research Network Working Paper No 2, University of Sussex, Brighton.

Todorov, Antony (1999), *The role of political parties in Bulgaria's accession to the EU*, Sofia: Centre for the Study of Democracy.

Torreblanca Payá, José Ignacio (1997), *The European Community and Central Eastern Europe (1989–93): Foreign Policy and Decision-Making*, Madrid: Centro de Estudios Avanzados en Ciencias Sociales.

Tóth, Tihamér (1998), 'Competition law in Hungary: harmonisation towards EU membership', *European Competition Law Review* 19, 358–369.

Tsebelis, George (1990), *Nested Games: Rational Choice in Comparative Politics*, Berkeley: University of California Press.

United Nations High Commissioner for Refugees (2004), *Asylum Levels and Trends: Europe and non-European Industrialized Countries, 2003* (Geneva: UNHCR).

Vachudová, Milada Anna (2001), 'The Czech Republic: the unexpected force of institutional constraints' in *Democratic Consolidation in Eastern Europe: International and Transnational Factors*, (eds) Jan Zielonka and Alex Pravda, Oxford: Oxford University Press, 325–362.

Vachudová, Milada Anna and Snyder, Tim (1997) 'Are Transitions Transitory? Two Types of Political Change in Eastern Europe since 1989', *East European Politics and Society* 11 (1), 1–35.

Wallace, Helen and Wallace, William (2000), *Policy-making in the European Union*, Fourth edition, Oxford: Oxford University Press.

Waltz, Kenneth N. (1959), *Man, the State and War: A Theoretical Analysis*, New York: Columbia University Press.

Weatherill, Stephen and Beaumont, Paul (1995), *EC Law*, Harmondsworth: Penguin Books.

Wedel, Janine (1998), *Collision and collusion: the strange case of western aid to Eastern Europe, 1989–1998*, New York: St Martin's.

Whitehead, Laurence (1996a), 'Democracy and Decolonisation: East-Central Europe' in *The International Dimensions of Democratisation: Europe and the Americas*, (ed.) Laurence Whitehead, Oxford: Oxford University Press, 356–392.

—— (1996b) (ed.), *The International Dimensions of Democratisation: Europe and the Americas*, Oxford: Oxford University Press.

Wiener, Antje (1998), *The Embedded Acquis Communautaire: Transmission Belt and Prism of New Governance*, EUI Working Paper RSC No. 98/35, San Domenico di Fiesole (FI): European University Institute.

Wilks, Stephen (1996), 'Regulatory Compliance and Capitalist Diversity in Europe', *Journal of European Public Policy* 3 (4), 536–559.

—— (1997), 'EU Competition Policy and the CEECs: the Institutions of a New Market Economy', Paper prepared for a workshop on 'State Strategies and International Regimes in the New Europe', Thorkil Kristensen Institute.

Winters, L. Alan (ed.) (1995), *Foundations of an Open Economy: Trade Laws and Institutions for Eastern Europe*, London: Centre for Economic Policy Research.

World Bank (1996), *World Development Report 1996: From Plan to Market*, New York: Oxford University Press.

—— (1997), *Poland: Country Economic Memorandum: Reform and Growth on the Road to the EU*, Report No. 16858-POL, Washington DC: World Bank.

Index